SACRED SYSTEMS

Sacred Systems

*Exploring Personal Transformation
in the Western Christian Tradition*

ERIC J. KYLE

◥PICKWICK *Publications* • Eugene, Oregon

SACRED SYSTEMS
Exploring Personal Transformation in the Western Christian Tradition

Copyright © 2014 Eric J. Kyle. All rights reserved. Except for brief quotations in critical publications or reviews, no part of this book may be reproduced in any manner without prior written permission from the publisher. Write: Permissions, Wipf and Stock Publishers, 199 W. 8th Ave., Suite 3, Eugene, OR 97401.

Pickwick Publications
An Imprint of Wipf and Stock Publishers
199 W. 8th Ave., Suite 3
Eugene, OR 97401

www.wipfandstock.com

ISBN 13: 978-1-62032-964-1

Cataloguing-in-Publication data:

Kyle, Eric J.

   Sacred systems : exploring personal transformation in the Western Christian tradition / Eric J. Kyle.

   x + 320 pp. ; 23 cm. Includes bibliographical references and index.

   ISBN 13: 978-1-62032-964-1

   1. Spirituality. 2. Spiritual life—Christianity. 3. Church history. I. Title.

BV4490 K94 2014

Manufactured in the U.S.A.

To Teddi, Katie, & Alex

Contents

Acknowledgments ix

Introduction 1

PART ONE: Early Non-Christian Influences

1. Philo of Alexandria's Contemplative Life 19

2. Iamblichus and the Mysteries 31

PART TWO: Early Christian Diversity

3. Gnostic Christian Formation 47

4. *Didache* Communities 57

PART THREE: Early Monastic Formation

5. Cassian's *Conferences* 74

6. *Philokalia* Formation 88

PART FOUR: Medieval & Renaissance

7. Franciscan Formation 110

8. Erasmus & Militant Christians 127

PART FIVE: Protestant Reformation

9. Francis de Sales' *Introduction* 144

10. Quaker Formation 160

11. William Law's *Serious Call* 176

Contents

PART SIX: Contemporary Movements

12 Dallas Willard's Renovating Heart   199

13 Personal Transformation at a Liberal Christian Seminary   217

14 Gerald May's Willing Spirit   240

15 Yale's Spiritual Self Schema (3-S) Program   248

PART SEVEN: Synthesizing & Summarizing

16 Synthesizing—The Sacred Systems through Three Lenses   267

17 Insights, Critiques, and Callings   298

Bibliography   307

Index   313

Acknowledgments

I would like to thank Frank Rogers Jr. for his support and guidance in formulating this project. I would also like to thank my family for humoring my many random musings as this work was carried out. This book is also done in gratitude to Reza Langari, Alexander Parlos, and especially Suhada Jayasuriya, who helped to stoke both my passions and education as a young engineer for the Feedback Theory upon which this text is based. In addition to our Beloved Creator, I would also like to dedicate this book in memory of Karen S. Reid without whose empowerment and courage this book might never have been completed.

Introduction

A Systematic Need

ALFRED GREW UP IN a Christian church that was committed to the discipleship of its congregants. Inspired by the passionately delivered sermons of his pastor, he felt the call to live a life that was more conforming to the Life and Spirit of Christ that was the focal point of these weekly orations. Alfred committed himself to trying to read the Bible from cover-to-cover. He prayed daily and sought to, as his religious community admonished, "do all things in Christ." In short, Alfred was beginning a more intentional process of spiritual formation for his own personal life.

As he grew, however, many challenges lay ahead. He struggled with the views of human nature that his community embraced that taught him that he was a "horrible, wretched sinner" and the struggles with guilt and intense fears that emerged as a result. Like many, Alfred also struggled with the dullness that can arise from praying the same sets of prayers day-after-day. He also struggled with questions of faith and the changes that his developing life brought. He wrestled with questions of meaning and purpose for his own life in light of the diverse religious context that he encountered in the neighborhood that lay just beyond the walls of his congregation.

More than these, however, Alfred struggled with how to help mentor others in their own religious and spiritual journey. You see, persevering in the midst of such trials, he now found himself to be the congregation's youth minister as a college student. While the weekly sermons of his community continued to inspire a committed and persevering faith, Alfred found little in them to guide him in working with the congregation's youth. What sets of ideals and goals should he be working with them toward? What kinds of support might he give to them as they encountered some of the very same struggles he had and continued to face? How was what he taught these youth weekly to be related to the larger multireligious context of their local community? How was he to decide what to do each week and how to evaluate whether these youth were truly progressing in the spiritual life or not?

It is questions such as these that illustrate the need for systematics. They are questions that prompt intentional reflection on the systems of spiritual formation that we use in our congregations, religious education programs, and retreat centers. Questions that ask how we can work more effectively toward the goals of our communities, how our beliefs influence our practices, how we can discern direction in light of context, and how we can assess spiritual progress are ones that prompt us to look at our formative efforts in more holistic and systematic ways. They prompt us to examine how our spiritual formation programs are interconnected and how they can be more effective. As we will see in the many pages that follow, viewing our spiritual formation programs from a systematic view can strengthen this work by helping to ensure closer connections between beliefs and practices, approaches and assessments, ideals and outcomes, providing greater clarity on the directions we are headed as well as insights into how we might continually adapt our efforts to ever-changing circumstances.

If we look at the historical and contemporary resources on spiritual formation, we find many that present systematic approaches. From early Jewish-Christian texts such as the *Didache* that present well-defined catechetical programs, to Renaissance authors such as Erasmus of Rotterdam who have offered detailed guidance on how to live a spiritually forming personal life in rigorous ways, to contemporary authors such as Dallas Willard who offer in-depth insights into the transformations of one's heart and soul, systematic texts in the Western Christian tradition abound. These texts can offer ministers and laypersons such as Alfred with much clarity, ideas, and guidance.

However, as this text will eventually assert, the spiritual formation systems that we use are always contextually influenced. In other words, Alfred can turn to some of these authors and communities for guidance, but it still remains for him to discern how these sources might help him with the particular youth that he is currently working with. It might be more helpful for Alfred, and others in this field, to therefore look to a set of systematic presentations of spiritual formation rather than trying to exactly replicate any one of these sacred systems. Instead, we can look for

Introduction

patterns and lessons learned across them that might help us to formulate and continually improve upon our own discipleship programs.

This book is therefore an attempt to explore views of and approaches to personal transformation in the Western Christian tradition from a systematic perspective. Our hopes here are to better understand how personal spiritual formation has been conceptualized and embodied by communities from across the Western Christian tradition. Such an exploration will not only help us to better compile a history of spiritual formation at the level of the individual for this religious tradition, but to also glean a better understanding of personal transformation so that we might engage this work in more informed and systematic ways.

A Systematic Landscape

In the edited book, *Mapping Christian Education*, "spiritual growth" is primarily understood as the "personal dimension of learning" while the work of religious education is asserted to focus more broadly to include relationships, whole communities, and the wider world.[1] Similarly, as we shall see later on, Dallas Willard asserts, "Spiritual formation, without regard to any specifically religious context or tradition, is the process by which the human spirit or will is given a definite 'form' or character."[2] For this set of contemporary authors, spiritual formation is seen primarily as a personal endeavor. More widely in our culture, it is common today to think of spiritual formation as primarily being oriented toward the level of the individual.

However, such person-centered views are not the only way to think about this field. As we shall also see in this book, a central theological position is the presence of God in every part of creation. In other words, it is asserted, the Spirit is formatively active within and throughout all that is. If we therefore took this theological position as the basis of our understanding of "spiritual" formation, we find a much broader definition to emerge. More specifically, we can understand the term "spiritual formation" to be the work of being "formed in the Spirit." Following the authors of *Mapping Christian Education*, and other religious education texts, we can therefore find God's formative Life to be at work not just at the level of the individual, but also in close relationships, in larger communities and organizations, and even in the wider ecosystems and cultures of which we

1. Seymour, "Mapping Christian Education," 20–21.
2. Willard, *Renovation of the Heart*, 19; see also ibid., 45.

are all a part of. If this is so, then spiritual formation can be seen as more intentionally happening at these other levels as well.

As this book is written for those working primarily in congregational and non-profit organizations, as well as researchers and theorists in this field, I assert that there are three primary levels toward which our congregational spiritually formative efforts can be focused. These three levels can be thought of as ever widening circles of community and relationship: with ourselves, with one another, and with larger immediate communities, neighborhoods, and organizations of which we are a part. The picture below shows these three levels. While not comprehensive, these levels are intended to illustrate a more systematic view of spiritual formation than the one expressed above and to further emphasize the point that this field can, and perhaps should, be focused beyond merely the level of the individual.

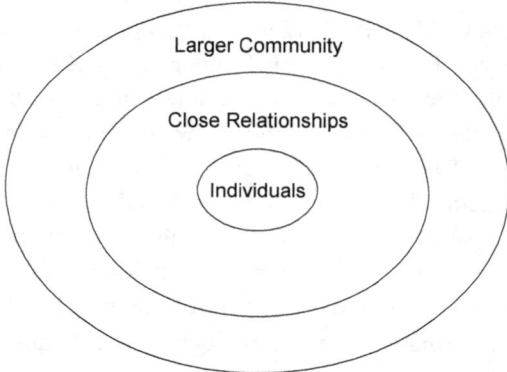

The first level is the one already mentioned, and that is the level of the individual. At this level, as the authors mentioned above have noted, our Western Christian focus is on individual persons and their growing personal life in the Spirit. It involves intentionality with both inner and outer aspects of each person's life for the purposes of helping them to grow in their personal spiritual life with God. It is a focus that is primarily concerned with each individual's private and public lives, helping them find and grow in their relationship with the God who is within, to, and beyond all that is, as we shall see in this book.

The second one is the level of close relationships and small groups. At this level, our spiritual formation efforts are focused more intentionally on the relationships that people have with one another. It is oriented toward nurturing relationships that are loving, just, giving, and healthy, attuned, intimate, etc.—i.e., relationships that are more reflective and manifesting of the Spirit. Such close relationships include the intimate ones we have with significant others, the mentoring partnerships that we choose, the small groups we are a part of, our families, etc. At this level, our formative focus is therefore on nurturing the life of God within and among these close relationships for, as we find Jesus to assert in the Gospel, "where two or three are gathered in my name, I am there with them."[3]

The third level that we can intentionally focus on in our local ministerial contexts, is the level of the wider community. For spiritual formators and pastors working in a church, this would mean focusing on the congregation as a whole. For leaders at a retreat center, this would be the large groups that come for a program. For those working in non-profits and engaging in community building and organizing efforts, this would be the organizations or neighborhoods they are working with. At this level, similar to the close relationship level, the focus lies in forming whole communities of justice, peace, harmony, order, compassion, et cetera for their political, social, and economic dimensions. Here, the minister's eyes are oriented not so much on the individuals, close relationships, and small groups that make up the community, though each of these are foundational, but rather more toward the overall dynamics of the larger community as a unified whole. This third level therefore focuses on the wider communities that we are in leadership with.

Of course, there are also even wider circles of influence and alternative formative foci that we can and should seek to address. We should seek to impact our cities, governments, and larger cultures. We need to actively pursue the health and vitality of our planet and its many, varied, and complex ecosystems. However, as spiritual formators working primarily in parishes and non-profits, many of us will formatively influence these wider circles mostly via our own local ministerial contexts. If we were a politician, however, then these wider circles could and should become the focus of our spiritually forming endeavors, for the Life of the Spirit, I believe, is active there as well. It is, however, these three levels—individuals, close relationships, and larger communities—that most spiritual formators will find themselves focused on in their congregational and non-profit or parachurch ministries.

Using this heuristic, and despite the intentional arguments for this broader understanding of spiritual formation, this book focuses at the level of the individual. Herein, we will be seeking to explore personal transformation as it has been systematically understood in the Western

---

3. Matt 18:20.

Christian tradition. While this work is congruent with the more narrow contemporary understandings of spiritual formation as being solely at the individual level, similar kinds of explorations are needed at the other levels as well. In the closing section of this book, we will hear of the need for much more research to be conducted in this growing field, particularly as an academic and more research-oriented discipline.

A Systematic Framework

At its heart, spiritual formation is essentially a feedback back system.[4] Feedback Theory has had wide ranging applications in such fields as engineering, theater and acting, and neuroscience-based approaches to formation.[5] In its most fundamental and simplified essence, "feedback processes," write professors of psychology Charles Carver and Michael Scheier, "involve the control and regulation of certain values within a system."[6] It is referred to as "Feedback Theory" because it is based on the assumption and/or observations that in order for a system to maintain or achieve these "certain values" it must have some way of monitoring its current values in relation to these desired ones. A very simple feedback loop may be pictured as follows:

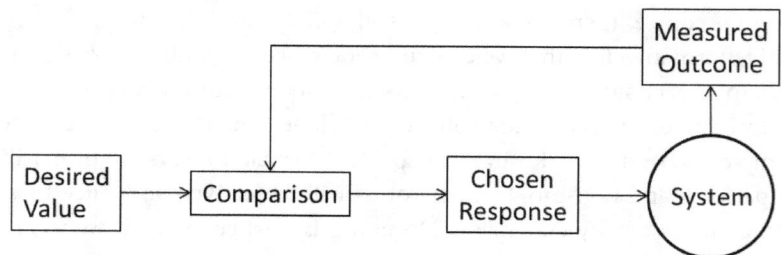

For example, a cruise control on a car must, through feedback, continually monitor the vehicle's speed in order to maintain the desired value set by the driver. If the car is traveling faster than this set speed, then the cruise control lets up on the gas. If the car is going too slow, it gives more

---

4. For discussions on the nature of feedback and its application to human systems, see such texts as Carver and Scheier, *On the Self-Regulation of Behavior*, chapter 2.

5. For examples of texts in these fields, see Franklin et al., *Feedback Control of Dynamic Systems*; Bilgrave and Deluty, "Stanislavski's Acting Method and Control Theory"; Dispenza, *Evolve your brain*, 292, 303, 26, 439–42.

6. Carver and Scheier, *On the Self-Regulation of Behavior*, 10.

Introduction

gas. In other words, the given system must have some way of gaining continuous feedback on what is currently happening so that it may compare this with the desired outcomes and appropriately alter its behaviors and actions in response.

In public education, for instance, there may be certain objectives that a teacher discerns are appropriate for her or his students. Based upon certain understandings of cognitive development, or other theories of human learning, she or he may then develop lesson plans of activities that are intended to help students to move toward these objectives. As most of us know, sometimes regretfully, educational classes do not stop here because the teacher is expected assess each student's progress. Tests, quizzes, projects, papers, reflection assignments, et cetera may be utilized toward these ends. Diagrammatically, this process might be envisioned to be something similar to the following:

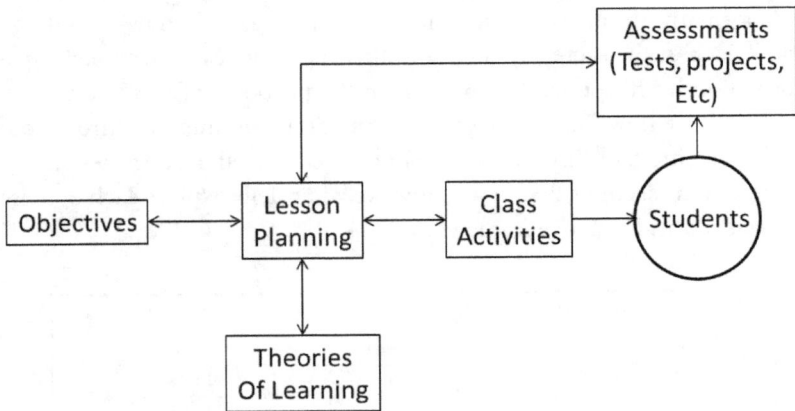

From this diagram, we can see that the educational objectives that a teacher has are central to her or his lesson planning as are the theories of learning that they are using. Based upon the planning and discernment processes that she or he practices, the activities that are used with the students are developed. Using a variety of assessments, the teacher then monitors and compares how students are doing in relation to the objectives that were chosen in the beginning. The outcomes of these assessments will therefore inform their ongoing lesson planning. As a result, the teacher might then decide to modify the objectives, alter their theories of learning, and/or utilize different class activities or even assessment tools. It is because these processes are at least partly dependent on the insights that assessments yield that they are a practical example of feedback theory in action.

In spiritual formation, we can likewise find this to be a basic architecture that may be used our field. Indeed, education may also be viewed as a spiritually formative activity.[7] Whether we're working with individuals, relationships, or communities, there is some set of ideals that we discern an invitation to partner with the Spirit to work toward. Given these goals, we then need to discern a set of approaches that we believe will help our constituents to grow toward/in them. As we engage in this formative work, we then need to continually monitor and evaluate the progress that is being made in relation to these ideals. This is the essence of all feedback loops. I therefore assert that the field of spiritual formation can be fundamentally approached as a feedback-oriented discipline.

Given this, we can propose a systematic "Formative Framework" for spiritual formation based upon feedback theory. The figure below captures this formative framework and will become the basis for how we will explore each of the sacred systems and their approaches to personal transformation in this book. Another one of the purposes of this book, then, is to explore how different spiritual formation communities throughout Western Christian history have embodied each of the categories shown below. In the sections that now follow, we will briefly explore each of these aspects of this formative framework.

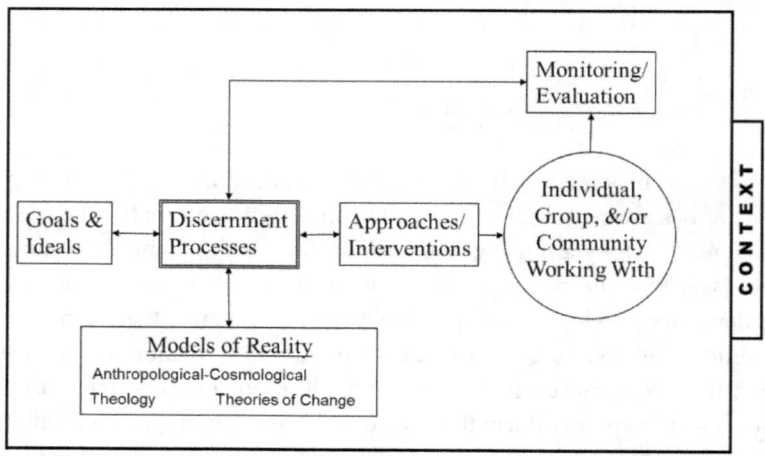

---

7. See such texts as Downs, *Teaching for Spiritual Growth*.

Introduction

Context

Context is, it seems, one of the most important aspects of any spiritual formation program, but also one of the most neglected or overlooked when developing spiritual formation programs. Especially in a historical study such as this one, it is very important to note the contextual influences of the time period and geographic location. As we shall see in the forthcoming chapters, spiritual formation programs sometimes are birthed and stand in both tension and harmony with the contemporary movements of their day. For instance, it has been asserted that the founder of the Society of Jesus religious order (more commonly known as the Jesuits), Ignatius of Loyola, formulated his Spiritual Exercises in light of and sometimes in opposition to the humanistic and Protestant Reformation movements of his day.[8] Someone studying his Exercises might not be aware of this and therefore not be able to fully appreciate how they were, in some ways, an attempt to meet the needs raised by these contextual factors from a distinctively Roman Catholic perspective.

It is therefore essential, in studying spiritual formation programs, that one understands, at least in a basic way, the contextual factors that contributed to the development and implementation of the program. These factors should include: 1) Who the programs are created for; 2) Who the approaches stand in opposition to (if applicable); and 3) Which movements, contemporarily and historically, the program embraces and to what extent.

Models of Reality

Of all of the categories that we will be considering for this historically explorative project, we can expect this to be the most diverse. Such diversity can be seen between 'post-structuralist' notions that view reality as nothing more than a "convergence among culturally and historically specific sets of relations,"[9] and others, such as Paul of Tarsus, who assert a "divine innateness" that is the presence of God's Spirit within us.[10] To help unpack and more clearly understand such diversity among the theories that are relevant for spiritual formation, we will explore three specific aspects of these models: Anthropological-Cosmological, Theological, and Theories

---

8. Modras, *Ignatian Humanism*.
9. Butler, *Gender Trouble*, 14. See also Sartre, *Nausea*, 25.
10. Paul, "Letter to the Romans," 63.

Sacred Systems

of Change. Each of these Models of Reality essentially strives to explain the nature of life, cosmos, the Divine, and transformation. These models form, as we shall see, a foundation of knowledge out of which spiritual formation systems emerge in dialogue with.

Anthropological-Cosmological Aspects

These aspects are fundamentally concerned with describing, explaining, modeling, et cetera the dynamics and complex interrelationships within creation. I term these aspects "anthropological-cosmological" because these models of reality often seek to detail both what happens within and among humans (anthropology), the happenings of creation as a whole (cosmology), and the intimate interconnections between the two. At the level of the individual, these would include the views of human nature that one has. For relationships, these models might describe what intimate relationships are and the complex interpersonal dynamics that accompany them. Such models, in the sacred systems that we will be exploring herein, will also include discussions of other realms of the cosmos, angels and demons, etc. Anthro-cosmological models therefore seek to explain the nature of life as it is being lived here on earth in relation to the wider cosmos of which we are all a part of.

Theological Aspects

While the anthro-cosmological aspects might detail the dynamics of individuals, relationships, communities, and creation as a whole, they do not necessarily or directly address the Divine or the God's relationship to them. We may therefore consider theological aspects as distinct from those models. Theological models are therefore taken to address the essence and nature of the Divine and seek to describe how God is present to creation and how creation relates to God. Even though not all spiritual formation systems might explicitly address these theological aspects, as we shall see with one of our contemporary "non-theistic" systems, I assert that all of them inherently have a theology contained within them as we shall see. It is therefore the intention of these reflections to uncover the explicit and implicit theologies that under gird the sacred systems that we will be reviewing.

Introduction

Theories of Change

Finally, we come to what is one of the most important parts of any spiritual formation program. Spiritual formation is fundamentally concerned with fostering some kind of intentional change in creation. In order to do this, however, one must have an understanding of how such changes occur and the processes by which they come about. Any models that address this are what I call "Theories of Change." Often, they flow directly from the anthro-cosmological models that one has. However, since spiritual formation is fundamentally a field that is focused on nurturing change, it is given a specific and separate focus here. These models are, therefore, a central part of what informs the discernment of what practices, actions, and guidance to offer to persons, relationships, and communities at any given time. These theories of change are therefore a necessary and integral part of any effective spiritual formation program.

Spiritual Formation Ideals & Goals

Most every spiritual formation program has a set of ideals and goals that they are actively seeking to nurture their constituency toward. Most, if not all, spiritual formation programs that I have both learned about and worked with over the years have some set of ideals, transformations, et cetera that their practices, theologies, worldviews, and communities are intentionally striving after. Some of these goals may be anthro-cosmologically based, such as emotional well-being, relational vitality, transpersonal development, or even "non-dualistic development" as found in Zen Buddhism.[11] Others may be more theologically centered, such as for Alfred who is seeking a more Christ-centered life. One of the keys to this category is therefore that each community is able to articulate the goals they are explicitly working toward and then to seek to tangibly move in those directions. It is therefore important to identify, as clearly as possible, what these horizons include.

Spiritual Formation Approaches

This is perhaps the most obvious of all of the categories. Every spiritual formation system seeks to bring about intentional, positive change through the use of specific approaches. Some of these approaches may be practices

---

11. For example, see Abe and LaFleur, *Zen and Western Thought*.

Sacred Systems

that nurture the general transformation of the individual, relationship, or community (such as worship services) or they may be very focused, such as meditative techniques that are intended to bring about specific states of consciousness.[12] These approaches, when utilized effectively, are chosen as a result of one's discernment processes and are intended to move one's constituency toward the intended goals. It therefore behooves us to explore the range of approaches to personal transformation that each of the sacred systems that we will be exploring utilizes.

Discernment

Just as lesson planning is for an educator, spiritual discernment should be the centerpiece for all formative endeavors in theistic ministries (i.e., those that have a concept of God as a central part of their worldveiws). For instance, once a community sets up a set of goals to work toward, they must then develop ways of discerning how to go about moving toward them. Spiritual discernment is absolutely essential in this, I assert, because each community's journey toward these ideals is as unique as they are. How does one know which practices to use for each person, relationship, et cetera at different stages of their journey? How does a minister, such as Alfred, know if someone in there group is experiencing a "dark night of the soul" or depression?[13] I assert that spiritual formators must develop methods and approaches to discern and answer such questions. They must therefore do so as they seek to guide their flock along the spiritual path ever moving in harmony with the unending and all-pervasive movements of God. As a result, we will be seeking to uncover some of the underlying processes and approaches to discernment that these different sacred systems seem to use.

Evaluative Techniques

As we have heard, the whole field of spiritual formation is one that inherently sets out to bring about some sort of intentional transformation. In order to do this, ministers must therefore have some ways of monitoring and evaluating the progress (or lack of), that their individuals, relationships,

---

12. For instance, see Anderson, "Intuitive Inquiry."

13. For discussions on this issue, see such texts as O'Connor, "Spiritual Dark Night and Psychological Depression"; May, *Dark Night of the Soul*.

Introduction

and communities are making. Doing so enables spiritual formators to provide better direction to their constituents and to continually modify their approaches in well-informed and clearly discerned ways. In addition, since discernment is inherently rooted in knowledge, this further establishes the need for effective techniques for observing and evaluating the Life of the Spirit within and to the moment-by-moment dynamics of the people that we are working with. For each of the sacred systems that we will be exploring, we will therefore be reflecting on the monitoring and evaluation techniques that they suggest and use.

Summary/Reflections

This formative framework seems to capture many of the essential aspects of any spiritual formation system. It is intended to provide a more systematic way of exploring sacred systems at any of the levels (individual, relational, etc.). As we shall see, this framework will provide us with insights into how each of its various aspects are interconnected with one another. By using it as a guideline for our explorations, we will see how the Models of Reality give rise to the Approaches that are utilized. We will note how the Ideals form the core of each sacred system. And we will better understand the nature and essence of each sacred system by stepping back and looking at each one's framework as a whole. In short, this formative framework is therefore intended to provide a systematic way of both exploring and learning from each of the systems that we will be considering in this book. As a result, it will be the foundational lens through which we view each personal transformation system herein.

THE SYSTEMATIC EXPLORATION AHEAD

With this formative framework in place, we finally turn to trying to identify what some of the major spiritual formation communities and movements throughout history have been so that we might identify which sacred systems of personal transformation to focus on for this exploration. To help us to do this, we turn to a series of different texts on the history of Christian spirituality.[14] Our hopes here are to identify the major and

---

14. Dupré, Saliers, and Meyendorff, eds., *Christian Spirituality*; Louth, *Origins of the Christian Mystical Tradition*; McGinn and Meyendorff, eds., *Christian Spirituality*; Raitt, McGinn, and Meyendorff, eds., *Christian Spirituality*; Rausch, *Radical Christian Communities*.

diverse movements of Western Christian spiritual formation throughout its history. These texts will not only serve as the source for our choices, but also as additional reference books for the exploration itself. Each of these texts covers major Western Christian spiritual movements, communities, and persons. From them, the following are the primary eras and movements that are addressed:

- Pre- & Contemporary non-Christian Influences (BCE–first century CE)
  - Greco-Roman
  - Jewish
- Jesus & the Early Christian Church (first–third centuries CE)
  - Diverse Communities (Matthew's, Luke's, Johannine, etc.)
  - Gnosticism
  - Martyrdom
- Early Monasticism (second–eleventh centuries CE)
  - Early Mothers & Fathers (Desert, Latin, & Eastern)
  - Monastic Communities (East, West, & Syriac Speaking)
  - Gregorian Reforms
  - Insular Traditions (Celtic & Germanic)
- Medieval & Renaissance (twelfth–sixteenth centuries CE)
  - Mendicants
  - Late Scholasticism
  - Medieval Mysticism
  - Devotio Moderna
  - Humanism
- Reformation (sixteenth–nineteenth centuries CE)
  - Protestantism
    - European
    - English
    - Americas
  - Roman Catholic
    - Counter Reformation
    - New Movements (French & Spanish)

- Orthodox/Eastern
  - Hesychast
  - Russian
- Modernity
- Contemporary (nineteenth century–today)
  - Mainline Protestant & Anglican
  - Evangelical Protestant (Pentecostal, Charismatic & Fundamentalism)
  - Roman Catholic
  - Eastern Orthodox
  - Unity Movements (Ecumenical, Interfaith, Liberation, New Age & Post-Modern)

From this, we can see that there is quite a bit more than what we could fully or adequately cover in a single book. As we move through the section introductions ahead, we will discuss which specific communities were chosen. With the need for systematics identified, a systematic landscape and formative framework laid out, and the major eras and movements identified, we are now ready to begin this informative walk through this history of personal transformation in the Western Christian tradition. Not only are we seeking theoretical insights into the nature of this field, but also for practical guidance on how we might further develop and refine our own sacred systems in the hopes that ministers such as Alfred might benefit from these endeavors.

PART ONE

Early Non-Christian Influences

THERE WERE TWO PRIMARY contextual influences that helped to shape the early Christian church. The first obvious influence was Judaism.[1] Jesus was a Jew as were his closest disciples. The primary scriptures and liturgies from which the early Christians drew were adopted from the Jewish religious tradition. Indeed, authors of Christian spirituality acknowledge that it is difficult, if not impossible, to understand the early church apart from this influence.

The second major influence of this early era that helped to shape Christian spiritual formation was the larger Greco-Roman culture of which both Christians and Jews were a part of.[2] The Roman Empire was a vast and powerful presence in this part of the world. As we shall see with Philo of Alexandria, the Empire had a system of Hellenization wherein its citizens were educated into Roman culture. Not only was the Empire prolific in the spread of its laws and religious practices, but also its philosophies as well, for which Platonism and its variations were central.[3] In addition, more and more converts to Christianity were "Gentiles," or non-Jews. This meant that the early church not only needed to address these new converts and speak to them in symbols, philosophies, and practices that they could understand but also that the beliefs and practices of Christianity would increasingly be formulated by them. For instance, Origen formulated his stages of the spiritual life in neoplatonic terms.[4] The

---

1. Burridge, "Jesus and the Origins of Christianity," 12; Sheldrake, *Brief History of Spirituality*, 13; Woods, *Christian Spirituality*, 4.

2. McGuckin, "The Early Church Fathers (1st to 6th Centuries)," 44–45; Sheldrake, *Brief History of Spirituality*, 27; Woods, *Christian Spirituality*, 48.

3. Chidester, *Christianity*, 5; Sheldrake, *Brief History of Spirituality*, 27, 31.

4. Sheldrake, *Brief History of Spirituality*, 35.

PART ONE: Early Non-Christian Influences

influence of Greco-Roman culture on early Christian spiritual formation can therefore not be overlooked.

Given these wider influences, it will therefore be helpful to better understand how personal transformation was understood by parts of these alternative traditions. While there are a few forms of personal transformation that we might look at, such as moral formation in Roman culture,[5] we have chosen two to focus on. For better insights into a Jewish view of personal spiritual formation, we turn to Philo of Alexandria and two of his short works: "Every Good Man Is Free" and "On the Contemplative Life or Supplicants." While, as we shall see, Philo might not be considered by some to be classically Jewish in a traditional sense because he was a Hellenized Jew, his works did go on to influence many early Christian thinkers such as Clement and Origen of Alexandria.[6]

A second text that we will be turning to is *The Mysteries of the Egyptians, Chaldeans, and Assyrians* by Iamblichus. This piece is very characteristic of some of the neoplatonic views of this era, many of which influenced early Christianity, particularly early monasticism as we shall see in the next part of this book. Not only, then, will Iamblichus' work provide us with insights into these worldviews, but it will also represent a very different systematic approach to personal transformation. It is therefore to these two sets of writings that we will now turn to in order to help us better understand the cultural contexts in which early Christian personal spiritual formation developed within.

---

5. For instance, see Malherbe, *Moral Exhortation*; Fitzgerald, *Passions and Moral Progress in Greco-Roman Thought*.

6. Jones et al., *The Study of Spirituality*, 95.

1

Philo of Alexandria's Contemplative Life

CONTEXT

OUR HISTORICAL JOURNEY BEGINS with Philo of Alexandria (20 BCE—50 CE). Philo was a wealthy Jew living in Alexandria and was a contemporary of Jesus and the early Christians.[1] Even though he was a devout Jew who defended his tradition, Philo was thoroughly "Hellenized," meaning that he was schooled in the Greco-Roman culture of his time, and he is considered to stand in the tradition of Middle Platoism. This brand of Platonism is considered to have a much clearer conception of God than did Plato.

In *Every Good Man Is Free*, Philo is speaking against those "who are slaves to opinions utterly under the influence of the outward senses"[2] and against those who "hesitate to get rid of that disease of the soul, ignorance."[3] Alternatively, in his text, *On the Contemplative Life*, Philo describes the life of monks who live in the desert and compares it to contemporary Hellenistic lifestyle, particularly as found among the rich during his day.[4] Both of these texts therefore seek to discuss what the nature of true soul freedom is all about, and how one may go about pursuing such a life. These two short texts by Philo therefore give us some insights into how personal transformation was conceived by him and therefore help us

1. Louth, *Origins of the Christian Mystical Tradition*, 17.
2. Philo of Alexandria, "Every Good Man Is Free," 11.
3. Ibid., 12, 55, 158.
4. Philo of Alexandria, "On the Contemplative Life or Supplicants," 20–21, 40–59.

PART ONE: Early Non-Christian Influences

to further understand how other contemporaries of the early Christians approached spiritual formation.

MODELS OF REALITY

Anthropological-Cosmological

Philo's anthropology in these two texts is fairly dualistic in nature. He asserts that the Greek heroes are of a higher nature than humans[5] and that every wicked person is a slave.[6] He asserts that there are two kinds of slavery: that of the soul and that of the body.[7] For those of the body, these include the wickedness and passions that people follow[8] as well as the anger and appetites to which people are slaves.[9] It is these enslavements that lead to the sufferings and tragedies in life, according to Philo,[10] and such things as covetousness, desire for glory, et cetera block our freedom and liberation from them.[11] For instance, Philo cites the great evils of those who molest young boys, something that was common in his day, to both the boys themselves as well as to society as a whole.[12]

In spite of such natural inclinations to slavery, Philo also asserts that no one is willingly a slave.[13] Women are therefore also included in the pursuit of freedom and virtue too,[14] and he directly addresses the common view of the caste system but nevertheless asserts that anyone is able to become free even though they might still be slaves in society.[15] Freedom from all forms of inner slavery is therefore central to Philo's anthro-cosmology.

Achieving freedom comes with education, knowledge, and reason, asserts Philo.[16] In discussing the impurities and slaveries of people, he writes, "Now when I speak of men not being pure, I mean those who have

5. Philo of Alexandria, "Every Good Man Is Free," 105.
6. Ibid., 1.
7. Ibid., 17.
8. Ibid., 17, 31.
9. Ibid., 45, 55–56, 57, 159.
10. Ibid., 55–56.
11. Ibid., 21.
12. Philo of Alexandria, "On the Contemplative Life or Supplicants," 60–62.
13. Philo of Alexandria, "Every Good Man Is Free," 36.
14. Philo of Alexandria, "On the Contemplative Life or Supplicants," 32, 68.
15. Philo of Alexandria, "Every Good Man Is Free," 35, 38–39.
16. Ibid., 46, 55.

either been utterly destitute of education, or else who have tasted of it obliquely, and not in a straight-forward manner, changing the stamp of the beauty of wisdom so as to give an impression of the unsightliness of sophistry."[17] For him, being enslaved and impure is related to one "not being able to discern that light that is appreciable only by the intellect."[18] Reason is therefore considered to be the "unerring law" and the "invisible mind" is asserted to be the true person.[19] As noted above, it is through the use of the intellect that virtues are acquired.[20] By acquiring virtue, humans become of a higher nature[21] for virtue protects one from attacks because it is an invincible fortification.[22]

To summarize and clarify, Philo asserts that when we allow ourselves to succumb to the passions and base desires of the bodies into which we have been born, we are enslaved and all manner of evil and suffering hence come forth. It is only the intellect, which is the higher part of ourself, that can liberate us from this inner bondage. Despite this obvious path to freedom and virtue, Philo finds the state of affairs in his day to be bleak as he asserts that "whatever is exceedingly beautiful is rare,"[23] the number of communities and people who are virtuous are rare,[24] and that cities are generally places of vice.[25] Nonetheless, there is hope as there are many in different cultures who are recognized and venerated as being virtuous according to Philo.[26] Such seems to comprise the general anthro-cosmology that Philo is working with in these two texts as he explores the growing personal life of freedom and virtue.

17. Ibid., 4.
18. Ibid., 5.
19. Philo of Alexandria, "Every Good Man Is Free," 46, 111.
20. Ibid., 106–7; Philo of Alexandria, "On the Contemplative Life or Supplicants," 26.
21. Philo of Alexandria, "Every Good Man Is Free," 129, 35.
22. Ibid., 151.
23. Ibid., 63.
24. Ibid., 63, 72.
25. Philo of Alexandria, "On the Contemplative Life or Supplicants," 19.
26. Philo of Alexandria, "Every Good Man Is Free," 74; Philo of Alexandria, "On the Contemplative Life or Supplicants," 21.

PART ONE: Early Non-Christian Influences

Theological

We have already seen how, for Philo, virtue protects one from attacks for it is an invincible fortification[27] and is a sure guide and defender.[28] Virtue is also the regulator of the whole of one's life and we need not fear because of it.[29] Philo goes on to assert that the love of freedom is firmly established in the soul[30] and the soul is able to distinguish between truth and falsehood.[31]

But where is God in all of this for Philo? How is God related to virtue and the soul? While he does not discuss the nature and role of God at length in these short texts, he does assert that the Creator has laid the roots of virtue very near—deep within us.[32] God, for Philo, gives divine guidance and revelation to people as well as divine inspiration[33] and God makes this nature of freedom to "never be subdued by external circumstances."[34] Finally, God is viewed by Philo as being "superior to the good, and more simple than the one, and more ancient than the unit"[35] and is the supreme Creator of all matter.[36]

Without stating it in so many words, God for Philo seems to be at least at the root of all freedom and virtue, as well as being active in creation as a whole. His portrayal of the desert monks, discussed below in the Spiritual Formation Approaches section, shows that one must strive to ever more fully be attentive to God in their growing life of freedom and virtue.

Theories of Change

As already discussed several times above, Philo is quite clear on how change comes about. Change has the goal of freeing one from their many enslavements through the acquisition and use of reason, education, and

---

27. Philo of Alexandria, "Every Good Man Is Free," 151.
28. Ibid., 152.
29. Ibid., 154.
30. Ibid., 113, 23.
31. Philo of Alexandria, "On the Contemplative Life or Supplicants," 10.
32. Philo of Alexandria, "Every Good Man Is Free," 68.
33. Ibid., 80.
34. Ibid., 149.
35. Philo of Alexandria, "On the Contemplative Life or Supplicants," 2.
36. Ibid., 4–5.

virtue.[37] It is by acquiring these that humans become of a higher nature.[38] By living such lives of contemplation and virtue, we can become citizens of higher and better living.[39] Such, for Philo, is the basis and nature of change, to retrain one's self to live ever more in accordance with the education, wisdom, reason, and virtue that we are growing into and thereby achieve the freedom that our souls inherently long for.[40]

However, this change does not come overnight. Change toward steadfastness in these comes about by a long hardening process where one is repeatedly tried and tested[41] through the fortification of reasoning[42] and through training up of one's self intentionally and over a long course of time.[43] There is therefore a need to slowly nurture people, step-by-step, into their freedom.[44] And it is through training, as the Essences and desert monks approached it, that freedom can be attained.[45] Philo's views of transformation therefore take a long-term perspective, one that requires the reordering and retraining of one's entire life from the inner slaveries discussed above.

Spiritual Formation Ideals & Goals

In both of these texts, Philo's hopes are of illustrating a better way of life than what is found in his contemporary Greco-Roman world, especially in the cities.[46] As a result, he spends some time describing what the ideal person is and how they live. Knowledge is asserted to be the goal of humankind,[47] with speculative philosophy being among the most beautiful and divine pursuits.[48] In *Every Good Man is Free*, Philo expends some

37. Philo of Alexandria, "Every Good Man Is Free," 46, 55, 109, 51–52.
38. Ibid., 129, 35.
39. Philo of Alexandria, "On the Contemplative Life or Supplicants," 90.
40. Philo of Alexandria, "Every Good Man Is Free," 36.
41. Ibid., 26.
42. Ibid., 27.
43. Ibid., 111.
44. Ibid., 160.
45. Ibid., 88, 106–7; Philo of Alexandria, "On the Contemplative Life or Supplicants," 20, 24, 30.
46. Philo of Alexandria, "Every Good Man Is Free," 63, 76, 84; Philo of Alexandria, "On the Contemplative Life or Supplicants," 20, 24, 30, 60–62.
47. Philo of Alexandria, "Every Good Man Is Free," 12, 14.
48. Philo of Alexandria, "On the Contemplative Life or Supplicants," 67.

effort in describing the ideal person as being truly free and what this really means. Such a free person is one who is independent,[49] the one for whom God alone is their leader,[50] and who cannot be compelled to do anything against their own free will.[51] They are people who are free from inner slavery to evils,[52] those who boldly speak out on behalf of their own freedom,[53] and those who have learned to disregard the commands of the "unlawful masters of the soul" (i.e., distorted temptations) and are free even from the fear of death.[54]

Such freedom Philo asserts is equally applied to slaves for even slaves can become masters of their masters in these inward ways.[55] Such freedom can be seen in those who have chosen death over slavery[56] and in those who choose not to have slaves because of their dedication to this freedom for all people.[57] For Philo, one is free when they can adapt their "circumstances and actions to the present occasion" and have an enduring spirit despite the good or bad of whatever may befall her or him.[58] They are those who can remain steadfast no matter what evils or threats may come[59] and they resist those who seek to guide and control them.[60] In short, achieving such freedom in one's self is a pinnacle for Philo's framework of personal transformation.

The achievement of virtue also holds a central place for Philo as an ideal to be sought after. He asserts that fame is sometimes "founded on the deeds of virtue deliberately performed, which very naturally make immortal those who practice them in a guileless spirit."[61] The wise only desire that which proceeds from virtue[62] and they do them voluntarily and

---

49. Philo of Alexandria, "Every Good Man Is Free," 19, 62.
50. Ibid., 20, 62.
51. Ibid., 60, 95–97.
52. Ibid., 64.
53. Ibid., 148–49.
54. Ibid., 22.
55. Ibid., 35, 104.
56. Ibid., 114–35.
57. Ibid., 143; Philo of Alexandria, "On the Contemplative Life or Supplicants," 70.
58. Philo of Alexandria, "Every Good Man Is Free," 24.
59. Ibid., 25–31.
60. Ibid., 40.
61. Ibid., 109.
62. Ibid., 60.

avoid all wickedness.⁶³ Such virtuous living is related to freedom for Philo when he writes, "a man is happy inasmuch as he bears within himself the foundation and complement of virtue and excellence, in which consists supreme power over all things, so that beyond all controversy and of necessity the virtuous man is free."⁶⁴ Virtuous people are also skillful in all the affairs that belong to life⁶⁵ and they do everything wisely⁶⁶ pursuing only the works of peace⁶⁷ and giving up their possessions to help humankind.⁶⁸ Virtue is seen by Philo as procuring God's love and attaining "the very summit and perfection of happiness."⁶⁹

Being a devout Jew himself, Philo turns to communities in his own religious tradition as examples of such virtuous and free living. He asserts that the Jews, who are possessed by the love of God and serve the living God, are no longer human but of God.⁷⁰ The Essences, for example, are those whom no one has been able to find anything wrong with them, but rather they have been seen by others as being truly free and rich (though materially poor).⁷¹ Finally, in a culture where banquets of drunkenness, violence, extravagance, use of slaves, indulgences, and entertainment are common place, all of which are revolting to Philo,⁷² he looks to those of the contemplative life and of those who truly love one another as being the more superior way of life.⁷³ For Philo, the love of God is the truer intoxicating "pure wine" of life.⁷⁴ Hence, do we find in Philo the centrality of cultivating true freedom, virtue, and the love of God for his views of one's positively developing personal spiritual life.

---

63. Ibid., 61.
64. Ibid., 41.
65. Ibid., 50.
66. Ibid., 59.
67. Ibid., 78.
68. Philo of Alexandria, "On the Contemplative Life or Supplicants," 14, 16.
69. Ibid., 90.
70. Philo of Alexandria, "Every Good Man Is Free," 43.
71. Ibid., 77, 91.
72. Philo of Alexandria, "On the Contemplative Life or Supplicants," 40–58.
73. Ibid., 59.
74. Ibid., 85.

PART ONE: Early Non-Christian Influences

SPIRITUAL FORMATION APPROACHES

Between both of these texts, Philo does spend some time discussing the approaches that can be used in helping one to move toward the ideals and goals he sets out above. These approaches seem to fall into at least five broad categories. The first category that he seems to address throughout these texts is the importance of community. For Philo, there is a need for associating with wise persons[75] and a need to withdrawal from the vices of the cities in order to contemplate and focus more fully on the virtuous life.[76] In *Every Good Man is Free*, he uses the Essences as an example of such a model of communal life. They are people who live in villages and shun cities in order to avoid its lawlessness[77] and they share all of their property in common and help one another as needed.[78] It is through such communal living that freedom is fostered and virtuousness cultivated.

The second broad category of approaches that Philo appears to address is wise spiritual guidance and education.[79] The eldest and wisest are to teach everyone else[80] while those who listen must do so with attentiveness to those who teach.[81] In the case of the Essences, Philo asserts that they sit and eagerly listen to elders of the community,[82] who explain scripture,[83] as well as teach about piety, holiness, justice, economy, politics, and what is good and what is bad. They do all of this in terms of the love of God, virtue, and humankind.[84] They also study moral philosophy[85] and look to their sacred texts as the source of wisdom and right living.[86] In his text, *On the Contemplative Life*, Philo further notes that the desert monks he is describing make use of the writings and examples of previous

75. Philo of Alexandria, "Every Good Man Is Free," 12, 30, 63; Philo of Alexandria, "On the Contemplative Life or Supplicants," 24.

76. Philo of Alexandria, "Every Good Man Is Free," 63; Philo of Alexandria, "On the Contemplative Life or Supplicants," 20, 24, 30.

77. Philo of Alexandria, "Every Good Man Is Free," 76.

78. Ibid., 85–87.

79. Ibid., 4, 12, 15, 54, 64; Philo of Alexandria, "On the Contemplative Life or Supplicants," 25.

80. Philo of Alexandria, "On the Contemplative Life or Supplicants," 31.

81. Ibid., 76–77.

82. Philo of Alexandria, "Every Good Man Is Free," 81.

83. Ibid., 82.

84. Ibid., 83.

85. Ibid., 80.

86. Ibid., 84.

the wise persons of their community so that they may imitate them.[87] It is this turning to the wise and experienced elders of one's community that the free and virtuous life is further nurtured.

The third broad category that can be seen emerging from these two texts is related to how one practically and tangibly lives their life. For Philo, wisdom and knowledge are not enough; one must also live their life properly.[88] As a result, one needs to be very active in life in cultivating their maturing life.[89] They need to nurture the tree which bears the fruits of wisdom, justice, courage, and temperance.[90] As a result, laziness and indolence are seen by Philo to destroy the seeds of virtue.[91] The Essences pursue works of peace,[92] have no slaves among them,[93] and seek to avoid all evils in life.[94] The desert monks, on the other hand, practice simplicity as the foundation of truth and therefore have adopted a simplicity in clothing, dwelling, and food.[95] Additionally, their feasts are simple compared to those he describes in the surrounding Hellenistic culture,[96] they live completely sober lives,[97] and they are even sometimes vegetarians.[98] These approaches all emphasize the concreteness and practicality of how they live out their virtuous life and are therefore central for Philo's approaches to nurturing such positive personal development.

The fourth category is related to asceticism. On this, Philo asserts that people have attained virtue by "looking on their bodies as if they belonged to strangers, or even to enemies . . .for through the love of knowledge having accustomed their souls from the very beginning to keep aloof from all participation with the passions, and to cling to education and wisdom."[99]

---

87. Philo of Alexandria, "On the Contemplative Life or Supplicants," 29.
88. Philo of Alexandria, "Every Good Man Is Free," 14.
89. Ibid., 69.
90. Ibid., 70.
91. Ibid., 71.
92. Ibid., 78.
93. Ibid., 79.
94. Ibid., 84.
95. Philo of Alexandria, "On the Contemplative Life or Supplicants," 38.
96. Ibid., 66–89.
97. Ibid., 74.
98. Ibid., 73.
99. Philo of Alexandria, "Every Good Man Is Free," 106–7.

Philo therefore emphasizes the need to keep the wicked passions of the body in check as one attains to the virtuous and truly free life.[100]

Turning to the desert monks, he claims that temperance is the foundation for all other virtues,[101] that fasting a common practice,[102] and that they strive to oppose "those feelings which nature has made mistresses of the human race, namely, hunger and thirst."[103] He also notes that some of the women monks are virgins out of love of wisdom.[104] Philo seems to be asserting, perhaps in response to the evils and ignorance of his day and culture, that asceticism is a necessary part of any growth in the free and virtuous life that he argues in support of.

The fifth and final category that is central to Philo's approaches to the maturing personal spiritual life is devotional practices. These practices were discussed most directly in *On the Contemplative Life*. Each desert monk, Philo asserts, has a sacred shrine in their home.[105] They try to keep their mind ever stayed on God, the divine virtues, and the divine powers, so much so that they are reported to even recite the "celebrated doctrines of the sacred philosophy" in their sleep.[106] One of their primary goals is to ever give thanks to God.[107] These monks engage in intentional prayer twice a day, once in the morning and once at night,[108] and devote their days to meditation and the practice of virtues and the rumination on scriptures and philosophies.[109] They have the desire to serve in the pursuit of the perfection of virtues[110] and they join together once a week for feast and fellowship,[111] and the singing of hymns together.[112] It is this well ordered life of devotion and contemplation, Philo asserts, that greatly helps them progress in the life of virtue and freedom.[113]

---

100. Ibid., 17, 31.
101. Philo of Alexandria, "On the Contemplative Life or Supplicants," 34.
102. Ibid., 35.
103. Ibid., 37.
104. Ibid., 68.
105. Ibid., 25.
106. Ibid., 26.
107. Ibid., 66.
108. Ibid., 27.
109. Ibid., 28.
110. Ibid., 72.
111. Ibid., 66–89.
112. Ibid., 84.
113. Ibid., 90.

Discernment

Of all the categories, this one is the least addressed in these two works of Philo. Nevertheless, he does assert that "the unerring law is right reason . . . one imperishable, and stamped by immoral nature on the immortal mind."[114] He also claims that the wise only desire that which proceeds from virtue[115] and that we must investigate the nature of the soul[116] in order to proceed in life and that one's work with others must be based upon the current stage of their development.[117]

As we can see from above, Philo seems to uphold the Platonic view that knowledge and reason are the primary goals of life.[118] Philo's approach to discernment seems to be one that is thoroughly rooted in one sitting in contemplation and using reason to decide how one should proceed in their spiritually maturing life. Indeed, Philo asserts that it is a life of contemplation of nature that makes one a citizen of heaven and of the world and therefore helps them to become "very acceptable to the Father and Creator of the universe."[119] It therefore appears that the faculties of reason and contemplation are the primary basis for Philo's approach to discerning how one should proceed along each step of their growing personal spiritual life.

Evaluative Techniques

As with Discernment, this category is not directly addressed by Philo. However, he does spend some length, especially in *Every Good Man is Free*, in discussing whether one is or is not virtuous based on the fruits of their actions. For example, he cites a number of examples of the many people who have chosen freedom over slavery and are therefore known by their actions to be truly free.[120] He also discusses the many poor governors and people who are given to passions and evil as clear examples of those who are not free.[121] I would therefore assert, that his primary mode of

---

114. Philo of Alexandria, "Every Good Man Is Free," 46.
115. Ibid., 60.
116. Ibid., 158.
117. Ibid., 160.
118. Ibid., 12, 14.
119. Philo of Alexandria, "On the Contemplative Life or Supplicants," 90.
120. Philo of Alexandria, "Every Good Man Is Free," 35, 50, 59, 74, 114–35.
121. Ibid., 4–5.

PART ONE: Early Non-Christian Influences

evaluating the spiritual progress of others is through observations of how they are concretely living their lives.

SUMMARY/REFLECTIONS

In summary, as the figure below shows, these two brief texts have provided useful insights into how Philo views and approaches personal spiritual formation. It is particularly interesting to see how he has blended Platonic anthropologies, of higher and lower selves, with the pursuits of freedom and virtue found in the Essence and desert monk communities. In essence, Philo has to some degree united elements of his Jewish religion with some Greco-Roman anthro-cosmological concepts. When we move on to early Christian approaches to personal transformation, we will continue to find this kind of melding happening for some of these communities as well. We should also note that the formation approaches Philo highlights are fairly comprehensive and that they are directly related to the ideals and goals he sets up. Overall, Philo offers a fairly well integrated systematic view of spiritual formation at the individual level.

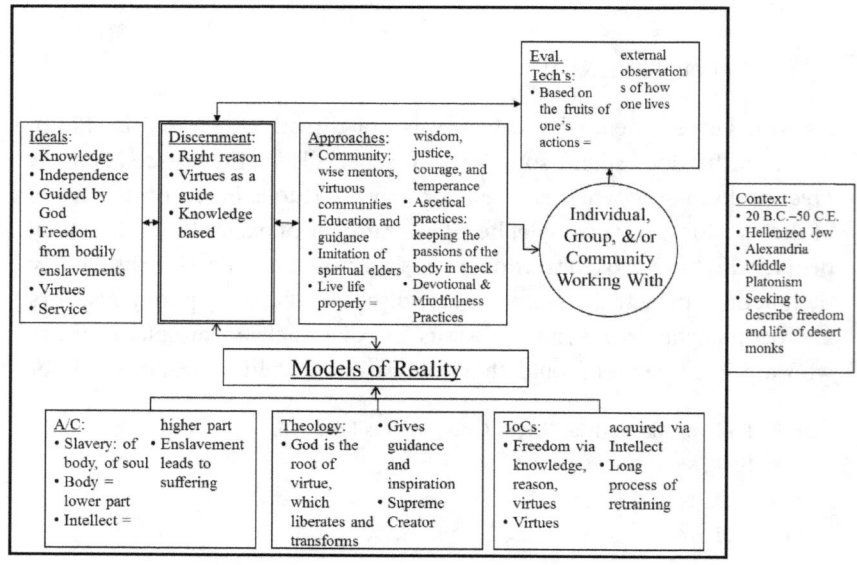

2

Iamblichus and the Mysteries

Context

WE CONTINUE OUR EXPLORATORY journey with Iamblichus (245–325 CE) who was a student of Plotinus and therefore a Neoplatonist, which was a popular Greco-Roman philosophical school during this time period. In his work *De Mysteriis Aegyptiorum* (On the Mysteries of the Egyptians), Iamblichus responds to a letter from one of Plotinus' other students, Porphyry, refuting the notion that contemplation alone can help one to achieve "divinization."[1] Instead, Iamblichus asserts that it is the neoplatonic rituals and one's interactions with angels (called *theurgy*, or magic, which is using rituals, plants, and animals to influence higher beings) that achieves this.[2]

In the letter to which Iamblichus is responding, Porphyry questions both the existence of lower gods and demons as well as the theurgists invocation of the lower gods for help, as well as their methods.[3] He questions what the connections are between the invisible, incorporeal gods and more visible and corporeal gods and demons[4] that were common in Greco-Roman religions. Porphyry also asks what divination is and how it is affected.[5] He also requests that some of "mystic" symbols be explained

1. Iamblichus, *Mysteries of the Egyptians*.
2. Louth, *Origins of the Christian Mystical Tradition*, 157.
3. Iamblichus, *Mysteries of the Egyptians*, 1–2, 8.
4. Ibid., 3–4.
5. Ibid., 5–7.

PART ONE: Early Non-Christian Influences

such as divinity being seen as "unfolded into light" or is "seated above a lotus."[6] Finally, he also inquires about the nature and relation of demons.[7]

It is in this larger Greco-Roman religious and neoplatonic context, and specifically to this letter from Porphyry, that Iamblichus writes and responds on behalf of his student, Anebo, to whom the inquiring letter was sent.[8] Iamblichus seeks to answer Porphyry's questions, but with an emphasis on the purification of the soul.[9] Iamblichus' work therefore represents some of the religious influences that early Christians, particularly Greco-Roman Christians (as opposed to Jewish Christians), might have been exposed to and familiar with. This work can therefore help us to better understand how some of the early Christian communities might have viewed and approached personal transformation during this early period. Finally, as we move through this historical Western Christian journey, we will hear many resonances with the beliefs and practices that are articulated here.

Models of Reality

Anthropological-Cosmological

Iamblichus' anthro-cosmology is very complex, and closely follows the Greco-Roman worldviews of his day. He begins by asserting that "an innate knowledge of the Gods is coexistent with our very essence; and this knowledge is superior to all judgment and deliberate choice, and subsists prior to reason and demonstration."[10] He therefore asserts that there is some interaction between what is human and material and what is heavenly and immaterial. Drawing on Greco-Roman cosmology, he expends some time unpacking the similarities and differences between the various levels of higher and lower gods, heroes and demons, and humans, views that are common in Platonic cosmologies.[11]

In this celestial hierarchy, heroes are leaders of humans and are from a different cause or origin than are the demons.[12] Demons are seen as

6. Ibid., 11.
7. Ibid., 15–16.
8. Ibid., 18.
9. Ibid., 22.
10. Ibid., 23.
11. Ibid., 23–24, 82–83, 99, 205, 68.
12. Ibid., 83.

Iamblichus and the Mysteries

being far from the "intelligible Gods,"[13] as these two are very different from one another.[14] On this, Iamblichus writes, "that which is divine is of a ruling nature, and presides over the different orders of beings; but that which is daemoniacal is of a ministrant nature."[15] Disorder and perturbations follow demons, whereas with the angels there is "efficacy of order and quiet."[16] Nonetheless, like angels, demons rule over certain, arcane, parts of creation.[17] His basic message in all of these discussions is that angels, and good celestial beings and heroes, are higher and more pure than are the demons. He writes, "Angels alone dissolve the bond of generation. Daemons draw souls down into nature; but heroes lead them to a providential attention to sensible works."[18]

With this framework in place, Iamblichus asserts the neoplatonic view that perfection and goodness flows through this hierarchical order from higher to lower beings, with higher beings giving of their goodness and energies to lower beings.[19] Within this framework, there are two extremes in this order: 1) the perfect and transcendent, which are higher and govern all things; and 2) the deficient and imperfect, which are lower and are ruled by the higher beings.[20]

Despite the deficiencies of lower, corporeal beings, "Each ['corporeal part of the universe'], likewise, by itself is capable of effecting different things, and produces certain different energies. They are also capable of effecting things much more numerous on each other."[21] In this, Iamblichus is basically asserting that different parts of creation comingle with one another and can cause effects that are neither from the gods nor from demons, but from the passions and lower natures of these lower parts.[22] As a result, some of the evil in the world comes about because one part unintentionally injures another part, like at a dance where two people accidentally bump into each other.[23] We can therefore see how distortions

---

13. Ibid., 76.
14. Ibid., 77.
15. Ibid., 78.
16. Ibid., 87.
17. Ibid., 282.
18. Ibid., 93, 95, 102.
19. Ibid., 32–34, 37, 68–69, 266.
20. Ibid., 36.
21. Ibid., 215.
22. Ibid., 220–23.
23. Ibid., 71.

and sin enter the world in this framework: from lower gods and demons in the hierarchy as well as from the things that creatures do that affect one another.

As it relates to human nature, we have at least two parts or our being in Iamblichus' framework: a body and a soul. Since humans are very low in his celestial order, divine bodies are viewed as being quite different from earthly ones. The celestial bodies do not "consist of things contrary and different,"[24] and instead are "things of a more excellent nature."[25] The human body, on the other hand, is seen to cause disorder and disharmonize to the divine harmony of the soul.[26] Iamblichus, in line with classical Platonic views, asserts that the body surrounds the soul on all sides with evil.[27] So low is his view of the body and of humanity in general that Iamblichus writes, "the human race is imbecile, and of small estimation, sees but a little, and possesses a connascent nothingness."[28] Not only must humans therefore struggle with the lowliness of the body, but also, so far as they participate in the sensible body, they may also be influenced by demons.[29] As a result, the defilements of the body fall on the body and humans must therefore be purified of them.[30]

The soul, on the other hand, existed apriori and was inserted into this organic human body, claims Iamblichus.[31] "The soul," he writes, "which ranks as a whole, presides over all the mundane body."[32] While residing in the body, Iamblichus also asserts that the soul is able to leave the terrestrial body and wander about creation to some extent.[33] As will be discussed below, liberation of the soul is central for his approaches to personal transformation.

Other noteworthy aspects of his anthropology are: there are two parts of the intellect: universal and partial;[34] and that humans have the possibility of a twofold life: one in the body and the other completely

24. Ibid., 67.
25. Ibid.
26. Ibid., 127.
27. Ibid., 170–71.
28. Ibid., 164.
29. Ibid., 198.
30. Ibid., 230.
31. Ibid., 40.
32. Ibid., 226.
33. Ibid., 224.
34. Ibid., 41.

separate from the body.[35] These views of the celestial hierarchical order, the interactions between its various levels, the relation of body and soul, and these other aspects of the person therefore all make up part of the anthro-cosmological foundation for his views of and approaches to spiritual formation.

Theological

Since his anthro-cosmology already includes much talk about the gods and their various relations to humanity, I have reserved discussions to the highest and most divine gods in Iamblichus' framework, and their relationship to creation, for this section. This is because, for him, some gods are material and other immaterial: the material adorn matter, while the immaterial utterly transcend it.[36] Nonetheless, all of these gods are good and participate in the good.[37]

While these distinctions may sound dualistic, Iamblichus rejects some of the dualistic understandings of his own time, asserting that the gods are not separated from the terrestrial world, nor are creatures separated from the celestial realms, for "terrestrial natures possess their existence in the pleromas of the Gods."[38] He asserts that the light and energy of the gods extends through all things while also being illuminated separately.[39] This divine energy is not drawn down to us, rather it is separate and "gives itself, indeed, to its participants, yet neither departs from itself, nor becomes diminished, nor is ministrant to those that receive it; but, on the contrary, uses all things as subservient to itself"[40] imparting only good and rendering "all things similar to itself."[41] On this, Iamblichus continues, "The energy of divine fire shines forth voluntarily, and in common, and being self-invoked and self-energetic, energizes through all things with invariable sameness, both through the natures which impart, and those that are able to receive, its light."[42]

35. Ibid., 118.
36. Ibid., 249.
37. Ibid., 68.
38. Ibid., 43.
39. Ibid., 46, 265.
40. Ibid., 159.
41. Ibid., 160.
42. Ibid., 208.

Hence, while the Divine does participate in creation, it also has its own immutable and separate nature as well,[43] utterly transcending creation as a whole.[44] In a similarly manner, the higher part of the soul, which is of the nature of the Divine, is itself incorruptible even though it is a part of corruptible creatures.[45] This light and energy has the purpose of drawing all things to be every more fully in accordance with its nature and essence; its sameness. Such an immanent-transcendent theology therefore informs how Iamblichus understands the human spiritual journey, and how personal transformation may be enacted, as discussed below.

Theories of Change

Given the utter lowliness and impotence of humans, and the intentions and powers of the higher beings to effect change in the lower orders, Iamblichus' basic theory of change seems to center around our becoming a participant with the gods.[46] A person, he claims, becomes united to the gods through sacred ceremonies, what he calls "theurgy."[47] On this he elaborates, "from supplication, we are in a short time led to the object of supplication, acquire its similitude from intimate converse, and gradually obtain divine perfection, instead of our own imbecility and imperfection."[48] Contemplation, for example, allows the soul to become "energized according to another energy" and is thereby liberated from this humanly realm;[49] one's will is therefore adapted to the gods and is "coharmonized" with them.[50] He further asserts that it is only by one becoming "adapted to divine participation" that humans come to "possess the Gods."[51] It is therefore, our comingling with the higher gods through theurgic practices that leads to spiritual changes in our life.

Such unions, however, can only be led by supernatural causes.[52] He asserts a twofold cause of them: "either from the gods being present with

43. Ibid., 49, 72, 147, 58, 60, 92.
44. Ibid., 227, 34, 332.
45. Ibid., 50.
46. Ibid., 59, 119, 23, 64.
47. Ibid., 62.
48. Ibid.
49. Ibid., 56.
50. Ibid., 57.
51. Ibid., 43–44.
52. Ibid., 73, 127, 34, 53, 64, 71–72, 78, 214, 70.

the soul, or imparting to the soul from themselves a certain forerunning light."[53] His basic claim here is that all things that are divine come from a divine cause.[54] Humans cannot make transformation happen of their own accord. It is, therefore, the "genuine lover of the Gods" who will ascend by giving themselves wholly and completely to the gods.[55]

Humans, however, are not wholly passive in this. We need to elevate our natures and participate in the higher natures, unions, and wholes that are a part of the celestial order.[56] Such purification comes about by our working to separate ourselves from the body[57] because the passions of the body only impede divine affiliations.[58] Part of this purification can happen via the intellect,[59] but part also happens by the works of the gods within us as well as our sacred practices, such as sacrifices. Explaining, Iamblichus writes, "the fire that is with us, imitating the energy of divine fire, destroys every thing which is material in sacrifices, purifies the things which are offered, liberates them from the bonds of matter, and renders them, through purity of nature, adapted to the communion of the Gods."[60] Hence, Iamblichus' central theory of change is related to the liberation of our souls from the passions of the body so that it can participate more fully with the higher gods. This change is primarily enacted by direct interactions with the gods, though each person must also work to purify themselves as well.

Spiritual Formation Ideals & Goals

One of the primary spiritual goals for Iamblichus, therefore, is union with the gods, with the invisible, and becoming one energy.[61] In light of his anthropology, he writes, "With respect to the soul, if it ranks as a whole, and does not belong to any particular species, it presents to the view a formless fire, extended through the whole world, which is indicative of the total, one, indivisible, and formless soul of the universe; but a purified

---

53. Ibid., 152.
54. Ibid., 170.
55. Ibid., 202.
56. Ibid., 74, 142.
57. Ibid., 118, 43, 46.
58. Ibid., 116, 279.
59. Ibid., 244.
60. Ibid., 247.
61. Ibid., 75.

soul exhibits a fiery form, and a pure and unmingled fire."[62] Such a united soul is one that is free, unencumbered by the things of the lower orders of creation. With this liberty, he claims, comes true happiness. Expanding on this, Iamblichus asserts, "the dispositions of the soul of those that invoke the gods appear to receive, when they become visible, a liberation from the passions, a transcendent perfection, and an energy entirely more excellent, and participate of divine love and an immense joy."[63] Such a soul, he goes on, additionally seeks to benefit human life.[64]

Other goals that Iamblichus highlights are achieving a purity in the ritual theurgic practices of his religious tradition,[65] as well as divination. He spends much time elaborating on the ins and outs of divination partly because Porphyry inquires about it. But it also seems that divination is a central part of this religious tradition. "Divination," for Iamblichus, includes divine inspiration,[66] dreams,[67] oracles,[68] and foreknowledge.[69] They are basically direct and pure encounters with the Divine in his framework.

As it relates to the ideals and goals he discusses about such divinations, they are considered to be divine, sent to humans from heaven.[70] They are therefore not a natural seed that is within us.[71] The ideal here is in our coming to know and hear what the higher gods say more directly, "a more perfect perception" as he puts it.[72] He asserts that "true divination was a solution of the divine part of the soul from the other parts of it,"[73] but that the symbols of art are also used by the gods to effect such divination.[74] In short, theurgists are seeking ever more direct contact, communion, and communication with the higher gods. Such, then, are the ideals and goals that his approaches to personal spiritual formation seek to achieve.

---

62. Ibid., 98.
63. Ibid., 101.
64. Ibid., 103.
65. Ibid., 260–63.
66. Ibid., 126, 40.
67. Ibid., 121.
68. Ibid., 140, 44.
69. Ibid., 112.
70. Ibid., 112, 13–14, 87.
71. Ibid., 189.
72. Ibid., 116–17.
73. Ibid., 127.
74. Ibid., 155.

Spiritual Formation Approaches

With this background and ideology in place, Iamblichus lays out some of the theurgical practices that help to affect the changes he describes and there are a number of different practices that he highlights. For instance, he notes some of the various practices utilized by some of the prophetesses to purify themselves: sacrifices, following the sacred laws in ceremonies, baths, fasting for three days, and retiring into a sacred place to receive prophetic inspiration. Through all these, he asserts, "God is entreated by prayer to approach, [and] becomes externally present, and that the prophetess, before she comes to her accustomed place, is inspired in a wonderful manner."[75] There are also intellectual and incorporeal modes of worship[76] and with these we honor the gods in more liberated ways.[77] There are also "supermundane" practices for the supermundane gods, which transcend bodies and matter and unite one to the gods by supermundane powers.[78] With all of these various practices mentioned, however, he focuses most of his discussions on sacred rituals, particularly sacrifices, as well as on prayers.

Rituals are intended to liberate people from their bonds, to heal and "save souls from the calamities with which the realms of generation are replete."[79] They are intended to help separate souls from their bodies to experience the things of the eternal.[80] One becomes united to the gods through these sacred ceremonies, and the gods are honored by them.[81] In alignment with his anthro-cosmologies, it is assumed that the gods send the sacred rituals and prayers for people to use,[82] that they really act through them both directly as well as through mediators,[83] and that the gods therefore create change in creation because they send the rituals and symbols for people to use to influence the gods.[84] Iamblichus is basically

75. Ibid., 144–45.
76. Ibid., 256.
77. Ibid., 258.
78. Ibid., 259.
79. Ibid., 54–55.
80. Ibid., 55–56.
81. Ibid., 62, 81.
82. Ibid., 63.
83. Ibid., 109–10, 278.
84. Ibid., 110.

claiming that since only the gods can effect transformation in humans, the rituals are given, imbued with, and enacted by the gods.

Nevertheless, humans also have an important part to play in them and therefore need to be of a special type. Priests conducting the rituals are considered to have two characters: their humanly one, and the one that is elevated. It is because of their more excellent character that they can invoke the powers of the universe.[85] For those who commit many offenses and/or partake of more corporeal living, however, are not able to invoke the gods to the same degree.[86] All practices, Iamblichus writes, "ought not to be exercised towards [the Gods] partially or imperfectly,"[87] for imperfect practices lead to imperfect results.[88] Superior beings, he asserts, will not come to participate in them unless the appropriate vessels, sacred sacrifices, and operations are used.[89] There are therefore sacred laws for these practices,[90] and the gods are considered to lead them.[91]

Of the rituals that are discussed, Iamblichus spends a significant amount of time discussing sacrifices. They are not just for honoring the gods, but have a much more purifying and necessary role in creation's functioning.[92] Elaborating, he writes, "Without them, we are neither liberated from pestilence, nor famine, nor sterility of fruits, nor obtain seasonable showers of rain, nor things of much greater consequence than these, I mean such as contribute to the purification of the soul, or an emancipation from generation."[93] They enact the purification and liberation that the soul needs, and are therefore absolutely essential for one's growing divine life. Such sacrifices transmit the "divine fire" that, he claims, "liberates us after the same manner from the bonds of generation, assimilates us to the Gods, causes us to be adapted to their friendship, and conducts our material nature to an immaterial essence."[94] As with all rituals, they must be done correctly,[95] and, when successful, they move us from lower to

85. Ibid., 207.
86. Ibid., 210–11, 18.
87. Ibid., 260.
88. Ibid., 261, 63.
89. Ibid., 267, 69.
90. Ibid., 264–65.
91. Ibid., 269.
92. Ibid., 232.
93. Ibid., 233.
94. Ibid., 247.
95. Ibid., 241.

higher gods,[96] unite a multitude of corporeal elements,[97] and effect healing, wholeness, and order to creation.[98]

Iamblichus also discusses a few different kinds of prayers.[99] These prayers are purported to yield three fruits: illumination, "communion of operation," and a "perfect plentitude of divine fire."[100] Prayers are central because "the continual exercise of prayer nourishes the vigour of our intellect, and renders the receptacles of the soul far more capacious for the communications of the Gods."[101] They also condition us to the gods, perfects us inwardly, draw "upward the manners of our soul, by divesting them of every thing foreign to a divine nature, and clothes us with the perfection of the Gods."[102] Prayer therefore makes us friends to the gods, imparts divine love and "inflames the divine part of the soul."[103] It is therefore through the use of such prayers, practices, rituals, and sacrifices that one's communion with the gods is affected and the individual is liberated from the body into the higher and more heavenly realms. Such is the fundamental basis that Iamblichus asserts in this text for his personal and communal spiritual formation approaches.

Discernment

Iamblichus does not explicitly address the ways in which a person in his religious tradition might go about discerning which practices, prayers, rituals, et cetera to use for which circumstances and at which stages of a person or community's spiritual journey. However, he does allude to methods of discernment at various parts of the text. For instance, he discusses the importance of knowing the differences between angels and demons [104] and between various dreams and their higher or lower sources.[105] He also spends some time discussing how to discern whether a divination comes

---

96. Ibid., 241, 49–50.
97. Ibid., 267.
98. Ibid., 253.
99. Ibid., 271–72.
100. Ibid., 272.
101. Ibid., 271.
102. Ibid.
103. Ibid., 272.
104. Ibid., 89–90.
105. Ibid., 115–16.

PART ONE: Early Non-Christian Influences

from the gods or from demons by detecting any falsehood in them[106] as well as how to discern between good and evil, or demonic, sources.[107] He further refers to the use of the sacred laws given by the gods to guide the various religious practices.[108] In short, Iamblichus' approach to discernment appears to be quite complex requiring specialized knowledge of both the sacred laws and the detailed anthro-cosmology that he outlines in his letter. Yet, its central features seem to include knowledge of rules, rationality, and divine inspiration.

Evaluative Techniques

Just as Iamblichus does not directly address discernment, he also does not appear to overtly discuss what evaluative approaches he might use for basing his discernment on. If I had to guess, based on the small discernment issues he does discuss, I would venture to assert that his evaluative techniques are primarily based on observations of the individual, the kind of pure or impure life they are living, how well they follow or violate the sacred laws, and how directed their lives are by this religious tradition's anthro-cosmology. As we saw above, Iamblichus places a great emphasis on living a pure life, one that is permeated by prayer, rituals, and sacrifices.

Summary/Reflections

Pictured below, Iamblichus' approaches to personal spiritual formation are therefore centered on helping people to ever more fully interact with and engage the higher gods. Such divining interactions not only purify and liberate the soul, but it also brings about transformation in the person's life. It is through the theurgic practices that one comes to such purifying divine interactions. Having a strong theology of the penetrating Light of the higher gods, these rituals are ultimately guided by the gods so that we might come to them more fully.

---

106. Ibid., 214.
107. Ibid., 224.
108. Ibid., 264–65.

Iamblichus and the Mysteries

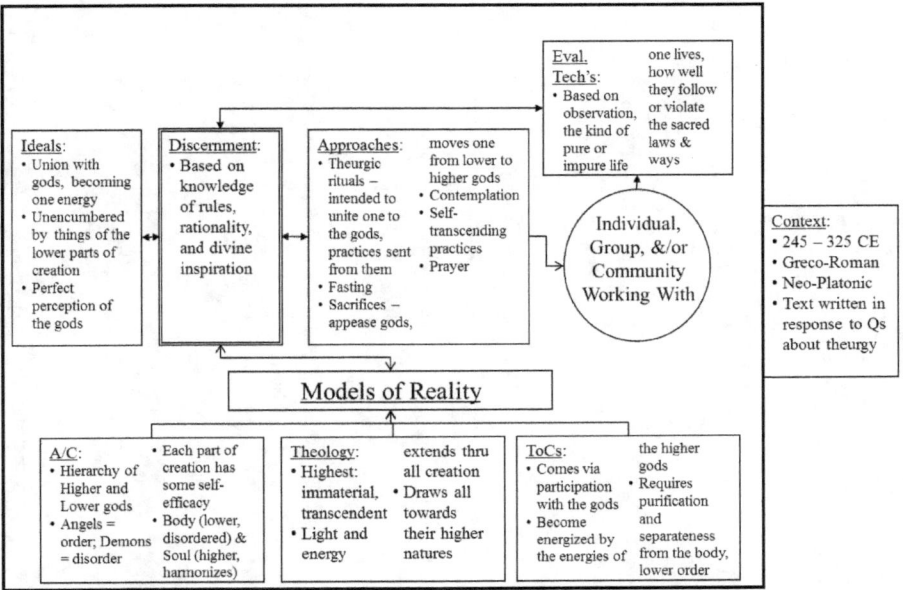

From a Christian perspective, Iamblichus' framework is quite fascinating. In some ways, it can sound very Christian when we think about the Eucharist and how it is asserted to help to do the work of salvation in our personal lives and our communities. In other ways, however, it is also very foreign to contemporary Christianity. Nevertheless, with humans being viewed as being so utterly distant, impotent, and defiled in comparison to the higher gods, the whole approach to personal transformation is logical in that it then is geared around trying to help us to come more and more into greater contact with these gods through the various practices that Iamblichus discusses. Obviously, many Christians might criticize and reject this system altogether because it does seem "magical" (i.e., humans trying to get the gods to bend to their desires). But Iamblichus is very clear that the prayers and rituals are, in their purest forms, given to humans by the gods to influence the gods for the betterment of creation. In that regard, and in some ways, it really does not seem all that different from how we in Christianity view some of our own rituals, prayers, and other spiritual practices (e.g., the Lord's Prayer and Communion). As we continue with our journey, we will find these and many other resonances with Iamblichus' view of and approaches to personal transformation. At any rate, it is Greco-Roman religions such as these that early Christians were exposed to during this era of Western history.

PART TWO

Early Christian Diversity

GIVEN THE CONTEXT DESCRIBED previously, these were times of great trials and tribulations for the early Church. Up until the early 300s, the Christians were a persecuted group for which martyrdom became an avenue through which some expressed their spirituality.[1] It was also a time of great diversity among early communities where religious doctrines and practices were still being debated and refined.[2] This was therefore an era of great change and challenge for the early church, where members sought to find direction and guidance from their communities.

For insights into how to live as a Christian, depending on their locale, disciples could have access to a number of different strands of Christianity during this era. For instance, there were many Jewish-Christian communities, which sought to reinterpret their Jewish tradition in light of Jesus of Nazareth.[3] As mentioned above, martyrdom was embraced by some of these followers as well. There were also a series of writings, from the "apologists," that sought to clarify Christianity as a reasonable and defensible religion.[4] Many of these communities also believed the end of the world was eminent, giving a distinctive character to personal spiritual

---

1. Chidester, *Christianity*, 76–77; McGuckin, "The Early Church Fathers (1st to 6th Centuries)," 39; Woods, *Christian Spirituality*, 33.

2. Chidester, *Christianity*, 43; McGuckin, "The Early Church Fathers (1st to 6th Centuries)," 43; Sheldrake, *Brief History of Spirituality*, 22; Woods, *Christian Spirituality*, 22.

3. Burridge, "Jesus and the Origins of Christianity," 25, 28; Chidester, *Christianity*, 44; McGuckin, "The Early Church Fathers (1st to 6th Centuries)," 43; Sheldrake, *Brief History of Spirituality*, 13; Woods, *Christian Spirituality*, 9.

4. Chidester, *Christianity*, 43; McGuckin, "The Early Church Fathers (1st to 6th Centuries)," 43; Sheldrake, *Brief History of Spirituality*, 22; Woods, *Christian Spirituality*, 22–23, 51.

PART TWO: Early Christian Diversity

formation as we shall see.[5] The deserts of North Africa saw the emergence, or adaptation, of hermetic and monastic forms of Christianity, which we shall take up in the next part of this book.[6] In addition, there were strands that reinterpreted Christian doctrine and practice in light of Platonic and neoplatonic worldviews.[7] Finally, as Christianity spread to the outer reaches of the Roman Empire, new and different brands of Christianity were developed in such faraway places as India and other parts of Africa.[8]

From amongst this great diversity, we choose two very different Christian communities by which to explore personal transformation. The first is Gnosticism with its more heavily laden neoplatonic version of Christianity. Looking to Hans Jonas' *The Gnostic Religion*, we will learn how some gnostics conceived of creation and sought to deepen one's growing spiritual life. In stark contrast to these more Greco-Roman influenced Christian communities, we will also be looking at the *Didache*, an early apocalyptic Jewish Christian text. To help us to further understand this very short writing, we will be using Aaron Milavec's book on the topic, which discusses not only this text but also early Jewish Christian communities more generally. From these sources, our hopes are to gain greater insight into how some of these many diverse early communities engaged in personal transformation.

---

5. Chidester, *Christianity*, 41; McGuckin, "The Early Church Fathers (1st to 6th Centuries)," 37; Woods, *Christian Spirituality*, 23.

6. Chidester, *Christianity*, 116–17; McGuckin, "The Early Church Fathers (1st to 6th Centuries)," 57; Sheldrake, *Brief History of Spirituality*, 41; Woods, *Christian Spirituality*, 57.

7. Chidester, *Christianity*, 40; McGuckin, "The Early Church Fathers (1st to 6th Centuries)," 44, 68; Sheldrake, *Brief History of Spirituality*, 27, 31; Woods, *Christian Spirituality*, 49.

8. Chidester, *Christianity*, 60; Holt, "Spiritualities of the Twenieth Century," 316, 19.

3

Gnostic Christian Formation

Context

IN HIS BOOK ON Gnosticism, Hans Jonas begins by giving the context in which Gnosticism arose: Under Alexander, cultures of the east and west mixed with one another.[1] With reason, or *logos*, as the ideal that evolved among the Hellenistic culture,[2] one could be *Hellenized* no matter what culture one was originally from.[3] From this Hellenized secular society, however, religious sects eventually began to emerge, primarily in competition with Christianity and other growing religions from within and outside.[4] The eastern side of the Hellenized world embraced dualistic realities,[5] as well as other ancient religious concepts such as "traditional astrological fatalism, traditional monotheism" but with a different view of them.[6] The religions from this eastern side became a new religious tide in the first century CE as Mystery Cults emerged.[7] Gnosticism was a part of this wave.[8] Gnostics, along with other religions of the time were: religious in nature, concerned with salvation, viewed God as transcendent, and

1. Jonas, *Gnostic Religion*, 4–5.
2. Ibid., 6.
3. Ibid., 7.
4. Ibid., 10.
5. Ibid., 21.
6. Ibid., 23.
7. Ibid., 25, 31.
8. Ibid., 26.

thoroughly dualistic.[9] Gnosticism, also similar to other religions in this wave, was a syncretism of the Hellenistic, Babylonian, Egyptian, Iranian, Jewish, and Christian movements of the time[10] and was, therefore, not just a Christian phenomenon.[11] It was in this pluralistic context of the Hellenistic world that Gnosticism existed.

Models of Reality

Anthropological-Cosmological

Similar to Iamblichus' and other Platonic frameworks, gnostic anthro-cosmology focused primarily on two aspects: 1) the larger cosmological framework, operations of the world (or the "cosmos"), and the gods; and 2) the nature of humans. As it relates to the larger cosmos, Jonas writes, "The universe, the domain of the Archons [the lower powers who rule], is like a vast prison whose innermost dungeon is the earth, the scene of [humanity's] life. Around and above it the cosmic spheres are ranged like concentric enclosing shells . . . The religious significance of this cosmic architecture lies in the idea that everything which intervenes between here and beyond serves to separate [humans] from god, not merely by spatial distance but through active demonic force."[12] It is the idea that creation is the work of lower gods who are each responsible for their own part of the cosmos and their purpose is to prevent souls from ascending through the various stages or circles of creation.[13] This is mostly done out of ignorance of God,[14] who is above them all, as will be further discussed below.[15] Not only do they not know this true God, but they also obstruct the knowledge of God.[16] Despite this bleak picture of the cosmos, some gnostics still held that there is a mixing of the light from God, or beyond, with the darkness of these imprisoned realms.[17]

---

9. Ibid., 31.
10. Ibid., 33; see also ibid., 207.
11. Ibid., 36.
12. Ibid., 43.
13. Ibid., 43, 117, 56–57.
14. Ibid., 133.
15. Ibid., 135, 251.
16. Ibid., 42, 132–33, 281.
17. Ibid., 162, 210.

Gnostic Christian Formation

Within this framework, then, humans are prisoners. Humans are considered to be composed of flesh, soul, and spirit,[18] though Jonas also seems to use soul and spirit interchangeably. The body and soul are the result of the cosmic powers/gods who imbue them with the passions and appetites of the lower spheres and are therefore subjected to the created prison. The spirit, on the other hand, is seen as having fallen from the beyond and is held captive by the body and its liberation, its awakening, only comes via knowledge.[19] This spirit is sometimes seen as the presence of an inner "Self," that is "the transcendent and true subject of salvation."[20] Salvation is viewed as a reuniting with this part of one's self.[21] However, while trapped, this spirit longs for freedom[22] for it is understood to be slumbering in matter; to be asleep.[23] "'Ignorance' is," therefore, "the essence of mundane existence."[24] It is an ignorance of one's spirit about itself and about the transcendent God[25] because of this slumbering. This spirit is also considered to be battled for by the various forces of creation.[26] Hence, God's true "Life" is seen as being trapped inside the body,[27] as well as within this cosmic prison, while the body is seen as being totally impure and not to be trusted along with the rest of the material and lower realms.[28]

Theological

As with Iamblichus' scheme, I have reserved this section for discussions of the most high God, the one that is not considered to be an intimate part of the system described above. Ultimately, God seen as being utterly transcendent.[29] Jonas writes, "The deity is absolutely transmundane, its nature alien to that of the universe, which it neither created nor governs and to which it is the complete antithesis: to the divine realm of light, self

---

18. Ibid., 44.
19. Ibid., 44, 176, 227, 82.
20. Ibid., 123.
21. Ibid., 124–25.
22. Ibid., 65–66, 150.
23. Ibid., 69, 92–93, 114.
24. Ibid., 45.
25. Ibid., 44.
26. Ibid., 283.
27. Ibid., 56, 63–64, 101.
28. Ibid., 72, 85, 115, 58, 267.
29. Ibid., 31, 34, 45, 49.

-contained and remote, the cosmos is opposed as the realm of darkness."[30] As a result, God is completely unknowable to creation as it currently is, requiring a special divine intervention in order to know anything of God.[31] Jonas continues, "The transcendent God himself is hidden from all creatures and is unknowable by natural concepts. Knowledge of Him requires supranatural revelation and illumination and even then can hardly be expressed otherwise than in negative terms."[32] Yet, God calls to us from beyond.[33] Though its Word confuses humans,[34] it nevertheless seeks to lead us via "the *reminder* of the heavenly origin . . . the *promise* of redemption . . . and finally the practical *instruction* as to how to live henceforth."[35] In this scheme, then, knowledge is considered to be the "original condition of the Absolute."[36] It is from this core theology that gnostics are given their name, which comes from the Greek word *gnosis*, meaning "knowledge," which is also the means by which one attains salvation.[37]

Theories of Change

With God being utterly transcendent and unknowable, all the lower realms basically being corrupted (of which the human body is constructed), and the goal being a complete liberation from it all, the fundamental gnostic theory of change and way to this salvation is centered on the acquisition of "knowledge," or *gnosis*.[38] The idea here is that God sends Divine Light down to humans thereby enabling them to share in God's existence.[39] Such knowledge from and of God not only liberates one from the body's corrupting passions, but is itself the "ultimate perfection" that transforms the soul.[40] In speaking about the relation between the knower and the known, Jonas writes, "There, the mind is "informed" with the forms it beholds and while it beholds (thinks) them: here, the subject is "transformed" (from

30. Ibid., 42; see also ibid., 101, 251, 71.
31. Ibid., 45, 138, 79, 251, 71, 88.
32. Ibid., 42–43.
33. Ibid., 74, 120.
34. Ibid., 76.
35. Ibid., 77, 81.
36. Ibid., 175.
37. Ibid., 32.
38. Ibid., 32, 34, 175–76.
39. Ibid., 35, 175, 284.
40. Ibid., 35, 284.

"soul" to "spirit") by the union with a reality that in truth is itself the supreme subject in the situation and strictly speaking never an object at all."[41] It is, therefore, by one's reception of Divine knowledge, that one is called, awakened, and finally liberated from all the lower realms.[42] There are also two additional purposes of this *gnosis*: it gives a magical quality to make the soul impenetrable and invisible to lower gods; and to give knowledge of how one can force their passage to the higher realms.[43] Gnostic transformation, which is "long and endless" and often confusing but also joyous,[44] is therefore rooted in one's communion with this knowledge.

This journey, however, is not considered to be made alone, especially in Christian versions of Gnosticism. A "transcendent savior" is believed to bring this "saving knowledge" from beyond these realms in which humans are imprisoned.[45] This savior comes to bring liberation[46] and He must descend and "assimilate himself to the forms of cosmic existence and thereby subject himself to its conditions."[47] For some gnostic Christians, such as Marcion, Christ saves us from the world and makes us children of the "alien" God by His blood literally being a "purchase price" of the creator to the lower gods.[48] For others, "Christos" is seen as establishing a new harmony into the cosmos by teaching the lower ignorant gods about the unknowability of God thereby bringing a new integrity to creation.[49] This savior is therefore a messenger of God, the bearer of the liberating *gnosis* that humans need in order to attain the God and realm that is utterly beyond creation. It is this acquisition of this *gnosis* that fundamentally undergirds the gnostic theories of change.

SPIRITUAL FORMATION IDEALS & GOALS

Gnostics pretty much have a singular focus when it comes to the aims of their religion. On this, Jonas asserts, "The goal of gnostic striving is the release of the "inner [person]" from the bonds of the world and [her or his]

41. Ibid., 35.
42. Ibid., 44, 74, 120.
43. Ibid., 168.
44. Ibid., 87–89, 153.
45. Ibid., 45, 228.
46. Ibid., 108, 22, 31, 89.
47. Ibid.,127; see also ibid., 222.
48. Ibid., 139.
49. Ibid., 185, 96.

PART TWO: Early Christian Diversity

return to [her or his] native realm of light."[50] It is to be "reunited with the divine substance";[51] a breaking through and awakening from the spirit's slumbering.[52] He continues, "It is no exaggeration to say that the discovery of this transcendent inner principle in [humanity] and the supreme concern about its destiny is the very center of gnostic religion."[53] Given the realm of prisons that the spirit is enclosed within, both cosmically and anthropologically, the goal is the gnostic ascent is through the concentric circles and one's self to the beyond where God dwells.[54] Being a thoroughly dualistic perspective, it is through this ascent, via a series of stages, that the immanence of the spirit attains to the transcendence of God.[55] This attainment therefore "involves a process of gathering in, of re-collection of what has been so dispersed, and salvation aims at the restoration of the original unity."[56] In short, the central spiritual formation goal of gnostic Christianity is a liberation of this imprisoned spirit into the realm of God that is utterly transcendent to and beyond all of creation.

Spiritual Formation Approaches

Knowledge of gnostic practices is historically sketchy, though we do know some of the approaches that were central for them. Because Jonas' work seemed to be lacking in detailing some of the gnostic practices and rituals, I have turned to another source on the gnostics by England's University of Exeter Professor Alastair Logan, and his book, *The Gnostics: Identifying an Early Christian Cult*.[57] I focused on his chapter entitled, "Gnostics Versus Catholics on Christian Identity: (2) Ritual and Lifestyle." In this book, Logan seeks to establish that Gnosticism was indeed a valid cult of the time in light of recent scholarly questions related to this issue.[58]

We know that gnostic practices were important since the acquisition of unknowable knowledge of God was considered to come via "sacred and secret lore or through inner illumination," either directly, or through a

50. Ibid., 44.
51. Ibid., 45; see also 166.
52. Ibid., 77–78, 80, 85, 114.
53. Ibid., 124.
54. Ibid., 153.
55. Ibid., 165.
56. Ibid., 59; see also 235.
57. Logan, *Gnostics*.
58. Ibid., 5.

savior.[59] Such knowledge, Jonas asserts, was not just related to gnosis, but also to the way of life that gnostics should live. On this, he writes, "On the practical side, however, it is more particularly "knowledge of the way," namely, of the soul's way out of the world, comprising the sacramental and magical preparations for its future ascent and the secret names and formulas that force the passage through each sphere."[60]

Of these practices and lifestyles, according to Jonas' book, we know a little. There were primarily two ways of life that gnostics used to approach moral life: in an ascetical way, and in a libertine way.[61] In the more commonly followed ascetical way, one avoids further contamination from the world, which is considered to be utterly base and corrupt, and therefore seeks a minimal contact with it.[62] It is also a way of not supporting the works of the lower, or this worldly, gods and the corruptions they encourage through such earthly things as food, marriage, sex, etc.[63] As one gnostic text, *The Hymn of the Pearl*, puts it, "The ascent starts with the discarding of the impure garments."[64] Such asceticism is seen to aid one's liberation from the clutches of these lower realms.

The less popular approach to living the gnostic way, was known as the libertine way. While the ascetical way seeks to negate the things of the world, the libertine way considered one, who has received gnosis, to be above and completely free from it.[65] While the ascetical way seeks very high standards of morality, the libertine way assumes that one whom is free from the prison of the lower realms is considered to also be free from moral law.[66] Hence, in contrast with the contemporary Hellenistic emphasis on virtues, libertines had no virtue formation in their system because of distrust and disinterest in the things of this world.[67] They claim that no laws on behavior or order are issued from God.[68] Instead, say the libertines, such morals, law, and virtues are given by angels and gods of the lower realms to lead humans into "servitude" to them thereby further

---

59. Jonas, *Gnostic Religion*, 35; Logan, *Gnostics*, 83.
60. Jonas, *Gnostic Religion*, 45; see also 284.
61. Ibid., 46, 270–71.
62. Ibid., 46, 231–32, 66, 68; Logan, *Gnostics*, 83, 84.
63. Jonas, *Gnostic Religion*, 144, 227, 31, 75; Logan, *Gnostics*, 83, 85.
64. Jonas, *Gnostic Religion*, 121.
65. Ibid., 46.
66. Ibid.
67. Ibid., 267.
68. Ibid., 271.

PART TWO: Early Christian Diversity

imprisoning them.[69] It is these two ways, but primarily the first, the gnostics sought to craft their lives around in pursuit of the liberation that their spirits longed for.

As it relates to some of the practices and rituals that gnostics used, they centered on creating a union of sorts between the individual and the knowledge of God. Gnostics used practices and instructions to induce "visionary states,"[70] used ceremonies enacting the souls ascent through the various stages of the cosmos,[71] emphasized the importance of knowing the names of the lower gods as a way of overcoming them,[72] and made use of mystical prayers to overcome the lower demonic influences and extinguish the passions.[73] These ceremonies were also thought to help make one's soul invisible to the lower gods so that it could ascend more quickly.[74]

As it relates to specific practices and rituals, we know of at least three that were significant. First, baptism was seen as a central ritual, one of the purification rituals adapted in addition to their ascetical practices.[75] It was considered to be a way that Christ descends and transmits knowledge to a person[76] and the Holy Spirit awakens them in this rite.[77] A part of the baptisms were five anointing rites, similar to what is found in the *Didache,* that were intended to block out the five senses from this world.[78] Secondly, they had a similar anointing rite of death-bed that was intended to protect the person from the lower gods, making them invisible to them just before their departure into the higher realms.[79] Lastly, and in contrast with other Christian communities that emphasized the Eucharist, gnostic Christians had no interest in communion because of its earthly elements and emphasis on the humanness of Jesus and instead emphasized exorcisms.[80] However, despite all of these various rituals, Logan writes, "What most profoundly formed the basis of regular meetings of the Gnostic cult

69. Ibid., 273.
70. Ibid., 167.
71. Ibid., 166.
72. Ibid., 168.
73. Ibid., 282.
74. Ibid., 135.
75. Logan, *Gnostics,* 78.
76. Ibid., 79, 81.
77. Ibid., 83.
78. Ibid., 79.
79. Ibid., 80.
80. Ibid., 82.

Gnostic Christian Formation

community and held it together was not a weekly eucharist, but the studying, reading aloud and commenting on one of the Gnostic 'scriptures.'"[81]

Discernment

With so little information in existence on gnostic practices and lifestyles, there is nothing that I came across in either Jonas' or Logan's texts concerning how a gnostic spiritual formator might discern which practices and lifestyle were appropriate for a specific person in a given leg of their journey. I would imagine that, like Iamblichus' system, there was probably at one time, either orally or in written form, a set of sacred codes, rules, regulations, etc., that gnostic mentors and disciples would follow as they ascended into the higher realms while still on earth.

Evaluative Techniques

This was another aspect that was lacking as well, and I think it goes hand-in-hand with the Discernment processes discussed above. If there were codified regulations to follow related to which practices and spiritual formation ways to use when, these would probably also discuss Evaluative Techniques. But, I didn't seem to come across any of them in these readings. However, for the ascetical way, we can conjecture that the progress of an individual might be gauged on the extent to which they were freed from their earthly passions. But this is merely conjecture at this point.

Summary/Reflections

Being influenced by a neoplatonic cosmology, Gnosticism is in some ways very similar to Iamblichus' system, with complete liberation from a corrupted creation as the goal, and the practices and lifestyles emerging out of these models of reality. These spiritual formation systems have a consistency between their beliefs and practices, something which is important for a integrated and coherent systematic formulation. Given their anthrocosmology and God's relationship to it, as shown below, gnostic Christian spiritual formation approaches sought to achieve what the goals of their system proclaimed: namely, a complete liberation from the lower imprisoning realms via practices, lifestyles, and community gatherings that were

81. Ibid., 81.

PART TWO: Early Christian Diversity

intended to help people shed their connections with this corrupted material realm and put them in a liberated communion with the utterly transcendent God via the *gnosis* that they sought via their approaches. While many gnostic views and practices were rejected and even challenged by other Christian communities, some of their neoplatonic concepts were shared by others such as early monastics as we shall see in the next part of this book.

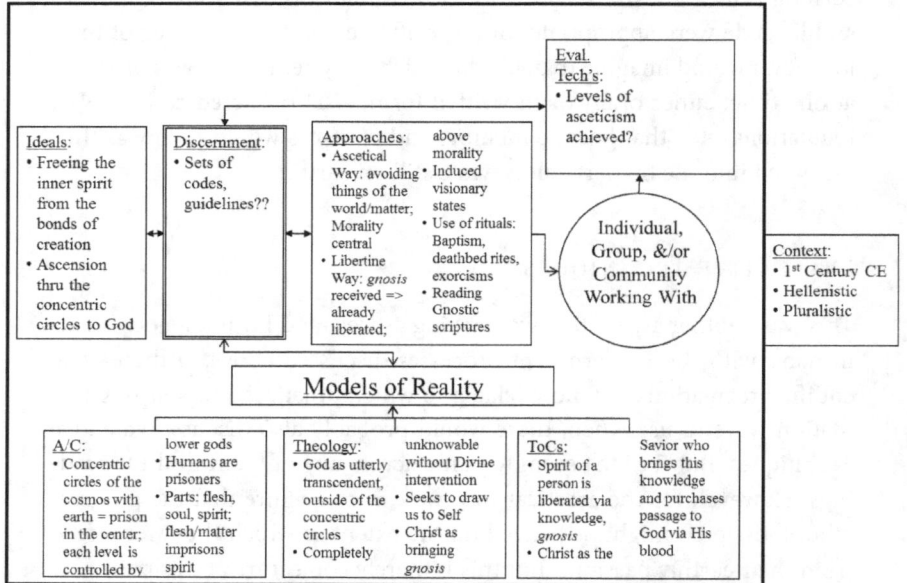

4

Didache Communities

CONTEXT

THE *DIDACHE* IS A Jewish Christian text from the first or second century, probably from Egypt, that is intended to lay down rules and conduct for a rural congregation.[1] In probable competition with the many gnostic movements in Christianity of the time, which was discussed in the last chapter, it has two parts: the first gives a code of morals, while the second is "a manual of Church Order."[2] Most likely, the first part was an independent document to which the second part was later added,[3] or both were independent documents that were brought together by a scribe with some editing and additions.[4] As stated, this document seems to have been intended to help guide rural congregations in their embodiment of the Jewish Christian faith,[5] as well as helping to lead Gentile converts to follow "the Way."[6] It is from this text that we have a better understanding of how the earliest Jewish Christians conceived of themselves and welcomed others into their midst.[7] It is also from this text, and other resources, that Aaron Milavec outlines what he believes to be "the Way" that these early Jewish Christians lived. It is from this text and Milavec's commentary on it

---

1. Richardson, *Early Christian Fathers*, 161, 63; Milavec, *The Didache*, vii.
2. Richardson, *Early Christian Fathers*, 161, 66.
3. Ibid., 164.
4. Ibid., 165; Milavec, *The Didache*, 235.
5. Richardson, *Early Christian Fathers*, 166; Milavec, *The Didache*, 61, 289.
6. Milavec, *The Didache*, vii, 98.
7. Ibid., vii.

that we will seek to better understand what spiritual formation might have looked like for Early Jewish Christian communities such as these.[8]

Models of Reality

Anthropological-Cosmological

Being a very short document, there is not much that the *Didache* offers in the way of its worldview. With Milavec's help, however, some clear points do seem to emerge. The *Didache* understands life in terms of a twofold understanding: the way of life, and the way of death,[9] where the path of life is the one that God made and intends for us.[10] Humans are seen as being made in the image of God [11] for God "pitches a tent" in the hearts of the members of the community.[12] As a result, all members of the *Didache* communities were treated as being equal. For instance, once established as disciples, women and men were given the same kind of training and discipleship.[13] Similarly, masters and slaves alike were also seen to be called by God equally.[14] As it states in the *Didache*, "[God] does not come to call [anyone] according to [his/her] social status, but [God calls] those whom the Spirit has made ready."[15] In spite of these radical views of equality for the time, members were not allowed to give Eucharist to those who were not baptized, for as the Lord said, it is asserted, "Do not give what is holy to the dogs."[16] *Didache* communities, as will be discussed later, made very strong distinctions between the "elect" and the unbaptized.

This is pretty much all that we know of their anthropology, which isn't much. This is mainly because the *Didache* communities lived in much anticipation of the coming kingdom of God, which will only come once.[17]

---

8. All Didache references will be noted according to Milavec's number/labeling system. For instance, a reference to the first sentence of the Didache would be footnoted: "Didache," 1:1.
9. Milavec, *The Didache*, 61, 108; "Didache," 1:1.
10. Milavec, *The Didache*, 94.
11. Ibid., 165.
12. Ibid., 386–87; "Didache," 10:2.
13. Milavec, *The Didache*, 81, 410.
14. Ibid., 164, 407.
15. "Didache," 4:10.
16. Ibid., 9:5.
17. Milavec, *The Didache*, 329, 31, 671, 74.

Being very apocalyptic, the *Didache* communities believed that the last days would become increasingly worse,[18] followed by a period of testing and destruction,[19] until finally the coming of truth and the Lord.[20] In these last days, those unfit for the kingdom will be destroyed[21] while only the "elect" will be saved.[22] Also in these end times, God will come in glory,[23] and the dead will be raised.[24]

Oddly enough, compared with contemporary understandings of the end times and the "anti-Christ," there are no references to Satan. In fact, they have, according to Milavec, been intentionally removed from their texts.[25] Instead, sin is seen to come into the world via a slippery slope in which such things as lust, use of local diviners, and "double-mindedness" leads to adultery, idolatry, and death, respectively.[26]

It is, therefore, these primary anthro-cosmological views of paths of life and death, the "elect" and the unbaptized, and the coming of the kingdom in the last days, that fundamentally guides the whole of the *Didache*'s approaches to "spiritual formation."

Theological

As it relates to God and God's relationship to creation, the *Didache*'s views are quite Jewish in nature. God is seen as being the supreme creator,[27] the one through whom all things happen.[28] As the *Didache* asserts, "apart from God, nothing happens" for God created all things.[29] Their views of God were also both transcendent and immanent in conception. God is seen as being in heaven and not on earth in some ways,[30] yet God is also

18. "Didache," 16:3–4.
19. Ibid., 16:5.
20. Ibid., 16:6–8.
21. Milavec, *The Didache*, 651.
22. Ibid., 898.
23. Ibid., 655.
24. Ibid., 659.
25. Ibid., 332.
26. "Didache," 2:4, 3:2–3.
27. Milavec, *The Didache*, 108.
28. Ibid., 155.
29. "Didache," 3:10, 10:3.
30. Milavec, *The Didache*, 320.

understood to be present in the events that God shapes,[31] like the child who is in the womb of its mother as well as one's journey out of bondage and slavery.[32] For the *Didache* communities, therefore, God is immanently found within the fabric of life.[33] This includes both the calling and training processes of *Didache* novices,[34] as well as God being present as the host of the eucharistic meals.[35] In tune with the *Didache*'s views of the equality of all, God has no regard for social status,[36] for God's name is to be made holy in all things.[37]

As it relates to Jesus, He is simply seen as the messenger for the message, which is the "way of life." He is viewed as being the one who pioneered this "way."[38] As the *Didache* repeatedly asserts, "knowledge and faith and immortality" were revealed through Jesus.[39] With their central focus being on God the Father, the *Didache*'s views of Jesus are therefore quite low. There is no theology of the cross in this document,[40] nor is there any understanding of the eucharistic elements being the "body and blood" of Jesus.[41] As with its' anthro-cosmological views, the theology of the *Didache* is quite simple and sparse.

Theories of Change

With such apocalyptic expectations, one can imagine that concern for personal and social transformation was not very central. Indeed, as Milavec writes, "The *Didache* did not offer any plan for world transformation ... The time was too short. The members were too weak. The society was too out-of-step with their ambitions. All they could do was take care of each other, work at their trades, and celebrate their daily lives until the Lord comes."[42] All fundamental change, therefore, was primarily rooted

---

31. Ibid., 865.
32. Ibid., 866.
33. Ibid., 868.
34. Ibid., 848, 56.
35. Ibid., 382.
36. Ibid., 165.
37. Ibid., 333.
38. Ibid., 355, 855.
39. "Didache," 9:2, 9:3, 10:2, 10:3.
40. Milavec, *The Didache*, 652.
41. Ibid., 354.
42. Ibid., 868; see also ibid., 91.

Didache Communities

in the belief that God would bring the transformation that individuals and communities needed when God comes in the end times.[43]

While the *Didache* communities therefore did not have a theory of change for long-term, inner or communal spiritual formation as we might have hoped, they do offer insights into how novices were to be formed into the Way. "If you are able to bear the whole yoke of the Lord, you will be perfect" the *Didache* proclaims.[44] However, this is not "perfection" as is commonly used today. Instead, it is a perfection in the living of the Way. Again, the goal was to be on a Way that "enabled adherents to attain that 'perfection' that would be expected of them by the Lord on that last day."[45]

In order for such perfection to come about, initial conversion required a "reorientation of the soul of an individual"[46] as the novice entered the community. Once they begin gathering with the community, deep learning for the novice then comes about primarily by prolonged contact with a master.[47] Milavec offers a flowchart of the progress that a typical novice would move through according to the *Didache* : moving from calling to apprenticing to transformation to full incorporation into community culminating with their baptism.[48] While God is ultimately the one who perfects, protects, gathers, and sanctifies,[49] it is practicing righteousness and the Way that leads to a life in God.[50] Training was therefore the central way of transformation in the novices life.[51] In some sense, then, the *Didache*'s primary theory of change might be categorized as a "works righteousness" theory wherein one comes to be transformed by repeatedly living the Way within the supportive and guiding context of a *Didache* community.

Spiritual Formation Ideals & Goals

While the *Didache* does mention some of the spiritual formation ideals that are common for other programs, such as to love God and "love your

43. Ibid., 898.
44. "Didache," 6:2.
45. Milavec, *The Didache*, 475, 625, 845.
46. Ibid., 847.
47. Ibid., 88.
48. Ibid., 101.
49. "Didache," 10:5.
50. Milavec, *The Didache*, 151.
51. Ibid., 70–72, 75, 88, 92, 147.

61

PART TWO: Early Christian Diversity

neighbor as yourself,"[52] it really seems to have only one primary goal in mind, according to Milavec. This most central goal is, quite simply, for one to prepare for the coming of God's kingdom, the last days, by living the Way.[53] As stated above, only the "elect" will be saved in the last days. How does one become a member of the elect? By living the "Way" that Jesus pioneered. What Milavec terms "ordinary holiness"[54] is therefore what one needs in order to be fit for the end times so that they might be among the ones saved.[55] As Milavec writes, "The end-time scenario of the *Didache* urged vigilance and sustained effort to attain the perfection that the end time required."[56] The ends times were therefore viewed as bringing a righting of all things,[57] where "the gentle will inherit the earth."[58] The most central ideal for these *Didache* communities, therefore, was for each person to perfect themselves in the living of the Way so that they could be numbered among the ones saved in these final days.

Spiritual Formation Approaches

With such an ideal in place, it is therefore no surprise that the bulk of the *Didache*'s contents, and Milavec's book, is dedicated to outlining what this Way is and how one rightly lives it. The *Didache* essentially demands that a certain way of life be lived and this way is to be memorized and lived in all things.[59] As Milavec writes, the *Didache* "was bent on defining correct practice rather than hammering out correct belief."[60] Hence, its theology is given only to help orient people toward right action.[61] Milavec further claims that the *Didache*'s central question is: "What is the order of training for reorienting gentiles so that they can fully participate in the promises made to Israel and be gathered among the elect when the Lord comes?"[62] The *Didache* is seen as therefore passing on "the revealed way of

52. "Didache," 1:2.
53. Milavec, *The Didache*, 671, 892, 97.
54. Ibid., 625, 73, 864.
55. Ibid., 651.
56. Ibid., 673.
57. Ibid., 894.
58. Ibid., 897.
59. Ibid., 60, 163, 68, 244, 82, 382, 474, 847.
60. Ibid., 67; see also ibid., 108.
61. Ibid., 109.
62. Ibid., 845.

perfection"[63] in which the imitation of God is viewed as being important.[64] It is important that one's deeds match their words[65] and that they therefore continually guard themselves from all infractions, large or small.[66] The goal is to reach a place of development where, apart from God, nothing happens in the novice's life, and this comes via the practice of righteousness [67] as was discussed above.

While Milavec argues that *Didache* communities preached moderation in all spiritual practices,[68] there are also long lists in the *Didache* where many "you shall not's," such as murdering, corrupting young boys, having abortions, doing magic, lying, eating foods offered to idols, etc are codified and strictly prohibited.[69] They also used and adapted the Jewish Decalogue for gentiles in order to help them live the Way while still in the midst of Roman society thereby helping them set themselves apart from some of the more common Hellenistic practices of the day.[70]

In addition to following these shoulds and should nots, there were at least four other aspects and practices involved in this Way. One was the practice of confession and examination of conscience which served not only to help individuals in their journey, but also helped members of the community to be reconciled with each other.[71] Often performed communally,[72] confession was used as a weekly stimulus toward perfection [73] in preparation for Eucharist.[74] It was intended to help members continually be watchful, awake, and alert thereby helping to keep them in the way.[75]

Another practice was one's ever trusting in Divine providence by accepting all things as good because all things come from God.[76] Such trust

63. Ibid., 168, 475.
64. Ibid., 109, 90.
65. Ibid., 146.
66. Ibid., 147, 49.
67. Ibid., 151.
68. Ibid., 856.
69. "Didache," 2:2–3, 5:1–2.
70. Milavec, *The Didache*, 117, 28, 227.
71. Ibid., 167, 530, 41, 48–49, 68–69; "Didache," 4:14, 14:1A, 15:3B.
72. Milavec, *The Didache*, 531.
73. Ibid., 547.
74. Ibid., 543.
75. Ibid., 634.
76. Ibid., 157, 62; "Didache," 3:10.

means that vulnerability is required in all things as well—social, economic, religious, etc.[77] It means: one is to be nonviolent in one's prayers and actions;[78] loving, praying, and fasting for one's enemies and not judging them;[79] not resisting anyone, giving to others and helping those in need;[80] not being angry[81] and instead being gentle and long suffering.[82] This trust is also to lead members to cheerfully give tithes out of love for God as an expression of gratitude and an offer of piety.[83] Some of these tithes are to be given to prophets and/or beggars because the *Didache* communities considered being joined to the lowly and just as a central part of the Way.[84] Such distributive justice and giving to one another and those in need was therefore central for them,[85] and was an expression of their providential trust along with their pacifistic ideals.

Fasting was a third important practice in the keeping of the Way. The practice of fasting, and the grieving that often accompanies it, was a possible way of intensifying prayer and conversion, responding to the events of the day, of grieving the loss of one's previous identity, cleansing the body from impure foods, and training for the regular fasts of the community.[86] Most fasting was done in discretion and followed the Jewish fasts of the day.[87] Some of these fasts lasted an entire day, some during the day only, some only during the night, and some for days on end.[88] They were also intended to bring about increased communal solidarity.[89]

Finally, prayer was a central aspect of the life of those who sought to keep the Way. Members were admonished to pray the Lord's prayer three times per day.[90] It is also likely that, when prayed in worship, the Lord's Prayer was viewed as containing themes that were to be elaborated on

---

77. Milavec, *The Didache*, 891–92.
78. Ibid., 343, 47, 892.
79. "Didache," 1:3, 2:7, 11:11.
80. Ibid., 1:4, 1:6, 4:8, 5:2.
81. Ibid., 3:2.
82. Ibid., 3:7–8.
83. Milavec, *The Didache*, 109, 494–95, 500, 504; "Didache," 4:7, 13:3–4.
84. Milavec, *The Didache*, 519; "Didache," 3:9.
85. Milavec, *The Didache*, 108, 61, 90–91.
86. Ibid., 237, 43, 44, 53–58, 83.
87. Ibid., 296, 98.
88. Ibid., 296–97.
89. Ibid., 298, 300.
90. Ibid., 242, 308; "Didache," 8:2–3.

Didache Communities

by gifted leaders.[91] Being the central prayer of *Didache* communities, the Lord's Prayer "is the prayer delivered by the lord God in the good news delivered through his servant Jesus."[92] It is also believed that these communities made use of communal prayers and probably gathered together regularly in the mornings to pray.[93]

In support of these codified rules and practices, there were a number of spiritual formation supports that the *Didache* communities drew from in order to help novices to come to live in accordance with it. One of these was the central use of an intensive apprenticing program. The Greek word, "didache," basically means the systematic training that a mentor would give to an apprentice.[94] Viewed as a form of spiritual parenting, this was essentially a person-to-person way to transmit the gospel.[95] Novices were seen as coming to acquire from their mentors the necessary performance skills over a long period of time via trial and error wherein the mentor demonstrated the Way of Life to the novice.[96] With these relationships seen as being essential for spiritual transformation, novices were expected honor and meditate on what they were learning from their mentors and thereby achieve the mastery their teachers exhibited.[97]

In such mentoring, there were two primary ways of training: telling people what must positively be done, and telling novices what must be avoided.[98] The community, as a whole, also had mentors in the form of leaders who were chosen by the community.[99] These leaders, who were be gentle, non-money loving, truthful, and tested/reliable, decided the matters of the community, helped reconcile conflicts, and prepared for the rituals.[100] These individual and communal mentoring processes therefore comprised the metaphorical "bread and butter" of the *Didache*'s approaches to novice formation.

Another support, which is already obvious, is the emphasis they placed on importance of community. In such vital communities, where

91. Milavec, *The Didache*, 336.
92. Ibid., 343.
93. Ibid., 334, 42.
94. Ibid., xi, 71, 354.
95. Ibid., 75, 92, 860.
96. Ibid., 70–72, 88, 147, 57, 62, 68, 243, 75, 582.
97. Ibid., 92, 360, 848; "Didache," 4:1–2, 4:9, 4:13, 11:1.
98. Milavec, *The Didache*, 65.
99. Ibid., 582–83; "Didache," 15:1.
100. Milavec, *The Didache*, 588–89, 600, 602.

PART TWO: Early Christian Diversity

"'the saints' met daily for work, for prayer, and for mutual encouragement and support," and empowerment, helped members to separate themselves from the undesirable practices and dispositions of the Greek and Jewish cultures they grew up in.[101] It is in the context of these communities that members hold one another accountable, reconciliation takes place, and the work of saving perfection in the Way occurs.[102] These communities also help members to prepare for and endure the abusive treatments that they will mostly likely encounter in their own families as well as in society.[103]

A final support that *Didache* communities used to help their members along in their perfecting of the Way, was through the use of rituals. These rituals also had the primary purposes of incorporating people into the community. The two most central rituals were baptism and Eucharist.[104] Trinitarian baptism was seen as the fulfillment of novice training in the Way. It was a signal of the permanent transformation of the individual, baptism was seen as ushering in a new way of living with one's self, one's world, and the Christian community of which they were becoming a part of.[105] It was also a way of overturning the social status inequalities of the day.[106]

While baptism incorporated members into the community, Eucharist was meant as a way of sustaining them. Eucharist was viewed as "the source and summit of the community's spirituality," a way of participating in the community as a full member.[107] As already mentioned above, it focused on the Father rather than Jesus. While the elements were not seen as the "body and blood of Jesus," eucharistic elements were not considered to be just a normal meal either for this meal was consecrated and separated from other ordinary food.[108] Sharing in this "brought the newly baptized into a sense of the common election and shared hope with those present" in the hope of Israel's messianic expectations as well as bringing nourishment for their souls.[109] It therefore also had the task of binding the

---

101. Ibid., 157–58, 68, 236, 50, 75, 302, 305, 308, 45, 582; "Didache," 16:2.
102. Milavec, *The Didache*, 396, 549–50, 53, 882; "Didache," 4:3, 14:2, 15:3A.
103. Milavec, *The Didache*, 113, 891.
104. Ibid., 232.
105. Ibid., 232, 36, 44, 67, 74, 83, 889; "Didache," 7:1–3.
106. Milavec, *The Didache*, 276.
107. Ibid., 232, 76; "Didache," 9:1–2.
108. Milavec, *The Didache*, 354, 58.
109. Ibid., 364, 72, 74, 414, 890.

Didache Communities

community more intimately together as it further joined them together in walking toward holiness and perfection in the Way.[110]

Taken together, these codified rules, the practices that were regularly engaged, and the supports that these *Didache* communities utilized, comprised the bulk of their spiritually formative approaches. These approaches had the purpose of helping members toward perfection in the Way so that they might be counted among the elect in the last days.

Discernment

With one of their fundamental beliefs being that there are only two ways in life, coupled with the hostile and pluralistic environments in which they lived, discernment related to spiritual formation holds a privileged place in *Didache* communities. Put simply, the crux of their discernment approaches centered around one's abilities to know whether or not any given practice, teaching, etc. was more in accord with the ways of life or the ways of death.[111] As this played itself out in the *Didache*, the main focus of such discernment had to do with traveling prophets, which were common in their day. In essence, knowing the difference between true and false prophets came by observing their habits. The true ones were those who do what they teach, will not be idle, and follow the *Didache*'s guidelines.[112] They will also not stay too long nor will they seek to gain leadership within the community itself.[113] Overall, it seems, their primary method of discernment was therefore comparing one's life with the codified rules, practices, and lifestyle that was set out in the *Didache* and passed on by mentors and the community as a whole. In this "works righteousness" system, discernment seemed to at least partly be a matter of comparing one's lived actions with those that were expected of all *Didache* community members.

Evaluative Techniques

While neither the *Didache* nor Milavec's book explicitly discusses the evaluative techniques used by *Didache* communities, it is quite obvious to that they primarily used the codified Way as the basis for observing

---

110. Ibid., 376, 81, 570.
111. Ibid., 387.
112. Ibid., 436–37, 65; "Didache," 11:5–6, 11:8, 11:10, 12:4.
113. Milavec, *The Didache*, 447, 50, 65, 69.

PART TWO: Early Christian Diversity

one's life and deciding on what spiritually formative steps to take next. For instance, since the *Didache* explicitly outlines certain shoulds and should not's, one method of evaluation would therefore be to look at the life of a novice/member and see whether or not they are adhering to these rules and this lifestyle. In a similar fashion, one could observe how closely or not each member is living the Way: do they pray three times a day, do they gather when the community gathers, do they tithe and spend time in solidarity with the poor, etc. In short, a "work righteousness" approach to spiritual formation lends itself nicely to evaluation because most of the criteria in these approaches, at least for the *Didache*, are concerned with external behaviors. This then allows one to easily know if they are likely to be counted among the elect or not—according to how accurately they are living the "perfect" Way.

Summary/Reflections

In this sacred system, as we can see below, the underlying models of reality are quite simple: the end is near, so follow this "Way" and you will be numbered among the "elect" when it arrives. Their methods of discernment, evaluative approaches, and their approaches all flow directly from these. There is a great simplicity, therefore, in seeking to follow a set of codified rules and practices. It is intended to be a formative process for novices, helping them to grow and be nurtured in the Way through community, mentoring, rituals, and prayers. These *Didache* communities therefore stand as an example of communities who turn to set of views and approaches that are clearly defined for their followers and the resulting spiritual formation system being clearly built based upon them.

Didache Communities

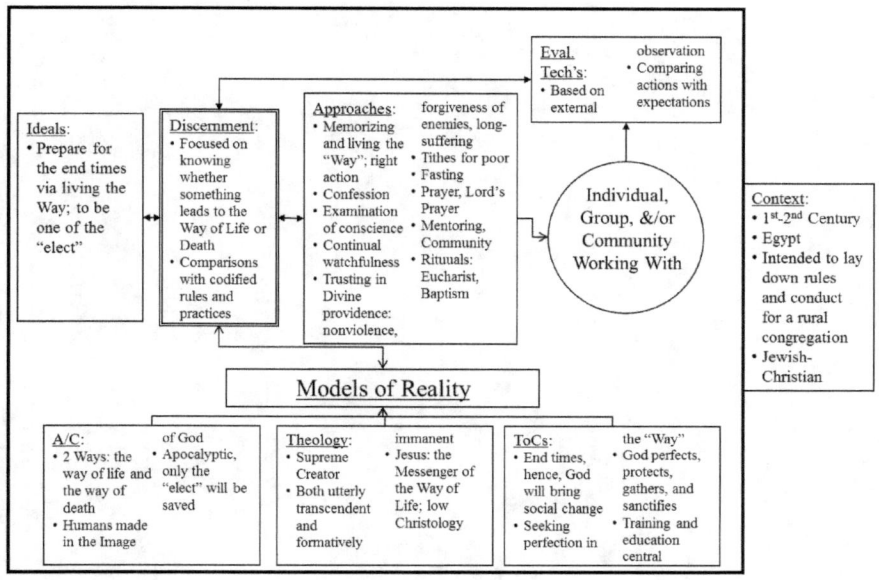

PART THREE

Early Monastic Formation

IN 313 CE, EMPEROR Constantine legalized Christianity in the Roman Empire for the first time.[1] Up until then, Christians had been, to varying degrees depending on local governance, a marginalized and sometimes deeply oppressed people.[2] A little more than sixty years later, under Emperor Theodosius, Christianity was declared the only legal religion in the Empire, thereby helping to usher in a new era in its history.[3] Rather than being a collection of widely scattered and diverse communities, Christian leaders now found themselves tasked with clarifying orthodoxy and orthopraxy (i.e., right thinking and right practice) increasingly throughout this era (and on into the next) and creating a more centralized hierarchy.[4] Though it had already been on this road from the very beginning, Christianity therefore found itself needing to become more of a unified institution in ways that it had not been so previously.

However, this new era in Western Christian history was marked by an even greater challenge that irrevocably shaped its future course: the Western Roman Empire collapsed roughly around 410 CE when Rome was sacked.[5] Germanic tribes invading from the north successively conquered more and more land pushing the Empire's protected boundaries all

---

1. Chidester, *Christianity*, 91; McGuckin, "The Early Church Fathers (1st to 6th Centuries)," 56, 58; Sheldrake, *Brief History of Spirituality*, 24.

2. Chidester, *Christianity*, 91; McGuckin, "The Early Church Fathers (1st to 6th Centuries)," 50; Sheldrake, *Brief History of Spirituality*, 24, 40; Woods, *Christian Spirituality*, 32.

3. Chidester, *Christianity*, 91; Sheldrake, *Brief History of Spirituality*, 40.

4. Chidester, *Christianity*, 91–92, 99; Sheldrake, *Brief History of Spirituality*, 26–27, 73–74; Woods, *Christian Spirituality*, 43, 55, 71.

5. Dales, "Celtic and Anglo-Saxon Spirituality," 88; McGuckin, "The Early Church Fathers (1st to 6th Centuries)," 32; Woods, *Christian Spirituality*, 73, 83.

PART THREE: Early Monastic Formation

the way back to its recently established capital of Constantinople.[6] There the Eastern Roman Empire (which became the Byzantine Empire), along with its own brand of Eastern Orthodox Christianity, continued to flourish for many more generations until it was eventually conquered by invaders in 1453 CE.[7]

Long before the collapse of the Roman Empire in Europe, however, there had already been a long history of women and men of different religious traditions—as we saw with Philo's text—journeying into remote places to live a life more centered on God.[8] Even early on in Christianity's history did such monastic and hermetic communities spring up.[9] The tendencies to want to, often in accordance with Platonic and neoplatonic worldviews as we shall see, separate one's self from the larger culture and live one's life more intentionally and religiously focused on God via monasticism took an increasing hold on some Christians as time went on.[10]

While these monastic communities were a significant part of early Christianity, they became essential to its survival after the fall of the Western part of the Roman Empire.[11] As the influence of the Empire lessened in these parts of Europe, local communities became more and more independent and self-sufficient as a feudal system of governance gradually took hold.[12] In this context, local monasteries became centers of education, culture, and food production.[13] They helped to preserve traditions, housed libraries, operated hospitals, furthered philosophy, theology, and science and acted as tutors and teachers for locals, particularly the upper and noble classes.[14] Monastic missionaries also played a central role in spreading Western Christianity and culture throughout Europe and

---

6. McGuckin, "The Early Church Fathers (1st to 6th Centuries)," 68; Woods, *Christian Spirituality*, 70.

7. Chidester, *Christianity*, 332; Sheldrake, *Brief History of Spirituality*, 67; Woods, *Christian Spirituality*, 91, 113.

8. Chidester, *Christianity*, 8, 116–17; Sheldrake, *Brief History of Spirituality*, 41.

9. Chidester, *Christianity*, 117; Sheldrake, *Brief History of Spirituality*, 42–45.

10. Farmer, "Saints and Mystics of the Medieval West," 91; Sheldrake, *Brief History of Spirituality*, 31; Woods, *Christian Spirituality*, 62–63.

11. Sheldrake, *Brief History of Spirituality*, 40–41; Woods, *Christian Spirituality*, 83.

12. Chidester, *Christianity*, 187; Woods, *Christian Spirituality*, 116.

13. Farmer, "Saints and Mystics of the Medieval West," 94; Sheldrake, *Brief History of Spirituality*, 40, 65; Woods, *Christian Spirituality*, 87.

14. Farmer, "Saints and Mystics of the Medieval West," 100, 105, 15; Woods, *Christian Spirituality*, 87, 102.

PART THREE: Early Monastic Formation

beyond and many monastic movements sought reform within the church.[15] It helped to shape the church's teachings, was the source of religious leaders, began the first universities in Europe, and helped to shape the local and general culture and direction of this part of the world.[16] Though the term is rightly contested, monasteries essentially were sources of light during these "Dark Ages."[17]

As a result, the influence of monasticism in Western Christianity cannot be overstated.[18] In addition to all of this, however, is the way of life that it offered to those who chose to become avowed nuns and monks within their walls.[19] Personal transformation as it was conceived of by many monastic communities has played in central role in how we think about spiritual formation right on through to today.[20] It therefore behooves us to look closely at a couple of examples of the ways of life that Western Christian monasticism embraced during this era.

While there are a number of resources that come to us from this era, we will be focusing on two texts from its earlier times. The first are the *Conferences* of John Cassian. This text has had a major influence on many monastic orders throughout the ages, particularly on Benedictine communities. The second text is the first volume of the *Philokalia*. This text is our one brief look into personal spiritual formation as it went on to influence a branch of Eastern Orthodox Christianity known as the hesychast movement.[21] While Eastern and Western approaches to personal transformation do have significant differences, they also share many similarities. Both of these texts are therefore intended to not only give us insights into monastic spiritual formation at the level of the individual but to also see some of the great diversity that there has and continues to be in Christianity as a whole.

---

15. Dales, "Celtic and Anglo-Saxon Spirituality," 76, 80; Farmer, "Saints and Mystics of the Medieval West," 94–95; Sheldrake, *Brief History of Spirituality*, 40–41, 62–63; Woods, *Christian Spirituality*, 87, 94, 100.

16. Chidester, *Christianity*, 167, 82; Sheldrake, *Brief History of Spirituality*, 81; Woods, *Christian Spirituality*, 99, 117.

17. Woods, *Christian Spirituality*, 87.

18. Sheldrake, *Brief History of Spirituality*, 40; Woods, *Christian Spirituality*, 86, 89.

19. Chidester, *Christianity*, 180–81; Sheldrake, *Brief History of Spirituality*, 40, 49–50, 60; Woods, *Christian Spirituality*, 84.

20. Chidester, *Christianity*, 180; Sheldrake, *Brief History of Spirituality*, 40.

21. McGuckin, "The Eastern Christian Tradition," 149.

5

Cassian's *Conferences*

Context

CASSIAN WAS BORN SOMETIME around 360 CE in what is present day Romania. He was educated in the Greek classics as a child and later left his "genteel" family to join a monastery in Jerusalem. He also spent as much as ten years in Egypt learning from some of the famous ascetics there. From there, he spent some time in Constantinople where he was "ordained to the diaconate" by John Chrysostom. After serving in the priesthood for some time, he left for Marseilles where he founded two monasteries. It was there that he spent the rest of his days, dying sometime around 430 CE. His works have gone on to influence such notables as Benedict of Nursia, Gregory the Great, and Thomas Aquinas.

His work, *The Conferences,* which I will be drawing from for this project, is by far the longest work we have from Christian antiquity. Cast in the genre of conversations that Cassian and his friend have with various desert masters in Egypt, this works draws from some of the major ascetical and philosophical movements of his day such as the Stoics and Augustine. This work focuses on matters of spirituality, one's spiritual development, battling demons, and the life which monks should live. Overall, the goal of the *Conferences* is a "purity of heart, and the end is the kingdom of heaven," and some describe Cassian as "a master of the inner life." With this context in mind, it is to Cassian's *Conferences* that we shall now turn in an effort to gain a better understanding of the system of spiritual formation described by these Egyptian monks. Given the length of this text, almost 800 pages in length, we will primarily be drawing from the conferences found in the first two (of three) parts.[1] It should also be noted that we will attempting to construct a more systematic understanding of personal transformation from the many gurus that Cassian and his friend interview, so there will be variations among them. Nevertheless, some common themes do emerge.

Models of Reality

Anthropological-Cosmological

The anthro-cosmology of these writings are very much reflective of the Greco-Roman views of the time and are similar to some of those we have already reviewed. The desires of the flesh are viewed as being at odds with the desires of the spirit[2] in a dichotomized world that was designed by God.[3] There is therefore a constant battle between the two.[4] As long as we are in "perishable flesh," it is asserted, we cannot be "inseparably united to [God]" and are therefore inherently limited.[5] One of the desert masters, for instance, in referring to Paul's discussion of flesh versus spirit, asserts that while flesh has many different meanings in Scripture, it is taken to mean "the will of the flesh and to its worst desires."[6] "Spirit," on the other hand, means "the good and spiritual desires of the soul."[7] Flesh therefore desire things of world, whereas spirit rejects the "honorable" things of the world.[8] Spirit is therefore taken as only nurturing goodness,[9] while others see the soul as a "light feather or plume" and "is naturally borne to the heavenly heights," but is weighted down by the passions of the earth.[10] It is this flesh versus spirit view that characterizes their approaches to personal transformation.

---

1. More specifically, I will be focusing on the following 11 conferences (there are 24 conferences in all): 1, 2, 4, 7, 9–11, and 13–16.
2. Cassian, *John Cassian*, 48, 158.
3. Ibid., 159, 376.
4. Ibid., 161–62, 334.
5. Ibid., 50, 54, 165, 379.
6. Ibid., 160.
7. Ibid., 161.
8. Ibid.
9. Ibid., 163.
10. Ibid., 331–32.

Human free will is then seen to be situated between these,[11] and is ever vacillating between the two. We can, at one time, be in spiritual bliss and, at another, be oppressed with sadness.[12] The source of such changeableness is to be found in our nature as humans. As one master asserts, "We believe that these wanderings of the soul which exist in the human race are not our own fault but nature's";[13] particularly the mind. The mind is observed to be ever changing,[14] which is why we need to keep it preoccupied.[15] Control of the mind's thoughts is also considered to be beyond us, but acceptance or rejecting of the thoughts that arise from it is not.[16] This is because the mind has the ability to see and grasp God by pure vision "in accordance with the character of our life and the purity of our heart."[17] In this framework, then, the grace of God and human free will are both an intimate and inseparable part of each other and therefore are both a part of our spiritual journey.[18] The core of this journey, as we shall see, therefore lies in one harnessing their mind and free will in accordance with the grace of God so that they may ascend to spiritual heights from the passions of the flesh.

As it relates to the world, it is viewed as being one of inequality in which demons are an intimate and struggling part. One monk highlights these inequalities when he asserts that as long as there is inequality in the world, we need works of charity.[19] In these inequalities and struggles, battles with the devil and demons are considered to be a part of life.[20] These demons and evil spirits are from the higher orders of angels[21] and many of them do different acts of mischief in the world.[22] However, they really have no genuine power over us,[23] except for those people who allow them

11. Ibid., 161.
12. Ibid., 156.
13. Ibid., 249.
14. Ibid., 250, 335, 86.
15. Ibid., 250.
16. Ibid., 56.
17. Ibid.
18. Ibid., 477–78.
19. Ibid., 49.
20. Ibid., 100, 56, 254, 57–58.
21. Ibid., 164.
22. Ibid., 269.
23. Ibid., 262.

to influence their lives.[24] Nevertheless, they do interfere with the workings of God and the angels.[25] These desert monastics assert that it is only with God and Christ's help that we can overcome and endure their continuous assaults and temptations.[26] We also need each other's help,[27] and the angels are there to guard and help us as well.[28] It is this anthro-cosmological framework, with its distinct emphasis on the power and use of the mind in congruence with the works and help of God, that fundamentally shapes the system of spiritual formation found in these desert monasteries.

Theological

Within this framework, God is "clearly perceived in the grandeur of the things that he has created."[29] The Trinity is able to penetrate and pour into all things[30] because "nothing is incorporeal but God alone, and therefore only to him can every spiritual and intellectual substance be penetrable because he alone is whole and everywhere and in all things."[31] God is therefore seen to be present in all things.

This everywhere present God, through God's "grace and mercy," always works for the good in us, though it also reproves and chastises.[32] As one of the masters proclaims, "the grace of Christ is at hand every day. It calls out . . . to everyone without exception."[33] God ever works with, calls out to, and forms even those who do not seek God.[34] God is therefore always there at hand to help[35] for the things of salvation are not possible without God.[36] However, God also understood to leave and test us[37] and the flesh/spirit struggles are viewed as being a part of God's designs as

24. Ibid., 254, 64.
25. Ibid., 351.
26. Ibid., 260, 345.
27. Ibid., 263.
28. Ibid., 514.
29. Ibid., 55.
30. Ibid., 256.
31. Ibid., 257.
32. Ibid., 157.
33. Ibid., 472; see also ibid., 74.
34. Ibid., 474.
35. Ibid., 379, 409.
36. Ibid., 470.
37. Ibid., 158, 484, 544.

mentioned above.[38] Also, while God does not give to those who are lazy,[39] no one is "ever tried without the permission of God" and everything that is "brought upon us by God" comes with the care of a "tender father" and "merciful physician."[40] The primary theological view of God, therefore, is an image of an omnipresent shepherd who ever works to nurture us along in our individual spiritual growth.

Theories of Change

These writings contain the most extensive reflections on the dynamics of personal transformation that we have encountered thus far in our explorations. This really should come as no surprise, however, for the purpose of these *Conferences* is for Cassian and his friend to seek out how to better and more effectively live out their personally growing spiritual lives. Throughout this text, the various monks assert that one can only attain true and lasting progress with divine help.[41] As one advisor admonished, we need God in both sadness as well as in joyous times lest we be snatched away in either. Hence, we should ever cry out, one of these monks asserts, "O God, incline unto my aid; O Lord, make haste to help me."[42] He continues his admonishment by saying, "This verse should be poured out in unceasing prayer so that we may be delivered in adversity and preserved and not puffed up in prosperity . . . meditate constantly on this verse in your heart."[43] We therefore must cling to God in order to change and to "cut off the desires of this world"[44] for "it is up to us to conform humbly to the grace of God that daily draws us on."[45] Angels also help to open us up and change us,[46] and it is through such divine interventions that God slowly works with us, building us up in strength and uprightness,[47] even overcoming our weakness of faith.[48]

38. Ibid., 159.
39. Ibid., 468.
40. Ibid., 267.
41. Ibid., 83, 97, 376, 467–68, 75, 90.
42. Ibid., 380.
43. Ibid., 382, 84.
44. Ibid., 253.
45. Ibid., 469.
46. Ibid., 247–48.
47. Ibid., 485–86.
48. Ibid., 487.

However, progress, it was noted above, is a combination of both God and the human will.[49] We also recall that the mind is given a central place, for it is the mind that can be directly crafted to bring the perfections that these monks sought after. Again and again, these masters asserts that we need to remain steadfastly focused on, and ever mindful of, our end and goal, with our minds ever attached to divine things, ever watchful, ever praying to God unceasingly.[50] "By way of this goal," one monks notes, "I forget what is behind—namely, the vices of my earlier life—and I strive to attain to the end, which is the heavenly prize."[51]

By this constant focus, the mind "gains experience and learns with what things to equip its memory, to what purpose it should direct its unceasing flights, and why it should acquire the power to remain fixed in one place."[52] This mindfulness is necessary because "the human mind cannot be open to every thought, and therefore as long as it is not occupied with spiritual pursuits it will inevitably be wrapped up in those that it learned some time before."[53] These practices therefore have the intention of cultivating "a solid firmness of soul"[54] in which the "continual awareness of God"[55] is attainable by its practitioners.

For these monks, then, there is a direct correlation between one's ability to be mindful of God and the level of one's purity.[56] It is by these efforts, therefore, that the holiness of one's thoughts, the purity of one's heart, and the chastity of one's flesh is attained.[57] As one master advises, "You see, then, that it is in our power to set up in our hearts either ascents, which are thoughts that touch God, or descents, which sink down to earthly and carnal things."[58]

Following a line of thinking that parallels the flesh/spirit dichotomies, these monastics mindfully seek to shun all vices in the pursuit of the virtues. By virtue or vice, it is asserted, we make our hearts the abode of Christ or of the devil.[59] We therefore need to cultivate the virtues and be

49. Ibid., 479, 81, 85, 523.
50. Ibid., 43–44, 46, 253, 377, 79, 83, 475, 514, 20.
51. Ibid., 44.
52. Ibid., 250.
53. Ibid., 517.
54. Ibid., 386.
55. Ibid., 379.
56. Ibid., 374, 78.
57. Ibid., 56–57, 162–63, 247, 376, 77, 517.
58. Ibid., 250; see also ibid., 48, 512, 22.
59. Ibid., 51.

purged of all vices before perfect prayer can be attained, and goodness adhered to.[60] We must therefore know what the vices are and how to remedy them, and how to form the mind via the virtues,[61] remembering that doing both requires much effort.[62] Finally, in these pursuits, we must know that "there are three things that restrain people from vice—namely, the fear of Gehenna or of present laws; of hope and desire for the kingdom of heaven; or a disposition for the good itself and a love of virtue."[63]

As one therefore grows in mindfulness, the purging of vices, and the pursuit of virtues, the good things of God will then further come forth within one's self.[64] As one monk testifies, "once the mind's attentiveness has been set ablaze, it is called forth in an unspeakable ecstasy of heart and with an insatiable gladness of spirit, and the mind, having transcended all feelings and visible matter, pours it out to God with unutterable groans and sighs."[65] In order to attain this, however, we must give all, especially in our hearts, to God[66] for spiritual knowledge does not come to an impure mind.[67] Nonetheless, even though we might have achieved some level of progress spiritually, we can always regress and become "lukewarm."[68]

The overall theory of change that has emerged here, then, is one that seems primarily related to a retraining of the mind and heart. Through the practice of unceasing prayer and the various spiritual disciplines, one's mind will gradually come to ever be filled with thoughts that "touch" God. Alternatively, as one practices the virtues and shuns the vices, their hearts will inevitably come to be filled with the love and goodness of God.

It is essentially is a view of the soul, or person, as a pattern-formed person. Since a person is born into sinful flesh, according to this scheme, they have become habituated and patterned according to the vices of the world. Their theory of change, therefore, is one where these habits and patterns need to be reshaped through the continuous practices that they use, which will be discussed below. Such reshaping, they assert, is an unending process for if one stops living the monastic way of life, they will inevitably

60. Ibid., 329–30, 413, 18–19.
61. Ibid., 506.
62. Ibid., 253, 506.
63. Ibid., 411.
64. Ibid., 490.
65. Ibid., 385.
66. Ibid., 45.
67. Ibid., 514.
68. Ibid., 167, 263, 411, 523.

begin to descend back down into the lower and more vice-ridden realms of earth or the flesh.

With this said, the image of the soul as a feather, mentioned above, is an appropriate one for capturing the general gist of their theory of change. In order to ascend and grow spiritually, one needs the constant up-lifting breath of God that comes via mindfulness and the other personal spiritual disciplines. If one stops, the feather will immediately begin to fall back down toward sinful earth.

Spiritual Formation Ideals & Goals

As noted in the Context section above, the kin-dom of God is seen as being the ultimate end goal of a monk[69] as is the purity of heart and flesh; what is called holiness.[70] These monks assert that the end goal is eternal life and the salvation of all[71] for God made us to live forever; to be upright.[72] What these end goals mean more specifically, however, is not completely clear. Since these conferences were conducted by Cassian and his friend with different monks, the views on this subject appear to vary. At least one of these monks asserts that love is the most important thing when he states, "You see, then, that nothing is more precious, nothing more perfect, nothing more sublime, and—as I might say—nothing more enduring than love."[73] Others, however, assert that it is an "inner tranquility of the heart,"[74] "righteousness and peace and joy,"[75] or a "continual tranquility of mind and perpetual purity"[76] that is the true perfection or kin-dom of God. Still others point to the "the contemplation of divine things in perpetual purity of heart"[77] as being the ultimate ideal to be striven after.

While it may be argued that each of these views are basically asserting similar final goals, it is also important to keep in mind the quotable quote by one of the masters in relation to such discussions: "understanding's

---

69. Ibid., 42.
70. Ibid., 43, 44, 163, 247.
71. Ibid., 44, 343.
72. Ibid., 472, 78.
73. Ibid., 419.
74. Ibid., 571, 73.
75. Ibid., 51.
76. Ibid., 329; see also ibid., 76.
77. Ibid., 41, 47, 49, 159, 784.

highest function is to know that you do not know."[78] Nevertheless, these perspectives do seem to paint a picture of where these monastics were headed—namely, to a place of inner peace, purity, and stillness where God's all-pervading love dwells.

Spiritual Formation Approaches

With these goals in mind, a habit-centered theory of change in place, and with unending mindfulness of God as their one of their central means,[79] these monks employed a whole range of personal spiritual formation approaches to draw from and help to cultivate an increasingly perfected life. Such practices included: fasting, hunger, thirst, watchfulness, reading, vigils, labors, meditations, solitude, bodily deprivations, unceasing prayer, the "squalor of the desert," patience in tribulation, renunciations, pleading "tirelessly for internal chastity of heart and soul," serving God in the midst of taunting, and the unending pursuit of truth.[80] Ultimately, these many practices were used with the intention of cleansing one from the flesh, purifying one's heart, stabilizing one's mind, and solidifying one's soul.[81] With so many practices and disciplines, these masters stress that they are merely the "tools of perfection," not perfection itself[82] and do not necessarily guarantee a growing life of perfection.[83] And in all of these, a few of these monks stress moderation and discretion.[84]

With such an emphasis on prayer and mindfulness, some guidance is also given regarding them. According to at least one of the masters, there are four kinds of prayer: supplication, prayer, intercession, and thanksgiving.[85] A supplication is "a petition concerning sins,"[86] prayers are "those acts by which we offer or vow something to God,"[87] intercessions are made on behalf of others,[88] and thanksgiving prayers are what the mind "offers

78. Ibid., 159.
79. Ibid., 43, 46, 50, 52, 63, 377.
80. Ibid., 45, 163, 71, 247, 386.
81. Ibid., 45, 48, 247, 386.
82. Ibid., 46, 49.
83. Ibid., 171.
84. Ibid., 85, 101, 265.
85. Ibid., 336–37.
86. Ibid., 337.
87. Ibid.
88. Ibid.

to the Lord in unspeakable ecstasies."[89] In addition to these, there is also a "more sublime and exalted" kind of prayer in which "the mind, having been dissolved and flung into love of him, speaks most familiarly and with particular devotion to God as to its own father."[90]

In each of these kinds of prayer, there is an acknowledged need for silence and stillness within one's self when making them.[91] And, as was discussed above, it is through these kinds of prayers that one's personal spiritual journey progresses, purification comes, and God is ever more clearly perceived.[92] This of course assumes that our prayers are insistent, full of confidence, and unceasing.[93] Truly it is, that prayer was the very heartbeat of these communities.

However, it was also recognized that solitary prayers alone were not enough to help one in their spiritual lives. While these monks did assert that it is only by withdrawing from the world into the empty deserts where one can see the brightness of God and ascend to the virtues (though one monk did acknowledge that Jesus didn't need to do this),[94] community was considered as being crucial. In these monastic communities, monks would watch out and pray for one another,[95] and form vital friendships that were based on the "true and indissoluble love that grows by the combined perfection and virtue of the friends."[96] In addition to individual spiritual formation, these monks were therefore also involved in relational spiritual formation as well.

These communities also held spiritual mentoring to be central for helping one another to judge what is right and wrong.[97] In these conferences do we hear many discussions about what various monks think on different subjects, almost like these desert monks are constantly talking and comparing notes on the spiritual life with one another.[98] While much of this communally experienced mentoring was intended for novices,[99] it

89. Ibid., 338.
90. Ibid.
91. Ibid., 353, 512.
92. Ibid., 55, 374, 505, 12–13.
93. Ibid., 350, 53, 471.
94. Ibid., 169, 375, 512.
95. Ibid., 263.
96. Ibid., 557–58.
97. Ibid., 90–91, 93, 99, 512.
98. Ibid., 506–7.
99. Ibid., 513, 19.

PART THREE: Early Monastic Formation

was also asserted that "no one, however well-endowed with knowledge, should persuade himself with empty pride that he does not need anyone else's advice."[100] Community therefore was considered an essential part of one's growing spiritual life.

Finally, we find the centrality and importance of education and learning as being a vital part of their approaches. It was primarily an education in the wisdom and teachings of the ancients, as well as Scripture, and was considered vital for personal spiritual progress and avoidance of error.[101] Such learning begins by reflecting on things known, such as the lives of holy persons and matters of ethics, and then moves on to God alone.[102] This education, especially in the Scriptures which the masters quoted constantly, fosters one's individual growth.[103]

These, then, were among the primary approaches that these communities utilized in their pursuit of perfection in light of their models of reality and theories of change. They were intended help each person liberate themselves from the bonds of the flesh and sustainably elevate themselves to the heights of spiritual attunement. They seem to have the primary focus of keeping the mind stayed on God, purging the body of fleshy passions, and helping the individual to ever remain on the endless journey of eternal salvation.

Discernment

Throughout these conferences, discernment is a central topic of conversation. For instance, it is asserted that where there is peace, righteousness, and joy, there is the kin-dom of God, but where there is "discord and the sadness that produces death," there is the devil.[104] Also, with such an emphasis on keeping one's mind stayed on God, there is a need for tracing and discerning the origins of one's thoughts so that they will know how to deal with them.[105] Such discernment of thought is necessary because of the mind's susceptibilities distortions the truth.[106] "All the secret places of our heart, therefore, must be constantly scrutinized and the prints of whatever

100. Ibid., 564.
101. Ibid., 373, 511–12, 15.
102. Ibid., 47, 505, 12.
103. Ibid., 515.
104. Ibid., 51–52.
105. Ibid., 59.
106. Ibid., 60–61.

enters them must be investigated in the most careful way," advises one monk.[107] We must therefore ever measure the content of our thoughts against the goodness of God, and form our thoughts in the virtues.[108]

Such discernment does not only apply to our thoughts, but to all the other parts of our lives as well. Calling it "discretion," something which is only given by God through true humility and the guidance of elders,[109] it "avoids excess of any kind and teaches the monk always to proceed along the royal road and does not let him be inflated by virtues"; "it is called the eye and the light of the body in the Gospel."[110] Accordingly, all other virtues need the foundation of discretion in order to grow.[111] Discretion helps one to know whether an elder is truly spiritual or not,[112] and to what extent they are to partake in ascetical practices such as fasting.[113] Such discretion is therefore to be utilized in every aspect of the monk's life, and essentially acts as the compass through which Gods leads one to perfection.

We also find discernment being discussed in relation to the uniqueness of each person's journey according to their current development, gifts, and cultural and educational histories. For instance, the prayer's that one uses are dependent on "the degree of purity to which each mind has attained, and according to the nature of the condition either to which it has declined because of what has happened to it or to which it has renewed itself by its own efforts."[114] Hence, we must choose prayer accordingly,[115] for each prayer has a different purpose given the compunctions, joys, hopes, progress, et cetera that one is currently experiencing.[116] Similarly, it is recognized that each person's journey is unique for there are different degrees of perfection[117] and God allows and accounts "for the salvation of the human race in numberless different manners and in inscrutable ways."[118] Finally, each person is considered to have different gifts and ministries[119]

107. Ibid., 63.
108. Ibid., 62, 506, 18.
109. Ibid., 84, 90–91, 93, 99, 102.
110. Ibid., 85.
111. Ibid., 87.
112. Ibid., 167–68, 538, 41.
113. Ibid., 101.
114. Ibid., 335.
115. Ibid., 336.
116. Ibid., 338.
117. Ibid., 418.
118. Ibid., 488.
119. Ibid., 507, 42.

for "it is impossible for one and the same person to shine simultaneously in all the virtues."[120]

These, then, comprise the understandings of discernment set forth in some of these conferences. It is a very robust approach to discernment that seems to rely on the consideration of one's personal histories and experiences, Scriptures, the wisdom and teachings of the ancients, local conditions, and the reflections of mentors and the community at large. All of these taken together seem as if they should allow for enough support and accountability to help keep one on an ever growing path, whilst simultaneously allowing for enough freedom and diversity that one is able to progress personally according to their own unique path. Overall, then, it seems to stand as a good model for providing guidance and sufficient nurturing for spiritual formation programs.

Evaluative Techniques

From the previous discussions, it is clear that there are at least two primary evaluative techniques that are being utilized in support of aiding someone in their spiritual growth. The first is their personal experiences and how they reflect on and encounter them in light of Scriptures, traditions, mentors, and their communities. By continually watching one's own thoughts and inner movements, they are better enabled to respond to what arises in their lives. The second one seems to be the external observations that mentors, spiritual friends, and the community-at-large makes of them. Through their sharing, mentors and friends are able to help evaluate and assess how things are going for one another and therefore offer critical insights and feedback. Similarly, the community-at-large can also observe the "fruits" of one's life as they share their lives together. Through both of these, internal and external, each person should be enabled to continually assess their progress and thereby make adjustments on a regular basis according to this system of personal spiritual transformation.

Summary/Reflections

These desert monks strove for a way of life that genuinely and continuously nurtured individual (as well as relational) spiritual growth of those in their midst as we can see below. As a result, their approaches are quite

---

120. Ibid., 508.

holistic and truly transformative. For them, a focus on mindfulness was one that was believed to be essential for any growing spiritual life. Interestingly enough, their views of how thought patterns are formed and changed are very resonant with the findings of some modern cognitive studies and theories, one of which we shall review later in this book.

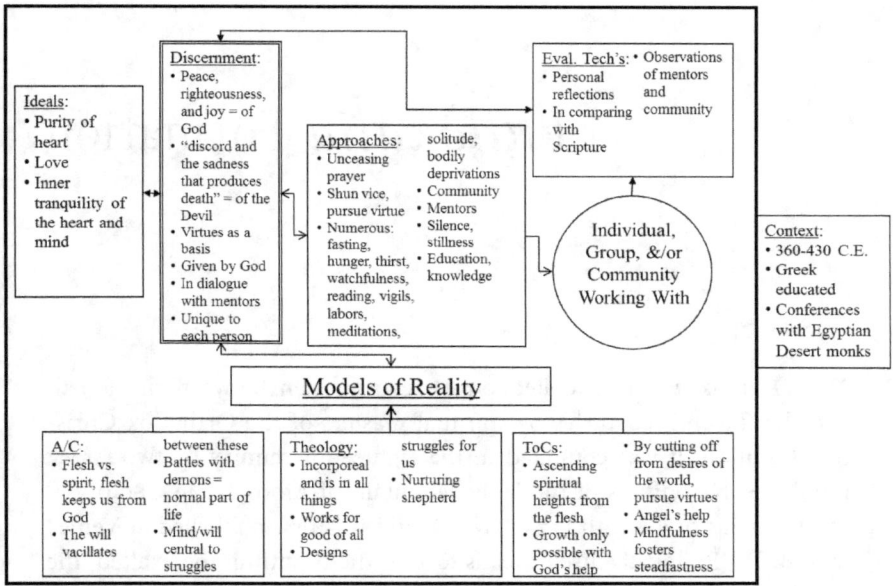

These *Conferences* therefore not only stand as a comprehensive system of personal transformation, and one that is still widely read today for guidance into the growing individual spiritual life, but also as an historical insight into how these communities lived and flourished during this era. We can also note how the neoplatonic worldviews that we have been encountering, and were so common of this time period, began to take on a more distinctively Christian flavor and form in these early desert monastic communities. As we shall see, their insights and lifestyles continued to influence how Western Christianity viewed and approached personal transformation for many centuries to come.

6

Philokalia Formation

Context

"The *Philokalia* is a collection of texts written between the fourth and the fifteenth centuries by spiritual masters of the Orthodox Christian tradition. It was compiled in the eighteenth century by two Greek monks, St Nikodimos of the Holy Mountain of Athos (1749–1809) and St Markarios of Corinth (1731–1805), and was first published at Venice in 1782."[1] "'Philokalia' itself means love of the beautiful, the exalted, the excellent, understood as the transcendent source of life and the revelation of Truth."[2] These texts were intended to help one along as they sought "purification, illumination and perfection."[3] There focus is help people to develop and sharpen their intellects, to become ever more watchful since this is considered to be the "hallmark of sanctity."[4] All in all, these texts are intended to be a guide to the contemplative life, particularly in the Eastern hesychast movement,[5] with its emphasis on silence and stillness. These texts are therefore intended for those who are thoroughly connected to the Eastern Orthodox tradition and monastic movements.[6] Nevertheless, this

---

1. *Philokalia*, 11.
2. Ibid., 13.
3. Ibid.
4. Ibid.
5. Ibid., 14–15.
6. Ibid., 15.

way of life and their goals of perfection are considered to be the vocation of every single person.[7]

For our purposes here, we will be focusing on parts of Volume I of the *Philokalia*.[8] Each of the authors in this volume primarily come from the fourth and fifth centuries (though one is thought to have lived in the sixth or seventh century). As with Cassian's *Conferences*, we will be attempting to synthesize a common framework from among multiple authors. In doing so, we again discover some common themes that emerge thereby giving us insights into the personal transformation systems of these writers.

Models of Reality

Anthropological-Cosmological

The anthro-cosmology found in these texts is largely neoplatonic. For their anthropology, body, soul, and spirit are considered to be the core attributes of humans and these are seen as being initially divided.[9] Because of Adam's sin, all souls are fragmented and split.[10] Some authors consider the soul to have three parts: incensive power (as in: "be incensed . . . against sin"), desires, and intellect.[11] For others, the lower part of the soul is considered to fundamentally be an appetitive part.[12] It is in this lower part that we find the passions that are common to all creatures and "lie concealed beneath our rational and spiritual nature."[13] These passions of the flesh, which can

---

7. Ibid., 16.

8. The entire *Philokalia* is four volumes total, more than 1,400 pages in length. We will only be focusing on those sections that seem most relevant. For instance, since we have already spent some time with Cassian's framework, we will be skipping this section. Also, we will not be reading the section by St. John of Karpathos as it seems less related to our efforts here as well as redundant to some of the other sections that we will be reviewing. Most of the rest of the text, however, is relevant to our pursuits in this book.

9. Ibid., 26.

10. Ibid., 261.

11. Ibid., 184.

12. Ibid., 47.

13. Ibid., 49.

PART THREE: Early Monastic Formation

never be fully satisfied,[14] are viewed as being distracting and evil,[15] leading to death and sleep,[16] and the higher intellect is blinded by them.[17]

Within this split between the lower and higher parts of the soul, and similar to what we found in the *Conferences,* good thoughts and bad thoughts battle against one another and we must therefore learn to recognize the difference between the two.[18] For instance, anger is seen as being a natural part of the intellect and our passions as well as this anger can help us toward purity. On the contrary, hatred of others is to be avoided.[19] The role of the intellect in this battle and the presence of free will allow us to choose as we wish between good and bad.[20] Nevertheless, the intellect is not be trusted since from the intellect comes evil and distractions.[21] As one monk writes, "When you sin, blame your thought, not your action. For had your intellect not run ahead, your body would not have followed"[22] since the body always follows the intellect.[23] Additionally, "the intellect changes from one to another of three different noetic states: that according to nature, above nature, and contrary to nature."[24] Hence, this author goes on to assert, nature is considered to be evil, but above nature are the fruits of the Spirit.[25] As we can see, the person is basically enmeshed in this struggle between good and evil; the passions of the lower part of the soul with the higher part. One must therefore choose which part/side they will follow.

Cosmologically, there are both angels and demons at odds against one another and against humans. Angels are considered to help and illuminate humans,[26] while the demons and evil spirits attack us in all kinds of deceitful ways.[27] Most of the cosmological discussions focus on these

14. Ibid., 53.
15. Ibid., 25, 36, 70, 117, 28, 31, 68, 201, 41, 69.
16. Ibid., 31, 210.
17. Ibid., 117.
18. Ibid., 42.
19. Ibid., 22.
20. Ibid., 254.
21. Ibid., 122.
22. Ibid., 118.
23. Ibid., 126.
24. Ibid., 132.
25. Ibid.
26. Ibid., 42, 59, 65.
27. Ibid., 22, 24, 43, 61, 63, 138, 71, 82, 261.

evil spirits as there are many different ones that tempt us in many different ways.[28] For instance, they wait for us to let our guards down so that they might attack and "drag [the soul] down mercilessly into all kinds of sin"[29] and they are seen by these writers to imprint things on our minds in the form of sensory things, both good and bad.[30] Nevertheless, they are all lower than God,[31] and if we can endure their assaults, they will eventually withdraw and give up.[32] Yet, for at least one of these authors, evil is seen as not really existing by nature because God makes only the good.[33] Instead, "when in the desire of his heart someone conceives and gives form to what in reality has no existence, then what he desires begins to exist."[34] It is therefore a view that evil is not real, but rather created by the choices that we one makes. It is also asserted that some "afflictions that come to us are the result of our own sins."[35]

This, then, is the anthro-cosmology that is found in some of these texts. It is one where great battles are being waged between good and evil both within one's own soul as well as in the heavens. From this foundational view of creation, and the theology that will be discussed next, their approaches to spiritual formation emerge.

Theological

Within this anthro-cosmology, God is viewed as being nothing but good[36] and "everything good is given by the Lord providentially."[37] God is "the source of every good virtue,"[38] though God also sends to us or allows trials in order to teach us.[39] However, God is not separately and completely transcendent, for God's grace dwells in the intellect[40] and we therefore need

28. Ibid., 38, 52, 58, 66, 116, 248, 82.
29. Ibid., 24; see also ibid., 37, 167.
30. Ibid., 40, 64, 194.
31. Ibid., 273.
32. Ibid., 25–26.
33. Ibid., 253.
34. Ibid.
35. Ibid., 126.
36. Ibid., 60, 110, 253, 75.
37. Ibid., 110; see also ibid., 21, 41.
38. Ibid., 113.
39. Ibid., 176, 286, 94.
40. Ibid., 280.

to discover this divine image within us.[41] God is also viewed as giving us "incensive power and desire" and energy.[42] If one strives after God, then God puts hope in them[43] and helps to save them.[44]

Similarly, the Holy Spirit unifies us and comes to help us.[45] God's role in creation, then, is not seen as being providentially active with humans only being passive recipients. "The Lord is hidden in His own commandments, and He is to be found there in the measure that He is sought," writes one of the authors.[46] God is therefore one who rewards a person according the efforts that they make and the faith that they have in God.[47] With all of this, Jesus is seen as being the model for the holy life.[48] It is this theology, one where God is present and active, but only to the extent of each person's efforts, that under girds the way of life that these monks pursued. It is one which asserts that if we will make the effort then this God of goodness will carry us forward.

Theories of Change

As with Cassian's text, the theories of change offered here are quite elaborate and extensive. The primary theory of change found here is that transformation takes time and effort, much like growing a crop.[49] Eventually, it is claimed, with consistently sustained effort the passions will fall away[50] and a state of grace and purity will follow.[51] As one writer admonishes, "escape from temptation through patience and prayer."[52] The idea that is asserted here is that change happens in cyclically reinforcing patterns. "Evils," one author asserts, "reinforce each other; so do virtues, thus encouraging us to still greater efforts."[53] "Sin is a blazing fire," another author

41. Ibid., 154.
42. Ibid., 48, 134.
43. Ibid., 23.
44. Ibid., 25, 63, 123–24, 30, 69.
45. Ibid., 26, 63, 278.
46. Ibid., 123.
47. Ibid., 127.
48. Ibid., 164, 268.
49. Ibid., 25.
50. Ibid., 47.
51. Ibid., 49, 181.
52. Ibid., 133.
53. Ibid., 116.

claims, "the less fuel you give it, the faster it dies down; the more you feed it, the more it burns,"[54] though sometimes evil also seems to grow on its own.[55] Hence, the primary theory of change is that the more things are nourished, the more they grow, whether they are good or bad.[56]

In light of this underlying theory, a hatred for all sin and all of the passions, which are seen as being evil, is therefore an imperative. As one monk writes, "If your heart comes to feel a natural hatred for sin, it has defeated the causes of sin and freed itself from them"; then union with God is achieved.[57] We must therefore also hate the passions of the world in order to be freed from them.[58] When we hate sin and the passions, it is asserted, then do we see them for what they are.[59] Similarly, we must hate the demons for then salvation will come.[60] One must therefore not talk to or entertain the thoughts of demons and they will eventually go away.[61] Such hatred therefore lends itself to the need to become truly penitent for all one's wrongdoings.[62] It is therefore by hating sin and the passions that the road to liberation can be more fully traversed.

However, a hatred of the passions is not enough, for one must come to be fully purified of them in order to achieve a fuller union with God. While submission to the passions is sometimes viewed as being a result of laxity, ignorance, or lack of faith,[63] freedom from them is what is needed in order for a life of stillness and higher prayer to blossom.[64] As it is written, "When the soul has been purified through the keeping of all the commandments, it makes the intellect steadfast and able to receive the state needed for prayer."[65] Such dispassion, however, can only come via a complete denial of one's self[66] for the "soul will not desire to be separated from the body unless it becomes indifferent to the very air it breathes."[67] When

---

54. Ibid., 119.
55. Ibid., 132, 57.
56. Ibid., 122, 42, 49, 233, 93.
57. Ibid., 23; see also ibid., 62.
58. Ibid., 117, 35, 38, 49, 277.
59. Ibid., 25.
60. Ibid., 44.
61. Ibid., 43.
62. Ibid., 111.
63. Ibid., 139, 75, 81.
64. Ibid., 32, 145.
65. Ibid., 57.
66. Ibid., 59.
67. Ibid., 269.

this happens, then does unity with God come[68] and "love increases as [the soul's] fear diminishes, until it attains perfect love, in which there is no fear but only the complete dispassion which is energized by the glory of God."[69] With hatred of sin leading to purification, purification is seen as leading to a full life in God.

As was stated at the beginning of this section, however, such transformation takes both time and intentionality, and many of these author's assert that it is their spiritual practices that lead to such change.[70] For instance, fasting is seen to purge us of sins as it "exalts the soul, sanctifies the mind, drives away the demons, and prepares [us] for God's presence."[71] "Spiritual reading, vigils and prayer bring the straying intellect to stability"[72] while prayers and vigils "uproots the causes of evil within [the intellect] through humility and confession before God and our neighbour"[73] and we must live the commandments in order to seek the "energies of the Spirit."[74] Again, one of the primary goals of all these efforts is stillness, which "helps us by making evil inoperative."[75] We can therefore see how the slow process of change happens for these authors: one must hate sin and the passions and then be purified of them through the extensive and continual use of the spiritual practices.

With such an emphasis on the need for a strong intellect to help free the soul from the passions through these practices,[76] these writers almost universally assert the spiritual practice of watchfulness as being most necessary for bringing about such change. As was noted above, it is up to the intellect, which stands between the lower and higher parts of the soul, to continually choose the good and thereby liberate the soul. Watchfulness, it is therefore claimed, "guides us to a true and holy way of life. It teaches us how to activate the three aspects of our soul correctly, and how to keep a firm guard over the senses. It promotes the daily growth of the four principal virtues, and is the basis of our contemplation."[77] If one is not

68. Ibid., 57–58.
69. Ibid., 258.
70. Ibid., 36, 60, 147, 238.
71. Ibid., 36.
72. Ibid., 54.
73. Ibid., 149.
74. Ibid., 130.
75. Ibid., 128.
76. Ibid., 23, 25, 26.
77. Ibid., 162.

watching, then provocation from evil can come, to which we then become attached to, followed by our assent to this evil within us, until finally we act on it and embody the evil ourselves.[78] Watchfulness is therefore asserted throughout this text to help us to stop this slippery slope before it ever starts.[79] It is therefore a necessary practice for purification for it frees us from passions and darkness.[80] In alignment with the theory of change stated above, one monk writes, "Continuity of attention produces inner stability; inner stability produces a natural intensification of watchfulness; and this intensification gradually and in due measure gives contemplative insight into spiritual warfare."[81] And this inner stability comes from a watchfulness, not just for evil and the passions, but also for one's own conscience, which "will [then] be our guardian, showing us each thing that we must uproot."[82] The continual watchfulness of the intellect therefore leads to sustained and on-going transformation in one's personal life.

In light of this emphasis on spiritual practices and their necessity for fostering genuine transformation, however, "the kingdom of heaven is not a reward for works, but a gift of grace prepared by the Master for his faithful servants . . . [for] a faithful servant is one who expresses his faith in Christ through obedience to His commandments," as one monk asserts.[83] In other words, many of these writers claim, we therefore need God's help,[84] for doing God's will overcomes all things.[85] With God being seen as an active participant in our transformation, God begins to "paint the divine likeness over the divine image in us" as we begin to perceive and turn to the Holy Spirit.[86] Disciples are therefore encouraged to cast their passions before the Lord,[87] because it is "through continually invoking Jesus the peacemaker against [unseen enemies], [that the mind] remains

---

78. Ibid., 170.
79. Ibid., 22–23, 61, 163, 70, 87, 233, 48.
80. Ibid., 39, 43, 162, 69, 93, 258, 70.
81. Ibid., 163.
82. Ibid., 22; see also ibid., 25, 115, 23.
83. Ibid., 125.
84. Ibid., 122, 23, 27, 30, 31, 47, 53, 59, 66, 79, 86, 260.
85. Ibid., 113, 23.
86. Ibid., 288.
87. Ibid., 41, 179.

invulnerable."[88] God's help and light are therefore needed in all of these efforts in order for true and lasting change to come about.[89]

This, then, is how transformation is considered to occur by these authors. At its core, it is a theory that views change as coming only with intentionality and effort, though it is entirely under girded and guided by God's grace. It is one that seems to assert that each person must engage the spiritual practices to fullest of their abilities trusting that God will meet them in these efforts and bring the attainment of the ideals they are seeking. Though it does not seem to be stated explicitly, their views seem to suggest a view that God's will ultimately acts through our own will; through our own intentional and effortful choices. By doing so, their theory of change goes, does personal transformation gradually and assuredly come about.

Spiritual Formation Ideals & Goals

There appear to be three basic ideals that these writings claim need to be unceasingly sought after. The first is a unity with God,[90] wherein one only seeks for God's will and ways.[91] Such unity, however, is not only with God, but also within one's self. Again do we see this parallel between what is happening within one's self with what is happening in the cosmos. Unity is to therefore additionally be achieved among one's soul, body, and spirit.[92] Speaking of this, one monk writes, "When they become one through the energy of the Holy Spirit, they cannot again be separated."[93] It is this unity of one's own being, as well as with God, then that these monks sought through their stringent ways of life.

A second ideal is related to the achievement of a life of stillness.[94] Such stillness ultimately comes by destroying desires and passions for,[95] it is asserted, "peace is deliverance from the passions."[96] As one monk writes, relating this stillness to love, "Of all the commandments, therefore, the

---

88. Ibid., 164.
89. Ibid., 265, 87.
90. Ibid., 23, 36, 57–58, 62, 253.
91. Ibid., 60, 113, 42, 77.
92. Ibid., 23.
93. Ibid., 26.
94. Ibid., 31–32, 33, 59, 184, 203.
95. Ibid., 39.
96. Ibid., 123.

most comprehensive is to love God and our neighbour. This love is made firm through abstaining from material things, and through stillness of thoughts."[97] Such stillness is considered essential because it leads to the highest forms of prayer[98] and such prayer, which is free from thoughts, is the ultimate weapon to fight evil with.[99] Such contemplative prayers are also considered to be pure prayers of stillness and nothingness. As one writer asserts, "When you are praying, do not shape within yourself any image of the Deity, and do not let our intellect be stamped with the impress of any form; but approach the Immaterial in an immaterial manner, and then you will understand."[100] Repeatedly is this recommendation to be free from all forms and shapes in prayer made in this text.[101] Such stillness, as we shall see more clearly below, is central to their spiritual formation approaches.

A third and final ideal that is mentioned by these authors has to do with ever keeping one's mind stayed on God. "A true monk," it is claimed, "is one who has achieved watchfulness; and he who is truly watchful is a monk in his heart."[102] Such mindfulness of God is considered crucial for "the [person] who always dedicated [her or his] first thoughts to God has perfect prayer."[103] These, then, are some of the central goals and ideals that these texts highlight for disciples to consistently work toward: unity, stillness, and mindfulness.

Spiritual Formation Approaches

To help foster this change, there are a number of spiritual approaches that these authors highlight that includes the need for watchfulness, prayer, ascetical practices, education, community, and others. The purpose of these is to "do everything possible to attain stillness and freedom from distraction, and struggle to live according to God's will, battling against invisible enemies"[104] and one is to engage all of these regularly, as a complete way of

---

97. Ibid., 145.
98. Ibid., 60.
99. Ibid., 165.
100. Ibid., 63.
101. Ibid., 68, 177, 249, 75.
102. Ibid., 190.
103. Ibid., 69.
104. Ibid., 33.

PART THREE: Early Monastic Formation

life, until the day that they die.[105] It is through these intentional approaches that one attains to the goals that they are seeking as discussed above.

Concerning watchfulness, given the central emphasis for personal transformation that it has, one is to be watchful at every moment,[106] ever examining themselves,[107] striving unceasingly to be mindful of God.[108] There are at least four types of watchfulness with the first including a scrutinizing of one's every thought.[109] Another type involves "freeing the heart from all thoughts, keeping it profoundly silent and still."[110] Yet another kind of watchfulness entails continually calling upon Jesus for help.[111] This type of watchfulness seems related to admonishments that we must also keep the good before us,[112] continually calling God's blessings to mind[113] and God's good nature as well as Christ's life.[114] As was mentioned previously, our conscience, once purified, must also be our guide and we must listen and follow it at all times.[115] Finally, one should ever keep "the thought of death in one's mind."[116] Such watchfulness might also include keeping "hell in mind" as well, doing nothing to displease God,[117] for we must hate and avoid all manner of evil,[118] as defined by these authors.

Related to this watchfulness is the centrality of prayer for these communities. Readers are encouraged to unceasingly pray[119] with attentiveness seen as being most essential to prayer.[120] We are to meditate on troubles and struggles whenever they arise,[121] and to "pray with fear, trembling, effort,

---

105. Ibid., 190.
106. Ibid., 24, 25, 28, 39, 48, 63, 121, 62, 82, 92.
107. Ibid., 26.
108. Ibid., 59, 120, 59, 63.
109. Ibid., 118, 64.
110. Ibid., 164.
111. Ibid., 165.
112. Ibid., 148.
113. Ibid., 148, 52.
114. Ibid., 155–56.
115. Ibid., 23, 115.
116. Ibid., 35, 53, 165, 78.
117. Ibid., 23, 36.
118. Ibid., 24, 27.
119. Ibid., 22, 27.
120. Ibid., 60, 71, 163.
121. Ibid., 59, 66, 123, 40.

Philokalia Formation

with inner watchfulness and vigilance,"[122] seeking a purity in our prayers where there is "nothing extraneous in our intellect when we are praying to [God]."[123] "Prayer is communion of the intellect with God,"[124] "the ascent of the intellect to God,"[125] "the intellect's true and highest dignity"[126] where one "becomes equal to the angels through prayer."[127] Prayer is also asserted to be "the mother of the virtues: for it gives birth to them through union with Christ."[128] We must therefore repulse all cares and doubts that arise during prayer[129] and all knowledge of created things[130] for "prayer is the flower of gentleness and of freedom from anger . . . the fruit of joy and thankfulness . . . the remedy for gloom and despondency."[131] There are many different methods of prayer,[132] one central one being the Jesus Prayer for some of these writers.[133] Ultimately, it is asserted, "there is no perfect prayer unless the intellect involves God"[134] and we must therefore use prayer always so that we may always be with God.[135]

In addition to watchfulness and prayer, most of these writers discuss the need for ascetical practices to attain their goals. There are two primary sets of ascetical practices that seem to emerge in these texts. The first is that each person must live a life that is impoverished of the world[136] living on only what one really needs to survive.[137] Such poverty includes keeping a sparse diet[138] and fasting in order to help purge one's self of sins and

---

122. Ibid., 37.
123. Ibid., 24.
124. Ibid., 57.
125. Ibid., 60.
126. Ibid., 65.
127. Ibid., 68.
128. Ibid., 128.
129. Ibid., 58.
130. Ibid., 140.
131. Ibid., 58.
132. Ibid., 111.
133. Ibid., 168–69, 92.
134. Ibid., 128.
135. Ibid., 133.
136. Ibid., 202.
137. Ibid., 246.
138. Ibid., 32, 35–36, 191.

PART THREE: Early Monastic Formation

cultivate self-restraint.[139] It also includes sleeping on the ground[140] and only wearing clothes that are needed for the body's care.[141] Such an impoverished ascetical life is thought to help further one along in their personal spiritual journey by helping to foster the mindfulness that was so central for these authors.

A second kind of ascetical practice is related to one ever practicing the virtues. In this vain, detachment is seen as a central virtue by most of these authors[142] for "detachment is the mark of a perfect soul."[143] One should also not try to hide their faults,[144] but rather examine themselves constantly.[145] Through this, one can further seek to avoid doing every kind of evil, thereby exercising self-restraint[146] because self-control is considered to be "common to all the virtues."[147] Additionally, one should not seek revenge or rebukes against others[148] and not concern themselves with the sins of others.[149] Rather one should seek to nurture a patient acceptance of whatever may come[150] for "without affliction, virtue has not been tested."[151] Such are the virtues of long-suffering and forbearance,[152] forgiveness and "acts of compassion,"[153] that are being grown by these efforts. Finally, one should cultivate humility, courage, and gentleness[154] as well as the love and fear of God.[155] In all of these virtues, and all actions, one's motives are what is really important.[156] Hence, we must ever practice the virtues and

---

139. Ibid., 36, 39, 267.
140. Ibid., 39.
141. Ibid., 32.
142. Ibid., 27, 31, 33, 59, 60, 67, 153, 85, 201, 28, 36, 41, 53, 61.
143. Ibid., 244.
144. Ibid., 113–14, 258, 95.
145. Ibid., 123, 51, 83.
146. Ibid., 127, 54, 74, 253.
147. Ibid., 266.
148. Ibid., 59, 67, 118, 19.
149. Ibid., 114.
150. Ibid., 111, 13, 21, 29.
151. Ibid., 114; see also ibid., 25–26, 43.
152. Ibid., 39, 135.
153. Ibid., 39.
154. Ibid., 66, 134, 43, 92, 206, 92.
155. Ibid., 255–56.
156. Ibid., 112.

the things of the Scriptures,[157] and we must live what we believe and not just talk about it,[158] assert many of these monks.

The need for education and acquisition of spiritual knowledge is also stressed in these texts.[159] There is an expressed need for one to engage in spiritual readings,[160] a need to learn and follow the commandments,[161] and a need for education of truth.[162] We must also seek to learn from the criticism of others[163] and recognize that "knowledge of the truth grows the more we hope in Christ."[164] This is because, as one writer claims, "Every word of Christ shows us God's mercy, justice and wisdom and, if we listen gladly, their power enters into us."[165] As their powers enter into us, it is claimed, we gain "the power to discriminate without error between good and evil."[166] Hence, education and spiritual knowledge are essential for one's growing spiritual life for the help to enlighten the intellect toward the better ways of life.

Finally, community holds an important place in their spiritual formation approaches. Some of these authors asserted the necessity of avoiding the worldly minded, including even one's own family,[167] by leaving the towns and villages[168] and only associating with spiritual friends.[169] It is in these cloistered and far-removed communities that one could find the help they need to fight the effects of the demons and the passions.[170] Such communities were also places where spiritual guidance, direction, education, and mentoring could be found since it is too dangerous to make the spiritual journey alone.[171] These communities were therefore seen as a central and necessary part of one's journey with God.

157. Ibid., 22, 116, 46.
158. Ibid., 125–26, 29.
159. Ibid., 151, 87.
160. Ibid., 53, 110.
161. Ibid., 112, 32, 293.
162. Ibid., 114, 59, 72.
163. Ibid., 119.
164. Ibid., 137.
165. Ibid., 144.
166. Ibid., 254.
167. Ibid., 33, 229, 40.
168. Ibid., 214.
169. Ibid., 34.
170. Ibid., 45.
171. Ibid., 158, 215–16.

PART THREE: Early Monastic Formation

While there are other approaches that they mention in these texts, such as the centrality of having faith,[172] finding work to keep one's self busy,[173] and ever deepening one's self-understanding,[174] the approaches discussed above seem to be the major ones discussed throughout these texts. It is through the use of these various and diverse approaches that these monastics sought to achieve the union they desired in the ever growing stillness of their lives.

Discernment

With the purpose of education being to enable novices to discriminate between good and evil,[175] discernment therefore had a central role in some of these texts. At its core, for some of these authors, discernment was fundamentally concerned with such discrimination. As one monk asserts, "As hesychasts, we should discriminate between virtue and vice with discretion and watchfulness; and we should know which virtues to practise when in the presence of our brethren and elders and which to pursue when alone."[176] It is through such discrimination and discernment that one can come to be freed from evil. This same monk goes on to note, "When a [person] has an exact knowledge about the nature of thoughts, [she or he] recognizes those which are about to enter and defile [her or him], troubling the intellect with distractions and making it lazy. Those who recognize these evil thoughts for what they are remain undisturbed and continue in prayer to God."[177] Such discernment therefore enables one to stop the cycle of evil and passions before they ever start.

With this as the foundational understanding of discernment, advice is then given on how to know when something arising within one's self is coming from God, or angelic sources, and when something is coming from demonic sources.[178] For instance, it is asserted that dreams from God are filled "with spiritual gladness" while dreams from demons "do not keep the same shape or maintain a constant form for long."[179] In its

172. Ibid., 110, 15, 45, 47.
173. Ibid., 35, 258.
174. Ibid., 278.
175. Ibid., 280.
176. Ibid., 27.
177. Ibid., 24.
178. Ibid., 39, 42–43.
179. Ibid., 264.

Philokalia Formation

more absolute form, and in accordance with their ideal of stillness, some authors go so far as to assert that all sensory thoughts and images are from demons or the passions and therefore only a state of pure nothingness in prayer is to be trusted and sought.[180] Such discernment is not to only be applied to one's inner life, but also to one's outer life and spiritual practices. For instance, one of the authors discusses how to distinguish true from false teachers,[181] while another talks about the use of moderation in fasting.[182] These are examples of how discernment is to be continually applied to both one's inner and outer life.

Overall, the process of discernment that seems to emerge here is one that is fundamentally concerned with one being able to know whether or not something is from God or from demonic sources. In accordance with their anthro-cosmology, and even their theology, such discernment seems to be based upon their views of all things of the world being evil and all things from beyond being good. If this is true, it is no wonder, then, as to why many of these monastics sought to retreat from the world of their time to live in the isolated communities they created and shared with one another.

Evaluative Techniques

As with most of the other systems that we have considered thus far, evaluative techniques do not seem to be explicitly discussed. It is clear from their discernment approaches and from their spiritual formation practices that any such techniques were probably and primarily internal observations. As was discussed above, by watching the thoughts and desires that arise within one's self, as they arise, an individual could know the nature of the thought's essence; whether it be angelic or demonic in nature. Also, since stillness was so central to their ideals and goals, one can gauge the extent of their progress by the level and extent of one's undisturbed prayer. In addition to this, with their emphasis on education and close communal mentoring and accountability, the observations that one's community make also likely helped these monks to continually monitor and evaluate their personal progress. Not only could they compare their progress to that which is presented in their sacred texts, but they could also compare experiences and stories of one's journey with one another. Taken collectively,

180. Ibid., 40, 64, 177, 94, 249.
181. Ibid., 204–5, 17.
182. Ibid., 266.

PART THREE: Early Monastic Formation

these internal and external observations and influences seemed to comprise the bulk of their monitoring and evaluative techniques.

Summary/Reflections

As we can see, this system of personal transformation is very similar to the one found in Cassian's *Conferences*. No doubt many of these monks shared similar ways of life. What we found more prevalent in these writings, though, was the more extreme emphasis on stillness as being one of the primary goals of their efforts as compared to the monks in Cassian's text. These authors seemed to hold that a pure apophatic state of nothingness is the only sure place where one can flee from the passions and demons of the world and be more fully united with God. Their system then seems to revolve around the cultivation of this most central ideal of stillness, one that resonates with their anthro-cosmology and theology (i.e., the world and its passions are evil and God is beyond all of it).

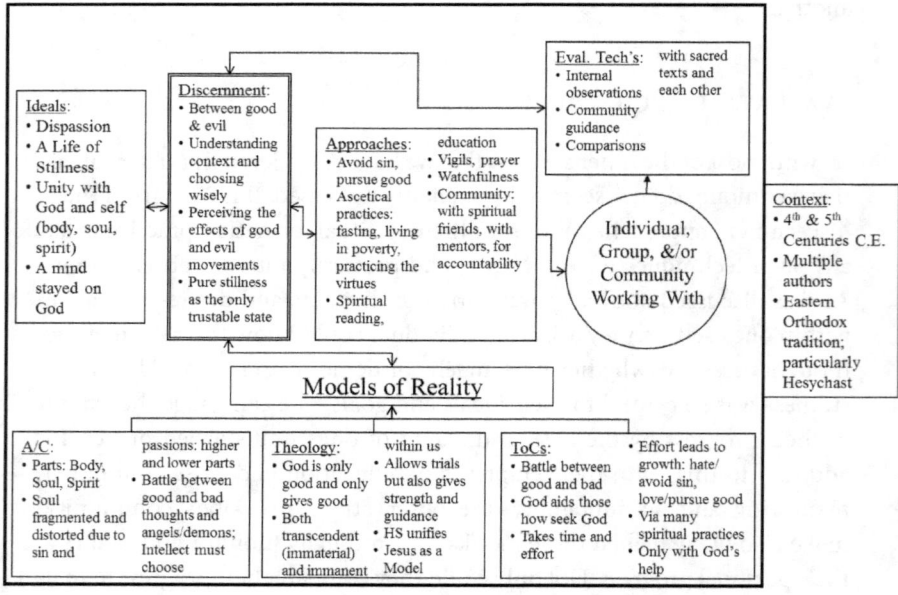

What we can also take from their system is the comprehensive way of life of watchfulness and intentionality in cultivating an ever growing life with God. These were people who retreated away from their contemporary cultures in order to pursue the ideals that they sought through the rigorous ways of life that they cultivated. In some ways, then, the *Philokalia* and the *Conferences* stand as a challenge to many of our contemporary churches. I say this becuase it can sometimes seem that many Christians (including myself) are trying to have church and our pursuits of God revolve around our current lifestyles, contemporary culture, and our work rather than the other way around, which is essentially what these early monastics strove for. While the life of a lay person is obviously and necessarily different from that of many vowed monastics, there is nevertheless much we can still learn from them. As we continue on with our journey, we shall see how such monastic-like systems were modified and altered for laity.

PART FOUR

Medieval & Renaissance

WHILE MONASTICISM CONTINUED TO play a central role throughout the middle ages, becoming a dominant institution of power, many other movements were also prevalent during this era on throughout the Renaissance time period. The so-called Dark Ages were coming to an end as more and more laypersons became literate as time progressed, cities became established once again, and universities and other centers of education were established.[1] Reconnecting with Greek Classics, Scholasticism emerged and Christian thought and practice witnessed a new kind of systematics that focused on the use of logic and rationality with such thinkers as Anselm, Thomas Aquinas, and Bonaventure.[2]

While culture and life progressed in some ways, however, it also continued to be chaotic in others. Most likely transmitted via fleas, Black Death swept through the European population leaving anywhere from a third to half of local peoples dead in its wake.[3] These were also times when Christians sought to regain control of the Near East through the violent excursions of the Crusaders.[4] Warring did not only happen internationally, but also continued among local queen and kingdoms as is evidenced by Francis of Assisi's own life experiences as a young soldier.[5] As Christianity remained the dominant religious tradition in power, the pursuit

1. Farmer, "Saints and Mystics of the Medieval West," 90, 100; Sheldrake, *Brief History of Spirituality*, 73, 78, 81; Woods, *Christian Spirituality*, 128, 40.

2. Farmer, "Saints and Mystics of the Medieval West," 92–93, 105; Sheldrake, *Brief History of Spirituality*, 76, 102; Woods, *Christian Spirituality*, 127, 35–36, 45, 49.

3. Sheldrake, *Brief History of Spirituality*, 104; Woods, *Christian Spirituality*, 174.

4. Chidester, *Christianity*, 189; Farmer, "Saints and Mystics of the Medieval West," 95; Woods, *Christian Spirituality*, 125, 41, 67.

5. Chidester, *Christianity*, 187; Farmer, "Saints and Mystics of the Medieval West," 101; Woods, *Christian Spirituality*, 141, 46, 76.

PART FOUR: Medieval & Renaissance

of heretics became a dark part of the institution as inquisitions were held throughout Europe.[6] In addition, the Church saw schisms both within its own ranks, as there were at one time two recognized Popes in Europe, as well as an irreparable split at the time with the Eastern Orthodox Church in 1054 CE.[7]

Despite these difficulties, spiritual formation flourished throughout this time period as well, making it one of the most vibrant eras of Western Christian spirituality. Pilgrimages found widespread popularity as people travelled many miles to view and pay homage to the saints of previous generations.[8] Resources for laypersons also became more pervasive, no doubt partly due to the increase in literacy rates, and these often mimicked many of the prayer texts used in monasteries and devotionals to Mother Mary.[9] With institutionalization, however, often comes abuse and many reform movements sprang on to the scene both among clergy as well as within the walls of monastic communities.[10] New religious orders, such as an originally "dangerous" group of wandering evangelizing celibates known as mendicants, found their foothold and origins during this time period as well.[11] This era also saw the flourishing of certain apophatic and revelational forms of mysticism among women and men in such places as England and the German Rhineland.[12] Overall, this era was therefore marked by great trials but also by great gains in Western Christian history.

From among these many movements, we focus on two that will help us to better understand some of the different ways that personal transformation was conceived of and approached during this time period. The first is one of the two dominant groups of mendicants that emerged during this

6. Chidester, *Christianity*, 255; Farmer, "Saints and Mystics of the Medieval West," 110; Woods, *Christian Spirituality*, 144, 54, 77.

7. Chidester, *Christianity*, 161; Farmer, "Saints and Mystics of the Medieval West," 90; Sheldrake, *Brief History of Spirituality*, 101; Woods, *Christian Spirituality*, 127, 67, 74.

8. Chidester, *Christianity*, 199–200; Farmer, "Saints and Mystics of the Medieval West," 118–20.

9. Farmer, "Saints and Mystics of the Medieval West," 118, 21; Sheldrake, *Brief History of Spirituality*, 98; Woods, *Christian Spirituality*, 140.

10. Farmer, "Saints and Mystics of the Medieval West," 91, 94, 122; Sheldrake, *Brief History of Spirituality*, 73; Woods, *Christian Spirituality*, 117, 40, 43.

11. Farmer, "Saints and Mystics of the Medieval West," 100, 103; Sheldrake, *Brief History of Spirituality*, 74, 83; Woods, *Christian Spirituality*, 124, 44–45.

12. Farmer, "Saints and Mystics of the Medieval West," 107, 15–18; Sheldrake, *Brief History of Spirituality*, 93–97; Woods, *Christian Spirituality*, 132, 36, 52–53, 57, 63, 76, 79.

PART FOUR: Medieval & Renaissance

era. While the Dominicans played a central role in the church of this period, and Roman Catholic Church today, we will instead be spending some time looking at early Franciscan formation as it is captured in a couple of the writings of Bonaventure. The second comes to us from Erasmus of Rotterdam, who is considered one of the forbearers of humanism in the Renaissance time period. As with each of the communities that we are spending our time with, both of these are intended to help us as we think about personal spiritual formation in our own lives and communities.

7

Franciscan Formation

Context

BONAVENTURE WAS BORN, GIOVANNI Fidanza, in 1217 and was educated in Paris.[1] He was eventually elected minister general of the Franciscans only thirty one years after the death of Francis, and was later made a cardinal in the church.[2] Because of the turbulent times for the Franciscans in the era in which he lived, he wrote many works in defense of their order and the mendicant way of life.[3] Among these works were two biographies that he composed about Francis and his *Journey of the Soul to God*, which describes the "Franciscan mystical journey" to God.[4] While his *Journey* was important for describing the centrality of contemplation for Franciscan spirituality, it was his biography, which emphasized compassion, that was one of the most widely distributed and embraced devotional texts of this era.[5] In order to gain insight into Franciscan spiritual formation of this time period, we will be turning to both of these texts by Bonaventure for this project.[6]

1. Hellmann, "Christian Spirituality," 41; Moorman, "The Franciscans," 304–5.
2. Hellmann, "Christian Spirituality," 41; Moorman, "The Franciscans," 305.
3. Hellmann, "Christian Spirituality," 41.
4. Ibid., 42, 43; Moorman, "The Franciscans," 305.
5. Hellmann, "Christian Spirituality," 43.
6. However, we will not be reading Part II of Bonaventure's *Major Life* as it is related to miracles that happen after Francis' death and does not seem as relevant for our purposes here.

Models of Reality

Anthropological-Cosmological

In *Journey*, Bonaventure depicts creation in ways somewhat reminiscent of Neo-Platonism. For him, some parts of creation "are merely corporeal, while others are partly corporeal and partly spiritual," while still "others are wholly spiritual."[7] Similarly, some things are corruptible and changeable, like terrestrial things, while others are changeable and incorruptible, such as celestial things, while still others are unchangeable and incorruptible, like supercelestial things.[8] Such views seem to also be found in his *Major Life*, where in prayer we ascend to the heights of God, while in preaching we must "descend to the level of humans."[9] This neoplatonic view of higher and more spiritual things being up while lower and more earthly things being down is therefore present in the Franciscan cosmology of this day. It is in this context that Bonaventure situates his "six stages of illumination" that lead up to union with God which will be outlined below.[10]

As it relates to the celestial beings, there is a battle going on in the heavens for the souls of humanity. In this scheme, "the ruling of the universe is attributed to the angels according to the command of the most high God."[11] Angels, it is asserted, help us on our way to God.[12] However, there is also the presence of the Devil who is ever "trying to snatch away" the souls of God.[13] Demons bring tribulations[14] but can only do what God allows them to.[15] Humans are therefore in the middle of this battle and these competing heavenly forces.

Because of this world view, Bonaventure considers himself to have been born a sinner for human nature is corrupted[16] and some people, he asserts in *Major Life*, are generally "hard-headed."[17] Bonaventure locates

---

7. Bonaventure, *Journey of the Mind*, 9.
8. Ibid.
9. Bonaventure, "Major Life," 721, 29.
10. Bonaventure, *Journey of the Mind*, 2.
11. Ibid., 11.
12. Bonaventure, "Major Life," 670–71.
13. Ibid., 654, 707, 18.
14. Ibid., 664.
15. Ibid., 678, 707.
16. Ibid., 636; Bonaventure, *Journey of the Mind*, 1.
17. Bonaventure, "Major Life," 635.

the origins of this sad status of humanity in the fall of the Genesis narrative. He writes, "According to the original disposition of nature, man was created fit for the quiet of contemplation and thus God placed him in the paradise of pleasure. But turning away from the true light to a changeable good, he and all his descendants were by his fault bent over by original sin, which infected human nature in a twofold manner: the mind with ignorance, and the flesh with concupiscence."[18] As a result, we must be cleansed in order to ascend to God[19] and the lower appetites need to be mortified and guarded against.[20] Francis therefore, Bonaventure writes, believed that "he was an exile from the Lord's presence as long as he was at home in the body."[21]

Nevertheless, God's image and presence works within humanity[22] and God gives gifts to the world through each of us.[23] Anthropologically, the mind/soul perceives in three ways: outside of itself, within itself, and beyond itself.[24] These three ways of perception come to comprise the essence of Bonaventure's stages of spiritual growth as we shall see below. He also asserts that there are six powers of our nature ("sense, imagination, reason, understanding, intelligence, and the summit of the mind")[25] and three powers of the soul (memory, intellect, and will).[26] Each of these becomes part of the means by which one ascends to the heights of God.

While this anthropology is discussed directly in his *Journey*, Bonaventure does not explicitly discuss them in his *Major Life*. Instead, it is the cosmology described above that seems to have a more central role, though it could be argued that the anthropology is implicitly there as well. Nevertheless, this anthro-cosmology, along with the theology that will be discussed next, does come to under gird the bulk of the Franciscan views of personal transformation that are found in these texts.

18. Bonaventure, *Journey of the Mind*, 7.
19. Ibid.
20. Bonaventure, "Major Life," 663, 66.
21. Ibid., 705.
22. Ibid., 635, 91; Bonaventure, *Journey of the Mind*, 6, 11, 25.
23. Bonaventure, "Major Life," 649.
24. Bonaventure, *Journey of the Mind*, 6.
25. Ibid., 7.
26. Ibid., 18–21.

Theological

While Bonaventure asserts the necessity of their being a Trinity,[27] it can also be found that there are at least three aspects of God that he discusses, explicitly or implicitly, in these two texts, one of which seems most central for the brand of Franciscan spirituality that he describes. The first is the utter transcendence of God who is ultimately beyond and above us.[28] Contact with this aspect of God represents, for Bonaventure, the highest stage of contemplation.[29] The second aspect of God is that of God's Being, or a perfect Spirit of sorts who "has memory, intelligence, and will."[30] However, this being, which appears to us as non-being,[31] "is within all things without being contained by them; it is outside all things without being excluded by them; it is above all things without being aloof; it is below all things without being dependent on them."[32] It is this Being of God that we grow within.

Such conceptions lead us into the third and, I assert, most central aspect of God for Franciscan spiritual formation: God's immanence. In this view, God is "in all things by His power, presence, and, essence,"[33] "the supremely excellent and most universal and sufficient cause of all essences."[34] It is because of this view that Francis can come to see that we are all sisters and brothers, animals and humans alike.[35] On this, Bonaventure writes, "The realization that everything comes from the same source filled Francis with greater affection than ever and he called even the most insignificant creatures his brothers and sisters, because he know they had the same origin as himself."[36] It these three aspects of God, particularly the immanence of God, that seems to guide Franciscan spirituality.

With this outlined, God's nature is conceived as being intimate, good, and ever helpful. God is depicted as the one from whom "all enlightenment flows" and "from Whom is every best and perfect gift," including

27. Ibid., 34.
28. Ibid., 6.
29. Ibid., 37–39.
30. Ibid., 21.
31. Ibid., 30.
32. Ibid., 31.
33. Ibid., 9, 11, 25.
34. Ibid., 31.
35. Bonaventure, "Major Life," 700.
36. Ibid., 692; see also ibid., 98.

PART FOUR: Medieval & Renaissance

visions.[37] Divine help is always there for "all who truly seek it with a truly humble and devout heart,"[38] and God inspired Francis "to profess the life of Gospel perfection and made him a leader and an apostle" to help others[39] leading him step-by-step all along the way.[40] God works to perform miracles in the world,[41] showers favors upon us,[42] and saves us from evils[43] by ever strengthening us.[44] God is ultimately the one who provides everything we need, especially when we have nothing.[45] God is therefore Goodness,[46] though God also brings adversity and illness upon us according to God's will.[47]

Jesus and Mary are also found to be a central part of Franciscan spirituality and theology. God guides humanity through Jesus, thereby working to "enlighten the eyes of our mind to guide our feet."[48] Jesus is therefore seen as the necessary mediator and Savior of humanity.[49] God sent Jesus,[50] and by this restored the fall of humanity. On this, Bonaventure writes, "taking on human form in Christ, [Truth became] a ladder restoring the first ladder that had been broken in Adam."[51] Jesus is therefore the one who guided Francis all throughout his life.[52] Mother Mary was also central for Francis,[53] and it is through these two mediators that humanity is restored and we are elevated to the heights of God and personal spiritual maturity.

---

37. Ibid., 637, 80, 724; Bonaventure, *Journey of the Mind*, 1.
38. Bonaventure, *Journey of the Mind*, 5.
39. Bonaventure, "Major Life," 631, 35.
40. Ibid., 637, 46.
41. Ibid., 632, 69.
42. Ibid., 635.
43. Ibid., 648.
44. Ibid., 703.
45. Ibid., 660.
46. Bonaventure, *Journey of the Mind*, 28, 33.
47. Bonaventure, "Major Life," 636, 702.
48. Bonaventure, *Journey of the Mind*, 1.
49. Ibid., 2, 7, 17, 23, 26, 37.
50. Ibid., 36.
51. Ibid., 23.
52. Bonaventure, "Major Life," 640.
53. Ibid., 699.

Theories of Change

While Bonaventure does mention the more traditional monastic stages of purification, illumination, and perfection,[54] his primary theory of change, as articulated in the *Journey*, are his six stages of illumination. Cast as three sets of two stages each, following the metaphor of the wings of a seraph, the three different meta-levels are as follows. The first level of illumination is related to one passing through the "vestiges which are corporeal and temporal and outside us."[55] By our experience of sensible things, he asserts, we can be led to "realize that there exists a first beauty, sweetness, and wholesomeness in that first Species, in which there is the utmost proportion to and equality with the One generating."[56] The basic idea here is that in this first level we come to see something of God in the sensible, created world which are "shadows, echoes, and pictures of that first, most powerful, most wise, and most perfect Principle, of that first eternal Source, Light, Fullness."[57]

In the second level of illumination, there is an entering "into our mind, which is the image of God, an image which is everlasting, spiritual, within us."[58] In this level, "Judgment . . . leads us in a still more excellent and more immediate way to a surer beholding of eternal truth" because it is abstracted from "place, time, and change."[59] Hence, what we judge about sensed objects is more infallible and unchanging because it is more reflective of God's essence and nature, which is unchanging and infallible.[60] So, for instance, apprehending numerical things about the sensed world brings us closer to God than do the sensible things themselves, Bonaventure asserts.[61] The goal of this level is to "reenter into ourselves, that is, into our mind, where the divine image shines forth."[62]

The final level is one where "we must go beyond to what is eternal, most spiritual, and above us."[63] Being most related to the transcendent

---

54. Bonaventure, *Journey of the Mind*, 26.
55. Ibid., 5–6.
56. Ibid., 14.
57. Ibid., 16.
58. Ibid., 6.
59. Ibid., 14.
60. Ibid.
61. Ibid., 16.
62. Ibid., 18.
63. Ibid., 6.

aspect of God discussed above, this is the level wherein the mind must "transcend and pass over, not only this visible world, but even itself . . . in this passing over, if it is to be perfect, all intellectual activities ought to be relinquished and the loftiest affection transported to God, and transformed into Him."[64] It is in this transcending of all things that there is an apophatic darkness and one must therefore "die and enter into this darkness,"[65] where one will have "reached something that is perfect."[66] This highest and most pure state of illumination is therefore one of the ideals wherein the peace, harmony, love and unity outlined above are fully realized and wholly integrated with one another.

While Bonaventure does not seem to discuss the inner dynamics and transformations that underlie one's personal progression through these stages, he does, through both texts, assert what is needed by one in order to make this journey. First is the necessity for desire and humility on the part of the disciple. He asserts that we must be desirous, "humble and pious," "contrite and devout," "lovers of divine wisdom," in order to make the ascent to God.[67] We cannot therefore be prideful.[68] Instead, we must have desires and affections for the Word in order to recover our spiritual senses.[69] We must, in short, love God.[70] There is, then, a need to raise our minds toward heaven, "to [acquire] a taste for the things of God."[71] Such affections and humility propel us through the stages of illumination without becoming stuck.

There is also a need for purification.[72] On this, Bonaventure proclaims, "First, then, O man of God, arouse in yourself remorse of conscience before you raise your eyes to the rays of Wisdom reflected in its mirrors, lest perchance from the very beholding of these rays you fall into a more perilous pit of darkness."[73] We need such purity because God's "grace of charity" "springs up from a pure heart and a good conscience and faith

---

64. Ibid., 37; see also ibid., 38.
65. Ibid., 39.
66. Ibid., 36.
67. Ibid., 2, 24; Bonaventure, "Major Life," 638, 39, 44, 71, 76.
68. Bonaventure, "Major Life," 649.
69. Bonaventure, *Journey of the Mind*, 24.
70. Bonaventure, "Major Life," 658.
71. Ibid., 636.
72. Ibid., 664; Bonaventure, *Journey of the Mind*, 25.
73. Bonaventure, *Journey of the Mind*, 2–3.

unfeigned,"[74] and these powers within us must be "cleansed by justice, trained by knowledge, and perfected by wisdom."[75] As Bonaventure explains, "Since happiness is nothing else than the enjoyment of the Supreme Good, and the Supreme God is above us, no one can enjoy happiness unless he rise above himself"[76] and when our minds are distracted, clouded by our senses, and drawn away by other desires, we do not enter more fully into God.[77] Hence, we need to be mortified of the lower appetites,[78] triumph over the Devil,[79] and be purified of lower desires through prayer and other disciplines.[80]

The final and most important thing needed in this ascent is, of course, God. It is Jesus' blood that cleanses us from our sins[81] for we need God's grace in order to "see the light of heaven" and this is done through Jesus.[82] We also need grace in order to progress generally[83] as God "purifies, illuminates, and inflames by the intervention of the Seraphim,"[84] as was mentioned above. As a result, contemplation of the attributes of God is needed in order for the mind to rise,[85] and the personal transformation approaches discussed below aid in such contemplation and the receiving of the help that God ever offers.

Overall, Bonaventure's theory of change therefore primarily seems to be one in which the soul ascends to the contemplative heights of the divine through a twofold process. The first is through the cultivation of love and humility toward all things related to God. The second is through purification and being released from the snares of this lower world and the treachery of the Devil. Taken together, along with the continuous help that God ever provides, the soul ascends through the stages of illumination that he has outlined.

74. Ibid., 7.
75. Ibid.
76. Ibid., 5.
77. Ibid., 23.
78. Bonaventure, "Major Life," 663.
79. Ibid., 737.
80. Ibid., 721.
81. Bonaventure, *Journey of the Mind*, 2.
82. Ibid., 7.
83. Ibid., 24, 38.
84. Bonaventure, "Major Life," 734.
85. Bonaventure, *Journey of the Mind*, 35.

PART FOUR: Medieval & Renaissance

While I have not made a detailed analysis of Bonaventure's *Major Life* in this way, it does seem that the six stages are basically the journey that Francis makes. He starts off with Francis coming to slowly be awoken in his noticing and desiring of the things of God, then progressing in his growing life of poverty, humility, and service, until he finally reaches ecstatic unions with God. Francis therefore seems to progress through each of the stages that Bonaventure outlines in *Journey*. Overall, then, it seems as if the soul's "memory, intellect, and will" are gradually being reshaped to focus on and desire only the things of God. Such a theory of change, if accurate, lays the foundation for the whole life that these early mendicants sought to live.

Spiritual Formation Ideals & Goals

With Bonaventure setting Francis up as "a shining example of Christian perfection," one to be imitated,[86] there are at least two categories of ideals that these texts depict. The first is related to peace, happiness, love, and unity. In this, peace is seen as a central goal[87] where "the true man of peace rests with a tranquil soul."[88] Additionally, happiness is what is loved most by the soul[89] and loving compassion is to be sought after by all people.[90] Such peace, happiness, and love should then ultimately lead one to a unity with God.[91] As it related to Francis and his uniting love for Jesus, Bonaventure writes, "No human tongue could describe the passionate love with which Francis burned for Christ, his Spouse; he seemed to be completely absorbed by the fire of divine love like a glowing coal."[92] Such unity, however, should also come between one's body and spirit, just as it did for Francis.[93] These goals of harmony, happiness, and peace must therefore inspire the Franciscan toward greater spiritual heights.

The second set of ideals is related to the imitation of Christ and service to God in all things. "Gospel perfection" is seen as a life of poverty,

---

86. Bonaventure, "Major Life," 671, 79.
87. Ibid., 657–58; Bonaventure, *Journey of the Mind*, 1.
88. Bonaventure, *Journey of the Mind*, 37.
89. Ibid., 21.
90. Bonaventure, "Major Life," 697.
91. Ibid., 688, 721.
92. Ibid., 698; see also ibid., 720.
93. Ibid., 737.

penance, and service.[94] In this perfection, one is to ever seek a purity of heart,[95] true faithfulness,[96] and a desire and humility toward God in all things[97] as well as to have an enduring gentleness and humbleness.[98] Such attitudes should then incline one toward seeing God in others, loving God in everything, and serving God according to God's will.[99] The core ideal here is to imitate Christ even in His passion and sufferings.[100] These two sets of ideals therefore make up some of the goals that Bonaventure highlights of early Franciscan spirituality in these texts thereby giving rise to the spiritually formative personal life that it sought to live.

Spiritual Formation Approaches

It is in consideration of Franciscan approaches to spiritual formation that their distinctive way of life and charism really reveals itself. Truly does it seem that this way is better understood via embodiment than it is via purer theoretical reflection. At the very heart of Franciscan life is prayer, which is to be done "long before and above all else."[101] Franciscans were therefore admonished to pray unceasingly to God.[102] In *Major Life*, Francis is depicted as praying constantly for God to guide him, as did others, and he "poured out his whole soul with groans beyond all utterance,"[103] ever attempting to keep himself in God's presence.[104] It is such prayers were intended to provide protection from attacks of the Devil, which were central to the cosmology that we explored above.[105]

There were also many different kinds of prayer that were used such as verbal and imagination prayers to address temptations and fears[106] as well

94. Ibid., 647.
95. Ibid., 652.
96. Ibid., 673.
97. Ibid., 638, 39, 44, 71, 76.
98. Ibid., 691.
99. Ibid., 691, 98, 722, 38, 39.
100. Ibid., 730, 37.
101. Ibid., 706.
102. Ibid., 710.
103. Ibid., 638, 40, 41, 47, 52, 54, 59, 62, 76, 87.
104. Ibid., 705.
105. Ibid., 718.
106. Ibid., 665, 68.

PART FOUR: Medieval & Renaissance

as the chanting of the Divine Office[107] and contemplation,[108] both of which were common for monastic communities of this time period. Sometimes Francis and others would seek solitude to "hear God's secret revelations,"[109] asserts Bonaventure, and they often had ecstatic experiences and visions.[110] Such a life of prayer resulted, for Francis, in prophecies and knowing the "secrets of men's hearts,"[111] and even a receiving of the stigmata (or crucifixion wounds) of Christ.[112] Praising God for all things[113] and in all things[114] is also asserted as being necessary as is seeing God in all things.[115] Prayer is therefore a central and necessary element in Franciscan spiritual formation at the level of the individual.

Almost as central, if not more so, was a complete renunciation of the world for a life of poverty, affectionately referred to as "Holy Poverty" and "Lady Poverty."[116] In *Major Life*, we find Francis rejecting the world[117] as well as himself[118] for poverty, which was considered by Francis to surpass all other virtues because "it had shown him how to regard himself as the last of all."[119] Put succinctly by Bonaventure, "poverty was [Francis'] profession."[120] In pursuit of such humility through poverty, early friars also made use of mortifications and penances.[121] Francis, Bonaventure writes, "mortified his lower appetites so strictly that he scarcely took enough food or drink to stay alive. In this way he would cloth himself with the armor of the Cross."[122]

107. Ibid., 709.
108. Ibid., 648, 729, 39; Bonaventure, *Journey of the Mind*, 7, 35.
109. Bonaventure, "Major Life," 643.
110. Ibid., 649, 51, 56, 61, 76, 706, 709, 36, 41.
111. Ibid., 713, 16.
112. Ibid., 731, 42.
113. Ibid., 643, 95, 738.
114. Ibid., 655, 95, 98.
115. Ibid., 698.
116. Ibid., 631, 39, 54, 57, 60, 80, 83.
117. Ibid., 638, 42, 47.
118. Ibid., 672.
119. Ibid., 684.
120. Ibid., 742.
121. Ibid., 640, 47, 57, 700.
122. Ibid., 663.

All of this, it is asserted, was done out of a need to "preserve perfect purity of soul and body"[123] and to watch for the temptations of the body,[124] something that was wholly in accordance with the anthropocosmology outlined above. While it needed to be done with discretion and temperance,[125] these practices helped early friars to embrace Christ's cross as their way of life.[126] It also enabled them be patient in trials with long-suffering.[127] Such a life of poverty was therefore central for them and applied not only to material poverty but also to a general poverty of spirit and life thereby nurturing the desire and humility before God that Franciscan ideals called for.

Closely related to the life of poverty was the need for one to practice the virtues.[128] In this, loving compassion was central,[129] as Francis really desired to give his "whole self" to others and not only money and other material items.[130] The virtue of keeping one's word[131] and being pure in one's deed[132] were also central virtues, as was denouncing evil wherever it was found.[133] Hence, the practice of virtues was also important for this way of life.

Along with the practice of the virtues, was a special emphasis to "preach repentance by word and example."[134] Early Franciscans were not just to live a life of purity by themselves, but to also reach out and encourage others in these ways of life as well. There were at least two primary ways that these friars did this. The first was through the help that they gave others, especially the poor.[135] They begged for and gave alms and money

---

123. Ibid., 664; Bonaventure, *Journey of the Mind*, 7.
124. Bonaventure, "Major Life," 666.
125. Ibid., 667.
126. Ibid., 662.
127. Ibid., 650, 737, 40.
128. Ibid., 659, 62–63, 711, 20; Bonaventure, *Journey of the Mind*, 7, 26.
129. Bonaventure, "Major Life," 688.
130. Ibid., 639.
131. Ibid., 636.
132. Ibid., 667.
133. Ibid., 725.
134. Ibid., 631, 53, 725.
135. Ibid., 635, 37, 91.

to help others,[136] and they helped lepers,[137] repaired old churches,[138] and we even find Francis living out his theology of immanence in the help that he consistently gave to animals.[139] Most central in this life of service, then, was the great emphasis that Francis gave to helping the poor and marginalized.[140] There were also many miracles that Francis was reported to have done in his efforts to help others.[141]

The second way early Franciscans shared their way of life was through their powerful preaching.[142] Well known is Francis' use of a real nativity scene,[143] and many other ways, all for the purpose of trying "to win for Christ the souls which the Devil was trying to snatch away."[144] There are also stories of Francis preaching to the birds, who seemed to listen to him.[145] In both of these ways of sharing their lifestyle with others, early Franciscans therefore embraced the need to avoid idleness, which is asserted to be "the root of all evil desires,"[146] and we find Francis, Bonaventure asserts, continually being occupied with the doing of good.[147]

While Francis was not theologically educated himself, though Bonaventure was, there is also an emphasis on the need for education. There was an expressed need for studying the Scriptures,[148] as well as for knowledge in general.[149] Scriptures are asserted by Bonaventure to help Francis in times of need[150] as well as providing guidance in times of conflict and indecision.[151] Francis also asserted a need, claims Bonaventure, to strictly follow "Christ's Gospel,"[152] which therefore requires a knowledge of these

136. Ibid., 639, 41, 85.
137. Ibid., 644, 737.
138. Ibid., 640, 45.
139. Ibid., 692–94, 97, 733.
140. Ibid., 635, 37, 44, 91, 737.
141. Ibid., 644, 59, 69, 87, 726, 46.
142. Ibid., 647, 722, 24.
143. Ibid., 711.
144. Ibid., 654; see also ibid., 704.
145. Ibid., 722–23.
146. Ibid., 650, 66.
147. Ibid., 729.
148. Bonaventure, *Journey of the Mind*, 25.
149. Ibid., 7, 35.
150. Bonaventure, "Major Life," 642.
151. Ibid., 646, 47–48, 729.
152. Ibid., 663, 81, 740.

passages. Francis' purity allowed him, it is asserted, to penetrate its depths even though he had never formally studied Scriptures in an institution.[153]

Just as important as this external learning, Bonaventure goes on to assert, is the need for self-knowledge as well, when he writes, "[The soul] could not love itself unless it knew itself, nor could it know itself unless it summoned itself to memory, for we do not grasp any thing with our understanding unless it is present to our memory."[154] Such "summoning itself to memory" therefore includes the all-important practice of confession and recalling of one's sins.[155] So, while education might not have had as central a role in early Franciscan life as did prayer and poverty, it was still considered a necessary part of their personally formative efforts according to Bonaventure.

A final spiritual formation approach at the level of the individual that these mendicants upheld and utilized with fervency was community. As it is well known, Francis was moved to found and grow his Religious Order.[156] In this Order, the importance of mentoring and setting an example for others in this new way of life was established,[157] with Francis being seen as one to be trusted, followed, and imitated.[158] To help with this, Francis established a rule of life, "necessary for their life in common,"[159] that focused on a "vow of poverty [and] the observance of the Gospel."[160] Such community was therefore one where early friars could hold each other accountable as well as support one another in the ways of life they ever sought to embody.[161] Community was therefore considered essential for these evangelizing mendicants of poverty according to Bonaventure's texts.

These approaches of prayer, poverty, virtues, serving & preaching, education, and community therefore comprised the core of Franciscan personal spiritual formation found in these two texts. It is through them that we find the unique charism that these early mendicants embodied in their profoundly compassionate and very simplistic ways of life.

---

153. Ibid., 711–12.
154. Bonaventure, *Journey of the Mind*, 18.
155. Bonaventure, "Major Life," 672, 91, 710, 14.
156. Ibid., 646, 48, 50, 53, 57.
157. Ibid., 650, 54, 67.
158. Ibid., 656, 735, 42.
159. Ibid., 650, 62.
160. Ibid., 682.
161. Ibid., 679, 91.

PART FOUR: Medieval & Renaissance

Discernment

As these texts were not intended to be systematic manuals on personal spiritual life, as were the *Conferences* and the *Philokalia,* there is not much explicit discussion of the processes of discernment. Nevertheless, there are a few examples that might shed insights into something of what this might have meant for early Franciscans according to these texts. In *Major Life,* there are a couple of stories relayed about Francis' encounters with the Devil and how he recognized it as such and therefore responded appropriately. In one such story, by God's inspiration, it is asserted, Francis realizes that the Devil was trying to tempt him into "half-heartedness" in doing penance. It is asserted that the sudden onset of fleshy temptations and desires confirmed this discernment.[162] In another story, when he was journeying with a friend, Francis and his companion found a large amount of money in the road and his companion told him to take it and give it to the poor. But Francis considered this to be "a trick of the Devil" because "what his companion wanted him to do—to take what belonged to another and make a present of it—was sinful, not meritorious."[163] Elsewhere, Francis admonishes the use of discretion in performing mortifications and penance.[164]

In each of these cases, the method of discernment appears to be a process of comparing what one is thinking about doing against what they believe is the image and/or will of God for each specific instance. In support of such discernment, Bonaventure asserts the true nature of each of the soul's faculties when he writes, "See, therefore, how close the soul is to God, and how, through their activity, memory leads us to Eternity, intelligence to Truth, and the elective faculty to the highest Good."[165] Discernment, in his framework, therefore includes the use of all of one's faculties in finding and following God in whatever situation arises before them on a case-by-case basis.

Evaluative Techniques

As with discernment, evaluative techniques are not formally discussed in these texts. However, it is clear from the numerous stories of Francis

162. Ibid., 665.
163. Ibid., 683.
164. Ibid., 667.
165. Bonaventure, *Journey of the Mind,* 21.

responding to the behaviors of his friars that observations and listening to one's confessions and discourses are central to this system of spiritual formation. Also, though such is not explicitly stated, it seems that self-observations were another central method of evaluating one's own current spiritual growth and direction. Indeed, the emphasis on self-knowledge and the many hours spent in prayer, as discussed above, lend themselves to these internal evaluative techniques. However, such internal reflections do not seem to be allotted the priority that they were given in the writings of the desert monks we considered previously.

Another possible and quite probable method of evaluation might have been the observations of one's deeds as made by others. As discussed in previous chapters, there was a noted emphasis on the doing of good works and not being idle. By looking at how a friar spent his time, a superior or other member of their community could therefore gauge how well they were following the rule set forth by Francis, and the Franciscan way of life more generally.

Summary/Reflections

At its core, pictured below, the Franciscan system of personal spiritual formation fundamentally seems to emerge out of its theology of immanence and the love and humility that was emphasized in relation to it. For Francis, spiritual life really seemed to be about coming to see, reverence, and serve Christ who is truly present within all things. Out of this simple, yet profound, theology of life seemed to come his life of poverty and loving service to all of creation. We can then see how the practices embodied by early Franciscans then naturally flow from these views and ways of life.

PART FOUR: Medieval & Renaissance

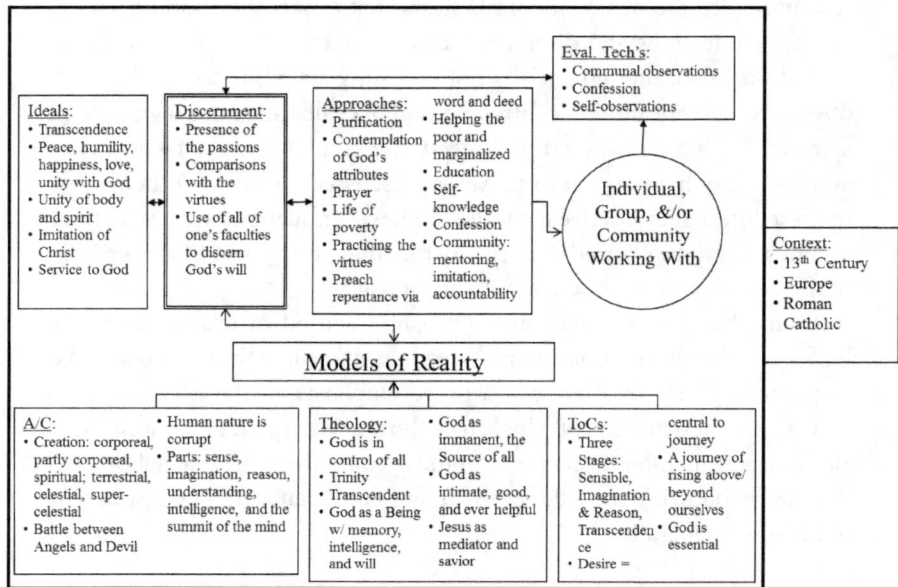

Francis' life can also stand as a testament to the simplicity and accessibility that a life with God can have for all people. One does not have to be highly educated, though Bonaventure was, in order to live a very simple life with Christ, as did Francis. While education, as we heard in this chapter as well as in previous ones, can and should help to correct errors, offer guidance and suggestions, et cetera to our personally growing spiritual lives, we must also remember that there is a simplicity about God, I believe Francis would assert, that is active within and appealing to every part of creation. We can therefore see, in comparing and contrasting Franciscan formation with our early monastics, great diversity in complexity and embodiment from one sacred system to another. Such diversity will become increasingly apparent as we continue in our explorations, particularly after the Protestant Reformation.

8

Erasmus & Militant Christians

Context

WHILE FRANCESCO PETRARCA IS known as the "father of humanism," Erasmus of Rotterdam (1466–1536) has been called the "Prince of Humanism," even though he was thoroughly Roman Catholic. Born out of wedlock, which was both an embarrassment and difficultly for him as a child, Erasmus was educated by the Brethren of the Common Life, who also influenced Martin Luther and John Calvin.[1] The Brethren's educational focus was "directed toward personal reform through a return to Christian inwardness" and Erasmus was troubled by their strict disciplinary tactics and he "later developed a deep-seated aversion to the monastic life" after spending some time in a Dutch monastery.[2]

He later served as a secretary to a bishop and then went on to the University of Paris where he was further frustrated with the then normal and extensive study of scholastic theology.[3] His interest and life's focus on theology was later reignited by Thomas More who encouraged him to study the early church fathers. His early studies resulted in his book, "The Handbook of the Militant Christian," which sought to liberate

---

1. Erasmus, "Handbook," 17.
2. Ibid., 18.
3. Ibid., 19.

contemporary theology through personal revelation, knowledge of the Gospel, and reverence for God.[4]

While many of Erasmus' works influenced the then growing reformation movement, Erasmus was troubled by their revolutionary spirit.[5] Refusing to become embroiled in the conflicts, though he did write against Luther, Erasmus continued his studies and translations of the early church fathers seeking a more pristine version of Christianity until the end of his life.[6] It is to Erasmus' early work, the "Handbook," whose whole purpose is aimed at making the reader pious,[7] that we will now be turning to for a better understanding of what personal transformation might look like to him.

Models of Reality

Anthropological-Cosmological

Being heavily steeped in both the New Testament, especially Paul of Tarsus,[8] and the early church fathers, Erasmus' anthro-cosmology is also very neoplatonic.[9] For him, there are two worlds: the visible realm, which includes earth and the stars; and the invisible "intelligible or angelic world" where "God dwells with the blessed."[10] The visible world corresponds to the corporeal part, "mere shadows of reality."[11] Hence, "the senses themselves cannot offer greater certainty."[12] As a result, Erasmus asserts, "the great majority of [humankind] is often deceived, for the world, like some deceitful magician, captivates their minds with seductive blandishments."[13] Many therefore think they have peace, but have instead really closed "their minds to reality,"[14] for to be still involved in the affairs of the world, he

   4. Ibid., 20.
   5. Ibid., 22.
   6. Ibid., 22–23.
   7. Ibid., 27.
   8. Ibid., 93.
   9. Ibid., 36.
   10. Ibid., 62.
   11. Ibid.
   12. Ibid., 37.
   13. Ibid., 29.
   14. Ibid.

asserts, is to only be a Christian on the surface.[15] Erasmus therefore embraces the neoplatonic notions of the world being evil and the heavens being good.

In this division between the invisible higher heavens and the lower visible earth, the world here below "is both contrary and hateful to Christ";[16] with the wisdom of the world seen as being false.[17] As a result, "life here below is best described as being a type of continual warfare,"[18] a "life-and-death battle,"[19] where we must ever struggle "for Life itself."[20] It is in this struggle that "our war is not between man and man, but within ourselves: The hostile battle lines spring forth in opposition to us from our very flesh itself."[21]

Erasmus' views of the person, as we can see, are also very neoplatonic in nature as he upholds the body-soul dualisms we have already seen many times. On this, he writes, "Man is a very complex creature composed of several contending parts: a soul, which may be likened to a sort of divine will, and a body, comparable to a dumb beast."[22] As with the neoplatonists and early church fathers, the body (or "Eve" of us all as Erasmus calls it) is the "carnal or sensual part of man."[23] The soul, on the other hand, is the means by which we ascend to the heights of the heavens and become one with God.[24] For the soul to die is therefore a much greater tragedy than the death of the body,[25] for the soul's death is everlasting.[26] We are to therefore work for the eternal life of this soul.

However, just as there is a battle between heaven and earth, there is likewise a conflict between the body and the soul that makes such eternal life difficult.[27] In this battle we are too weak as human beings to attain

---

15. Ibid., 66.
16. Ibid., 29, 52.
17. Ibid., 40.
18. Ibid., 28.
19. Ibid., 80–81.
20. Ibid., 31.
21. Ibid., 42.
22. Ibid.
23. Ibid., 29.
24. Ibid., 43.
25. Ibid., 32.
26. Ibid., 33.
27. Ibid., 43, 49–50.

the ideals, but we must still try.[28] Also, as similarly asserted by the neo-platonists, the mind can help us to rise above this world in such eternal pursuits and is therefore a central part of Erasmus' personal transformation system.[29] Erasmus also asserts the presence of God in the soul ever seeking its betterment and life.[30]

If this battle were not difficult enough, there is also the presence of the "enemy" in the world that humans must also struggle against. The "enemy of ours . . . intends to cast both the body and the soul into hell"[31] as it only want to destroy us.[32] This enemy, which is sometimes in the form of vice[33] and sometimes in the form of the harm that we do to ourselves[34] as well as being a force unto itself, continually attacks us and leads us away.[35] The enemy is also very deceitful and lays traps for us.[36] It is therefore in the midst of these three battle grounds (between heaven and earth, within one's soul, and with the enemy), that humans must continually work with God for the salvation of their souls.

Theological

In these battles, however, we are not alone, for we have the help of Jesus as well as God in both Being and Immanent forms. For Erasmus, Jesus is the one, alone, who grants peace and shatters "earthly folly."[37] He is the one who gave His life for us[38] and is the example that should ever be kept before our eyes.[39] Jesus gave us life to begin with and restored it to us through baptism, so we owe it all to Him,[40] and those who are not with

28. Ibid., 76.
29. Ibid., 43.
30. Ibid., 33–34.
31. Ibid., 31–32.
32. Ibid., 35.
33. Ibid., 29.
34. Ibid., 72, 90.
35. Ibid., 29, 35.
36. Ibid., 35, 82.
37. Ibid., 40.
38. Ibid., 31.
39. Ibid., 73, 80.
40. Ibid., 30.

Him are against Him.[41] Erasmus therefore holds a very high Christology, with Jesus being at the very center of his system.

We also find Erasmus speaking more generally about God in this text and the help that God offers. For him, God sees all, as do all the heavenly beings,[42] and God is always there trying to help us.[43] God is the one who opens things up in and for us[44] as God is all-powerful.[45] Regarding our struggles with temptations, God is considered to be "a loving Father teaching a future heir or punishing a beloved son."[46] With God, "the very highest reward will go to him who perseveres, just as the most severe punishment will be meted out to him who deserts."[47] This is because, Erasmus asserts, something good will come to those who endure.[48] Despite these potential punishments, God ultimately wants the highest good for everyone.[49]

This God, and Christ, claims Erasmus, is not just to be thought of as some far removed Being and Overseer, however. God is to also be found in charity, virtue, and goodness. On this, he writes, "Where God is, there is charity, for God is charity."[50] And again, "whenever you find truth and virtue, refer it to Christ,"[51] since "[God's] nature is virtue itself . . . He is the parent and authority of all virtue."[52] Finally, God is the "Author" of all our goods[53] as God's "very nature is to do good."[54] All in all, we can see theologically, that for Erasmus, God's Presence in the midst of the many conflicts of our existence is a very active one, where God is ever working for the good. Such is the bulk of the theological foundation that he sets out in this text.

41. Ibid., 31.
42. Ibid.
43. Ibid., 34.
44. Ibid., 38.
45. Ibid., 89.
46. Ibid., 76.
47. Ibid., 31.
48. Ibid., 49, 57, 82.
49. Ibid., 86.
50. Ibid., 33.
51. Ibid., 39.
52. Ibid., 40.
53. Ibid., 73.
54. Ibid., 72.

PART FOUR: Medieval & Renaissance

Theories of Change

Erasmus' primary theory of change seems to be very reminiscent of what we found in the *Didache,* with its emphasis on works righteousness and habit formation. For Erasmus, there two paths in life: the path of gratification of the passions that leads to death, and the path that, "through mortification of the flesh, leads to life."[55] As we have already noted above, we are to leave the visible, sensible, compound things along with the body and pursue instead the invisible, intelligible, and simple things of the spirit.[56] In this scheme, the paths of life and death are traveled via the habits that one has. For instance, in speaking of "evil men," Erasmus writes, "Their worldly wisdom leads inevitably to false presumption, which is followed by blindness of the mind, slavery to base appetites, and all other species of vice. The bad habits developed in this manner produce a dullness or insensibility of the mind, and the victim no longer considers himself a sinner."[57] Elsewhere, he writes, "remove [the soul] from the habit of sinning and it will be more capable of receiving God's grace, even though it is not yet perfect."[58] In short, habits of vice lead to death, while the habits of virtue lead to life.[59] Such habit forming approaches therefore seem to comprise the core of the theory of change that Erasmus articulates in this text.

With this theory of change in place, disciples are therefore to commit themselves to the ways of virtue and life, for it is by these ways that the rewards of God will come. As he asserts, "There is but one way to attain [the peace that Christ gives]; we must wage war with ourselves. We must contend fiercely with our vices."[60] We must therefore set perfection as our goal and pursue it with self-determination and perseverance, claims Erasmus,[61] and train ourselves to "gain control of [our] evil inclinations."[62] In this training and habit reformation, those who are spiritually mature welcome temptations because it helps them to better guard against themselves and cultivate the habits of life.[63] While such training may sound

55. Ibid., 54.
56. Ibid., 71.
57. Ibid., 41.
58. Ibid., 76.
59. Ibid., 85.
60. Ibid., 40.
61. Ibid., 47, 52.
62. Ibid., 47.
63. Ibid., 49.

tiresome and burdening, Erasmus asserts that "after you have overcome temptation and crucified your flesh with its evil desires, you will find true peace and tranquillity, and you will see that the Lord is sweet."[64] We will also, he asserts, eventually come to see how what we once cherished of the flesh was really transparent.[65]

Such change, for Erasmus, requires at least three components besides self-determination and effort. First, one must turn to God through prayer and receive the gentleness and humbleness needed for the journey.[66] One can also find remedies for all temptations in the Cross by our meditating on how Christ lived and what He endured.[67] Secondly, one needs knowledge in such habit forming because "it fortifies the mind with salutary precepts and keeps virtue ever before us."[68] It is also through such knowledge, especially of the Scriptures, that one can further receive help from God.[69] Finally, one must use reason in this journey since "the way of Christ is the most sensible and logical one to follow."[70] It is through such reason that we can restrain evil and be guided toward the virtues that we seek to cultivate.[71] These three elements are therefore intended to help one in their determined efforts to pursue the habitual paths of life that God ever lays before us. It is from this theoretical model that Erasmus' personal transformation approaches directly emerge.

Spiritual Formation Ideals & Goals

As it relates to the ideals that one should strive for, Erasmus does not seem to have too much to say in this fairly short text. He does write, "Peace is the highest good to which even the lovers of the world turn all their efforts."[72] In addition to such peace, eternal happiness is also purported to come to those who carry on and struggle in the battles through the dark nights of life.[73] He also asserts that a true Christian is one who attains the higher

64. Ibid.
65. Ibid., 57.
66. Ibid., 35, 41, 46.
67. Ibid., 80–81.
68. Ibid., 35.
69. Ibid., 37.
70. Ibid., 56.
71. Ibid., 45, 46.
72. Ibid., 40; see also ibid., 49, 78.
73. Ibid., 31, 49.

virtues of life,[74] and admonishes his readers to seek the praise of God rather than humans.[75] Finally, we find Erasmus claiming that the fullness of wisdom is to know one's self.[76]

Overall, Erasmus seems to be asserting an ideal of one successfully making the spiritual journey, traversing from body to spirit and from earth to heaven. If this is true, then the goal and ideal of one's life is to complete this transcending pilgrimage. Such an ideal, if accurate, is very similar to what we found in our studies of the early desert monks previously.

Spiritual Formation Approaches

In order to help one to attain eternal life for their soul, and the peace and happiness that comes with such salvation, Erasmus discusses at least six personal spiritual formation approaches that are essential for one's pilgrimage. First and foremost, one must desire Christ and they must desire perfection.[77] He asserts that a person's "actions are mere expression of [her or his] inner convictions"[78] and everything must therefore be done in service to Christ[79] looking only to Him as the sole archetype and guide.[80] As he proclaims, "Whatever things you find Christ's image in, join yourself to them."[81] We must also, Erasmus adds, always give thanks to God for the victories and gifts of our lives,[82] trusting and looking to God at all times.[83] Such devotional reverence is therefore a central approach for him.

Directly related to this are regular practices of prayer and meditation. For Erasmus, prayer is one of our most potent weapons in the battles of our lives,[84] for pure prayer can subdue the passions[85] and is a way to be strengthened internally.[86] One must beware, however, for prayers and ritu-

74. Ibid., 28.
75. Ibid., 87.
76. Ibid., 42.
77. Ibid., 69, 72.
78. Ibid., 71.
79. Ibid., 61.
80. Ibid., 58, 71, 73, 74, 88, 91, 92.
81. Ibid., 92.
82. Ibid., 34, 73, 89.
83. Ibid., 54, 64, 77–78.
84. Ibid., 35, 92.
85. Ibid., 35.
86. Ibid., 38.

als can still be done in pursuit of fleshy passions to.[87] Nevertheless, prayers and meditations, such as those on the life of Christ as mentioned above, can help fight against the vices and increase our love for Christ.[88]

A third set of spiritual formation approaches found in this text are related to ascetical practices. One must be prepared to lose everything in this struggle against the world for Christ's sake; we must "get out of [our] own self and let Him support [us]."[89] We must be dead to the world[90] and attack the enemy within.[91] As he writes, "The fleshpots of Egypt must be forsaken once and for all"; we must forsake the passions of the flesh.[92] However, all of this is to be done in moderation for some of the things of this life, such as in eating.[93] All of this is because we need to prepare and armor ourselves for this war,[94] never loosing hope because God is always on our side.[95] Such practices therefore become a central part of our habit forming armor in these struggles.

Closely related to this, and as noted above, one must also love and seek the virtues and hate all the vices.[96] Erasmus encourages his readers to reflect and meditate on the consequences of each, especially how detestable vice and sin is.[97] He advises us to emulate the virtues of the saints we revere[98] and not the vices or violence of others.[99] Be not revengeful or violent, he asserts, because if you do, "you only offer reasons to be treated in the same way."[100] Instead, he continues, we must only forgive[101] and ever put evil out of our minds right away[102] and in all things, we must

---

87. Ibid., 51.
88. Ibid., 79, 81, 84, 89, 91.
89. Ibid., 54.
90. Ibid., 65.
91. Ibid., 70.
92. Ibid., 54.
93. Ibid., 86.
94. Ibid., 30.
95. Ibid., 34.
96. Ibid., 61, 78–79, 83, 87.
97. Ibid., 79, 81, 84.
98. Ibid., 66, 92.
99. Ibid., 90.
100. Ibid.
101. Ibid., 91.
102. Ibid., 77, 85.

persevere.[103] In the practice of the virtues and the avoidance of vices, one must also use works of piety in order to ever stay with Christ rather than the world.[104] We must ever be giving of our self for our neighbors for their benefit.[105] Such pursuits will, as noted above, lead to the paths of eternal life according to Erasmus.

A fifth set of approaches is related to watchfulness. Each person, he asserts, needs watchfulness at all times "lest he expose God's fortress to demons."[106] We must therefore struggle and ever guard ourselves against the vices at all times,[107] always fortifying the mind [108] that can liberate the soul.[109] He writes, "The flesh will be overcome if we immediately reject evil thoughts and desires and turn our thoughts to what is of God."[110] Erasmus also notes that we need to guard ourselves especially for those things that we are most vulnerable to and these can change throughout our lives.[111] Such watchfulness is therefore also a necessary and central part of one's journey.

Finally, a sixth aspect of one's spiritually forming personal life has to do with the acquisition of knowledge. He argues that knowledge is one of our most potent weapons when it is turned to Christ.[112] "Let your study," Erasmus encourages his readers, "bring you to a clearer perception of Christ so that your love for Him will increase and you will in turn be able to communicate this knowledge of Him to others."[113] Such knowledge is found in at least three sources according to him. First, turning to Scriptures will ward off all attacks, hence, we should meditate on them day and night.[114] Taking them to be allegorical truth that is inspired by God, rather than literally,[115] one must seeking spiritual understanding by reading them with a clean heart, a "high regard for the revealed word," and

103. Ibid., 80.
104. Ibid., 36.
105. Ibid., 68, 72.
106. Ibid., 29; see also ibid., 39.
107. Ibid., 30, 77.
108. Ibid., 92.
109. Ibid., 43.
110. Ibid., 52.
111. Ibid., 45–46, 78.
112. Ibid., 35, 42, 58.
113. Ibid., 58–59.
114. Ibid., 36, 53, 93.
115. Ibid., 37, 53, 63.

with all humility.[116] A second source of knowledge comes from the writings of others, particularly the early church fathers,[117] though the Platonic "pagan poets" are also advisable.[118] Of the early Fathers, Erasmus writes, "their very thoughts constitute a prayerful meditation, and they penetrate into the very depths of the mysteries they propound."[119] Finally, we must turn to an understanding of ourselves as yet another essential source of knowledge.[120] All of these sources are intended to better enable one to pursue the path of life that leads to salvation.

These are the six primary personal transformation approaches that we find Erasmus addressing in this text. They each seem to clearly come out of his convictions for the worldview he proposes and his readings of the early church fathers. It is through these approaches, that one will cultivate the habits of virtue that ultimately lead to life according to him.

Discernment

Erasmus' discernment process primarily seems to be one of reflecting on the fruits of one's life in comparison with the image of God/Christ that one has. For instance, he suggests several signs to know if one's "soul is diseased or perhaps even dead": when the Word of God is sickening to us when we hear it; if we do acts of piety unwillingly; when we can't handle rebukes; when material loss troubles us; when one is no longer able to perceive truth; when we can't hear the inner divine voice; when one doesn't feel anything at the sight of the suffering of others; and when one's conscience doesn't feel remorse for the bad things that we have done.[121] It therefore seems that his discernment is at least partly a matter of one reflecting on how they are thinking, feeling, and acting.

But such discernment also seems to be set in relation to the image of Christ that we have. Erasmus admonishes his readers to see Christ as "charity, simplicity, patience, and purity" and the devil as "anything that deters us from Christ and His teaching."[122] So, for example, when we seek to do things for our self, then we "have fallen away from Christ and have

116. Ibid., 36–37, 38.
117. Ibid., 64, 92, 93.
118. Ibid., 36, 39, 93.
119. Ibid., 37.
120. Ibid., 42, 46, 89.
121. Ibid., 32–33.
122. Ibid., 58.

made a god out of" ourselves.[123] Or, he also claims in another example, there is loving one's spouse for fleshy reasons and loving them in Christ, i.e., because we see Him in them. This second kind of love is "spiritual love," asserts Erasmus.[124] It is, therefore, by comparing what one experiences and does against the image given by God through Christ that we can know if we are pursuing the ways of life or the paths to death in Erasmus' system.

In such discernment, as was noted a couple times above, the mind and reason also play a central role. We must be able to, he asserts, discern between the "dictates of reason and the promptings of passion"[125] and we must use reason and logic to guide our self as we'll come to find that Christ's way is the most logical one.[126] He further writes, "This then is the only road to happiness: first, know yourself; do not allow yourself to be led by the passions, but submit all things to the judgment of reason. Be sane and let reason be wise, that is, let it gaze upon decent things."[127] Reason and knowledge are therefore at the very heart of his discernment approaches, for, in summarizing Socrates' view, he claims that "virtue is nothing other than the knowledge of things that are to be sought after or of things that are to be avoided . . . Vice, then, can proceed from no other source than wrong opinions."[128] It is, then, by using reason that is based on the knowledge of what is right, which comes primarily from our image of Christ, that one can discern which ways one is to follow as they reflect on the ever manifesting fruits of their lives.

Evaluative Techniques

As we have already heard several times above, Erasmus emphasizes that we must know ourselves.[129] This seems to be the primary evaluative technique heralded by Erasmus in this text. Such evaluations are not to be made in isolation, as we have heard, however. Instead, they are to be made in light of Scripture, the early church fathers and other saints, and through the application of reason. Though he does not seem to explicitly mention

123. Ibid., 60.
124. Ibid., 51.
125. Ibid., 47.
126. Ibid., 56.
127. Ibid., 46.
128. Ibid., 71.
129. Ibid., 42, 46, 89.

it in this text, it can be hypothesized, based on his own early monastic formation, that community observations and reflections are yet another source of evaluations that one can use to help them on their spiritual journeys. Indeed, as we have seen, some of his reflections on how the personal spiritual life unfolds is based on his own external observations of others.

Summary/Reflections

This, then, is the spiritual formation system that we find in Erasmus' text, "The Handbook of the Militant Christian." In many ways, it seems like a blend of the *Didache* and the early monastic systems that we encountered earlier, which is not surprising as he turned to early texts of this type for his own studies and formation. It is very much a "hunker down and endure the battle" kind of a system of personal transformation. Much of Erasmus' views seem to emerge more out of his anthro-cosmology and theory of change rather than being more focused on the theology that he has, which wasn't all that developed. His focus seems to be more about the battle we are in the midst of and the determination that we must all have rather being than on one that is particularly focused on some specific aspect of God as we found with the Franciscan framework and its heavier emphasis on the simplicity and immanence of God in creation.

PART FOUR: Medieval & Renaissance

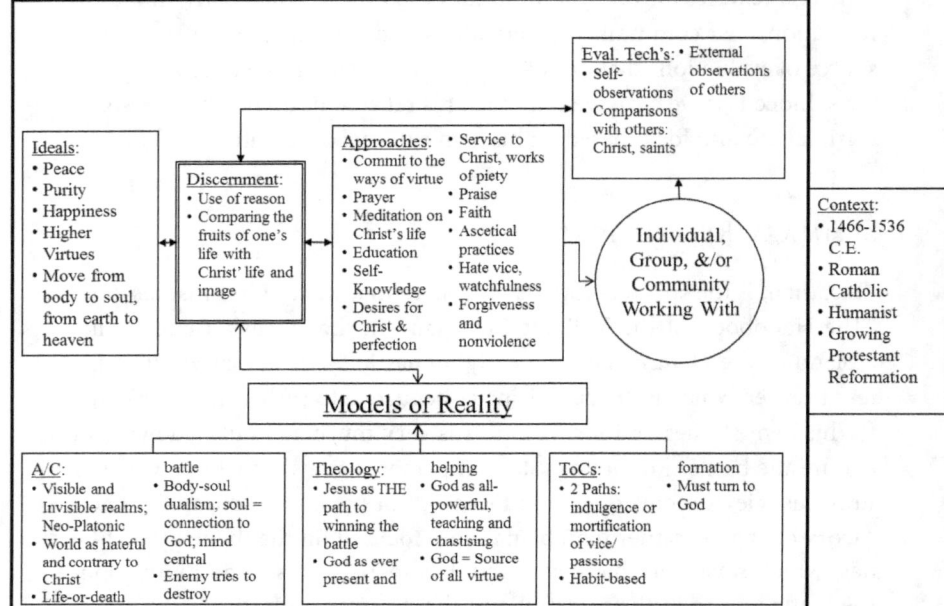

Based on this, we are beginning to see that there are at least two sources out of which spiritual formation systems emerge: one stemming from a part (or even the whole) of one's anthro-cosmology, and the other coming from their specific theological emphases. Erasmus' system seems to be more of the former than the latter with the core of his system being one that is based on a habit forming model of spiritual formation; i.e., we must train the soul in the virtues thereby conquering the vices of the body and then will we overcome evil and be united with God. The Franciscan framework, on the other hand, was more focused in many ways on a theology of God's immanence and participating with this theologically asserted aspect of God. As we continue in our explorations, we shall see that these systems of personal transformation seem to have a tendency to lean toward one of these more than the other.

PART FIVE

Protestant Reformation

WHEN MARTIN LUTHER HAMMERED his 95 theses against the Roman Catholic Church to the door of the Wittenberg Castle in Germany in 1517, he unwittingly sparked a firestorm that irrevocably altered the course of Western Christianity.[1] Aided by other "protesting" reformers (hence the name, Protestant Reformation),[2] the Roman Catholic Church found itself challenged not only theologically but also politically as nations such as England began to secede from the rule of Rome.[3] The result was an internal schism that spawned the Thirty Years War, one of the most devastating and taxing violent confrontations to sweep through Europe.[4]

Religiously and spiritually, this was a fervent time of new movements as people and communities were now more free to pursue their own interpretation of what it meant to be a Christian outside of the watchful and dominating influence of the Roman Catholic hierarchy.[5] The newly formed United States, for instance, was described as a "motley sampler" of approaches to Christianity where anyone "who has, or fancies that he has, some inward experience and a ready tongue, may persuade himself that he is called to be a reformer."[6] Translating the Bible into local vernacular

---

1. Chidester, *Christianity*, 313; Selderhuis, "The Prostestant Tradition in Europe," 170, 76; Sheldrake, *Brief History of Spirituality*, 110; Woods, *Christian Spirituality*, 186, 88.

2. Selderhuis, "The Prostestant Tradition in Europe," 175, 76.

3. Carmichael, "Catholic Saints and Reformers," 202; Chidester, *Christianity*, 315–16, 19, 31; Selderhuis, "The Prostestant Tradition in Europe," 170–71, 76; Sheldrake, *Brief History of Spirituality*, 116; Woods, *Christian Spirituality*, 186, 96.

4. Chidester, *Christianity*, 323, 26, 30; Sheldrake, *Brief History of Spirituality*, 107; Woods, *Christian Spirituality*, 188, 90, 228.

5. Chidester, *Christianity*, 325–26; Woods, *Christian Spirituality*, 185, 212.

6. Chidester, *Christianity*, 400–401; Graham, "The Protestant Tradition in

languages also became much more prevalent during this era as Luther and others, such as William Tyndale (whose translations became one of the primary bases for the King James version of the Bible), produced German and English versions.[7] Martyrdom also returned as an idealized way to live out the Gospel as both Catholics and Protestants persecuted one another.[8] Affective spiritualities, such as German Pietism and other strands, also emerged partly in response to the overly influence of Scholasticism of the previous era with its heavy emphasis on rationality and intellectual systematics.[9] In addition, this was an age of great preachers where traveling evangelists such as the founder of Methodism, John Wesley, is purported to have preached more than 42,000 sermons in his lifetime.[10]

On the Roman Catholic side, such diverse movements were no less dynamic. Many new religious orders, such as the Jesuits, Little Brothers of Jesus, and Vincentians, found their origins in this era.[11] An internal reformation also spread through Catholic ranks as people such as Teresa of Avila, Lorenzo Scupoli, and a reforming priestly order known as the Oratory of Jesus Christ strove to address many of the abuses that were noted by Protestants as well as by Catholics themselves.[12] New approaches to spirituality also found footing among Roman Catholic communities as imagination-based prayers, silent contemplative prayers, Sacred Heart devotions, and simple ways of living and working became more popular.[13]

America," 276; Sheldrake, *Brief History of Spirituality*, 166; Woods, *Christian Spirituality*, 228, 37.

7. Selderhuis, "The Prostestant Tradition in Europe," 177; Sheldrake, *Brief History of Spirituality*, 110; Woods, *Christian Spirituality*, 187, 227.

8. Carmichael, "Catholic Saints and Reformers," 215; Chidester, *Christianity*, 326; Sheldrake, *Brief History of Spirituality*, 115; Woods, *Christian Spirituality*, 193.

9. Chidester, *Christianity*, 400; Selderhuis, "The Prostestant Tradition in Europe," 179–80; Sheldrake, *Brief History of Spirituality*, 143; Woods, *Christian Spirituality*, 187, 221.

10. Chidester, *Christianity*, 401; Selderhuis, "The Prostestant Tradition in Europe," 195; Sheldrake, *Brief History of Spirituality*, 146, 67; Woods, *Christian Spirituality*, 228.

11. Carmichael, "Catholic Saints and Reformers," 203, 28, 41; Chidester, *Christianity*, 328; Sheldrake, *Brief History of Spirituality*, 122–23, 36, 56–57; Woods, *Christian Spirituality*, 205, 31.

12. Carmichael, "Catholic Saints and Reformers," 207, 14, 28; Chidester, *Christianity*, 327, 29; Sheldrake, *Brief History of Spirituality*, 129, 34; Woods, *Christian Spirituality*, 186, 200, 203, 206.

13. Carmichael, "Catholic Saints and Reformers," 204, 25, 33, 35, 38, 42–43; Chidester, *Christianity*, 328–29; Sheldrake, *Brief History of Spirituality*, 137, 57, 59; Woods, *Christian Spirituality*, 201, 11, 15.

PART FIVE: Protestant Reformation

In addition to this explosion of newer and more diverse forms of Western Christian spirituality, were the larger sociological movements taking shape during this time period. Women came to play an increasingly accepted role in both church and state.[14] Democracy, as a viable political system, also began to take hold.[15] Lay spiritualities, on Catholic as well as Protestant sides, found increasing support as literacy rates continued to rise and text-based resources were developed.[16] Finally, modern scientific methods became more prevalent as the likes of Pascal, Galileo, and Newton lived during this era and the Industrial Revolution began to take shape.[17] Increasingly throughout this period, and on into the next, would religion need to respond to the findings and assertions of modern science as we shall see in the final section of this book.[18]

With so much diversity on both Protestant and Catholic sides, we turn to three sets of writings in order to gain a sense of some the richness in approaches to personal transformation found during this era. We will first look to an imagination and affective-based strand of Roman Catholicism with Francis de Sales' *Introduction to the Devout Life*. Influenced by Ignatian spirituality, de Sales' text gives us insights into how some Catholic clerics sought to work with their lay communities. Next, we will turn to the Quaker tradition by pouring over the pages of dairies of such notables as George Fox, Isaac Pennington, John Woolman, and Rufus Jones. Finally, we will spend some time with William Law. Law was an Anglican whose text, *A Serious Call to a Devout and Holy Life*, which we will be focusing on, was intended for the upper classes that he worked with. Overall, these writings provide us with little more than a brief snapshot of the vast number of approaches to personal transformation in this era. However, they are an insightful source into some of this great diversity.

---

14. Carmichael, "Catholic Saints and Reformers," 202; Sheldrake, *Brief History of Spirituality*, 164–65; Woods, *Christian Spirituality*, 206.

15. Carmichael, "Catholic Saints and Reformers," 202; Sheldrake, *Brief History of Spirituality*, 156; Woods, *Christian Spirituality*, 230.

16. Chidester, *Christianity*, 313; Selderhuis, "The Protestant Tradition in Europe," 176; Sheldrake, *Brief History of Spirituality*, 106, 31; Woods, *Christian Spirituality*, 188.

17. Carmichael, "Catholic Saints and Reformers," 202, 36; Sheldrake, *Brief History of Spirituality*, 171; Woods, *Christian Spirituality*, 233, 35, 40.

18. Carmichael, "Catholic Saints and Reformers," 219, 23–24; Sheldrake, *Brief History of Spirituality*, 171; Woods, *Christian Spirituality*, 241.

9

Francis de Sales' *Introduction*

Context

FRANCIS DE SALES (1567–1622), by education, was a humanist who sought to bring universal holiness to all people, especially laity.[1] Raised by a noble Catholic family in a region that was predominantly Calvinist, he received both his education and spiritual direction from the Jesuits, making the Spiritual Exercises annually.[2] Living in the sharply divided world of his time, his "paramount aim was to restore unity of faith in his diocese and beyond."[3] His writings were almost solely focused on articulating a lived spirituality, a "mysticism in action."[4]

In his *Introduction to the Devout Life*, de Sales seeks to articulate to "Philothea" (or the soul) what is needed in order to ever grow in responsiveness to what love asks of us.[5] This text, which was a best seller in de Sales' lifetime, was originally advice that he had given to a devout woman and went on to influence such notable persons as Jeremy Taylor and Jean-Pierre de Caussade.[6] It is to this influential text that we will be turning

---

1. Stopp, "Francois de Sales," 380–81.
2. Ibid., 381.
3. Ibid., 382.
4. Ibid.
5. Ibid., 382–83.
6. de Sales, *Introduction*, xxxviii; Stopp, "Francois de Sales," 385.

Francis de Sales' Introduction

to better understand de Sales' personal transformation framework and thereby gain a better sense of this time period.

Models of Reality

Anthropological-Cosmological

Francis de Sales' view of the world is one that is seen as being in conflict with the spiritual life. As he writes, "Do what we will, the world must wage war upon us."[7] It is a world that "runs down true devotion, painting devout people with [A] gloomy, melancholy aspect, and affirming that religion makes them dismal and unpleasant"; a world that "sees nothing of that inward, heartfelt devotion which makes all these actions pleasant and easy."[8] It is out of this sinful world that one must rise up into a devout life.[9] The life of our souls must therefore be one that is unaffected by it. De Sales asserts that just "as the mother-of-pearl lives in the sea without ever absorbing one drop of salt water . . . a true steadfast soul may live in the world untainted by worldly breadth."[10] The world, then, is one that we must ever be at odds with as we grow spiritually.

In line with the humanistic and Ignatian views of his time, which "attach central importance to the human person and human values,"[11] de Sales asserts that humans were created to show forth God's goodness, to "work for Eternity,"[12] and that our souls are "noble and excellent" things.[13] However, just as we are in conflict with the world, so too are the parts of one's soul. Regarding these various parts, and their relationship with each other, he writes, "our souls have two parts, one inferior, the other superior, and the inferior does not always choose to be led by the superior, but takes its own line, it not infrequently happens that the inferior part takes pleasure in a temptation not only without consent from, but absolutely in contradiction to, the superior will."[14] So while we have a higher and more

---

7. de Sales, *Introduction*, 188.
8. Ibid., 5.
9. Ibid., 12.
10. Ibid., xxxviii.
11. Modras, "The Spiritual Humanism of the Jesuits," 11.
12. de Sales, *Introduction*, 19, 59.
13. Ibid., 234.
14. Ibid., 192.

reasonable part,[15] the soul is also tempted by natural inclinations and it is this darkness that often shrouds our heart that can lead us astray.[16]

Despite these tendencies, however, we also have the presence of God within us.[17] It is, says de Sales, the "Holy Spirit [who] enlightens our conscience,"[18] and God is the "Source of all holy thoughts."[19] Put more succinctly, de Sales asserts that God "is very specially present in [our] heart and mind, which He kindles and inspires with His Holy Presence, abiding there as Heart of [our] heart, Spirit of [our] spirit."[20] Nevertheless, by sin one can lose the help that God's grace ever offers to us.[21] It is this Holy Presence that helps the soul to rise within itself and from the sinfulness of the world into a more holy and devout life.

In addition to the difficulties laid upon the soul by its own natural temptations and by the world, de Sales asserts the presence of an "Evil One." With "sadness and melancholy . . . [as] his own characteristics,"[22] the Devil is one who tries to trick and catch us.[23] For instance, the Devil will use friendships to deceive and delude us[24] and "often inspires men with ardent desires from unattainable things."[25] This Evil One is asserted as leading a "troop of worldly men,"[26] and sometimes does things with the permission of God.[27] Through the use of meditations, de Sales also envisions Hell as "a dark city, reeking with the flames of sulfur and brimstone, inhabited by citizens who cannot get forth," with "torture in every sense and every member" and people are sent there to suffer because of their sins.[28] However, he also envisions Heaven as its opposite with images of a "lovely, calm night," a "glorious summer's day," a "sweet and precious place," with "countless inhabitants of that blessed country" who have great

15. Ibid., 168.
16. Ibid., 43, 151, 223.
17. Ibid., 81, 195.
18. Ibid., 40.
19. Ibid., 63.
20. Ibid., 50–51.
21. Ibid., 13.
22. Ibid., 204.
23. Ibid., 10, 208, 18.
24. Ibid., 133.
25. Ibid., 171.
26. Ibid., 34.
27. Ibid., 193.
28. Ibid., 29.

Francis de Sales' Introduction

and endless peace and joy.[29] Such views of heaven and hell, and the Evil One, therefore form a central part of the cosmology in which his anthropology is situated.

Theological

For de Sales, most of his theology focuses on God's relation to the individual. As mentioned above, God, through grace, "not only leads us to do well, but to act carefully, diligently, and promptly"[30] and it is God who ever helps to lead and sustain us.[31] God created us out of nothingness, purely out of God's goodness,[32] and God intervenes to change us, just as God did with the saints such as Bernard of Clairvaux.[33] God will therefore never allow temptations that are too hard for us, for they are intended to help us grow.[34] Because of God's sovereignty, we are not to judge, [35]for God will eventually "separate the evil and the good" and wickedness will be condemned as God will call us all to account for our actions.[36] But de Sales' views of this Sovereign God that is so active in our lives is not just confined to humans alone, but is also working throughout all creation. On this, he writes, "[God] is everywhere, and in all, and that there is no place, nothing in the world, devoid of His most Holy Presence, so that, even as birds on the wing meet the air continually, we, let us go where we will, meet with that presence always and everywhere."[37] In short, no matter where we are or what we are doing, good or bad, God is always there.[38]

As I will discuss more below, Jesus also has a central place in de Sales' spiritual formation system. For him, Jesus is "the light of the world," "the tree of life," and the "living fountain of Jacob's well," and "there is no way to God save through this door."[39] It is Jesus that we are to imitate, and it is to Him that we are to trust and leave all, even something as small as our pub-

29. Ibid., 30–31.
30. Ibid., 4.
31. Ibid., 37, 137.
32. Ibid., 17.
33. Ibid., 89.
34. Ibid., 194.
35. Ibid., 154.
36. Ibid., 27, 130.
37. Ibid., 50.
38. Ibid., 62.
39. Ibid., 47.

lic reputations.[40] For de Sales, God and Christ are actively present in one's life and all of creation as our souls ever seek to journey in the devout life.

Theories of Change

As we shall see, the assertion of our having good dispositions is a central goal in the system. de Sales asserts that these are necessary for change because a good heart is what leads to good actions.[41] It is a process of transformation that comes as our will turns the direction of the soul through the love that is nurtured in it. Put succinctly, he writes, "God desires to have us only for the sake of our soul, or the soul through our will, and our will for love's sake."[42] It is love, then, that lures the will toward God thereby leading the soul to perfection. If, on the other hand, the soul yields to fleshy temptations, it will only find destruction.[43] As he writes, "Our earthly nature easily falls away from its higher tone by reason of the frailty and evil tendency of the flesh, oppressing and dragging down the soul, unless it is constantly rising up by means of a vigorous resolution."[44] Change, then, can only happen by our concerted effort de Sales asserts.

The will therefore holds a central place for our personal transformation, as does perseverance, because we can change natural imperfections and natural tendencies by "cultivating the reverse disposition."[45] For example, one can counter vices with their opposite virtue: anger with gentleness, pride with humility, etc.[46] By continually exercising the will toward the things of God, one is able to attain to the devotional life that de Sales desires for all people. On this, he writes, "Now we are yet but as grubs in devotion, unable to fly at will, and attain the desired aim of Christian perfection; but if we begin to take shape through our desires and resolutions, our wings will gradually grow, and we may hope one day to become spiritual bees, able to fly."[47] Love, will, and continual devotion are therefore key ingredients to his theory of change.

40. Ibid., 107, 108.
41. Ibid., 210.
42. Ibid., 130.
43. Ibid., 40–41.
44. Ibid., 223.
45. Ibid., 43.
46. Ibid., 88.
47. Ibid., 190.

Francis de Sales' Introduction

However, as noted, such change does not happen in an instance, but rather through long gradual stages. "The soul which rises from out of sin to a devout life has been compared to the dawn, which does not banish darkness suddenly, but by degrees," and, de Sales goes on to assert, as we rise, we can always regress and fall backwards.[48] Generally, he claims, we start in the lower, imaginary stages of growth, "until God calls [us] up higher" to the more abstract thoughts and higher stages of contemplation.[49] One of the primary metaphors that he draws on as a model of such gradual progress is Jacob's ladder: "the steps themselves are simply the degrees of love by which we go on from virtue to virtue, either descending by good deeds on behalf of our neighbor or ascending by contemplation to a loving union with God."[50]

In this journey, purification is a necessary beginning step as "we need the pruning hook to cut off all dead and superfluous works from our conscience" and we need to be purged from all of our sins.[51] However, he adds, "we can never be altogether free from venial sin, at least not until after a very long persistence in this purity; but we can be without any affection for venial sin."[52] Again, he asserts the need for the transformation of one's affections and will as a central aspect of his change theory.

Finally, he also outlines three stages that either vices or virtues progress through as they enter into one's being: temptation or inspiration; delectation; and consent.[53] Vices and virtues both have their initial seed as either a temptation or inspiration within us in some way. Then, we take pleasure in either the vice or the virtue. Finally, we consent to its presence and manifest its fruits. As de Sales asserts, what we aim for is what we tend toward,[54] and knowing these steps can help one to recognize their progress and either encourage, as in the case of a virtue, or discourage it, as we should for vices.

This theory of change is therefore wholly in keeping with his goal of fostering love and devotion. As one comes to nurture and pursue the love of the virtues and goodness, which comes from God's work in our hearts as we heard above, the soul begins to rise to the heights that God desires

48. Ibid., 12.
49. Ibid., 53.
50. Ibid., 6.
51. Ibid., 11, 13, 40.
52. Ibid., 40; see also ibid., 199.
53. Ibid., 73–74, 190.
54. Ibid., 97.

for all of us to attain. Such personal transformation therefore comes partly by our ever attending to the inner vice or virtue movements within us and working to cultivate the will in a love for all the things of God. Overall, then, his theory of change seems to be one of a gradual growth through the intentional cultivation of one's will toward some desired aim.

Spiritual Formation Ideals & Goals

Regarding this particular text, de Sales claims that "my object is teach those who are living in towns, at court, in their own households, and whose calling obliges them to a social life . . . such persons are apt to reject all attempt to lead a devout life under the plea of impossibility."[55] For him, all people are therefore called "to bring forth fruits of devotion, each one according to his kind of vocation."[56] Throughout this text, he returns again and again to the centrality of each person living a devout life, as the name of it implies, as "our business is to become good, devout people, pious men and women; and all our efforts must be to that end."[57] Such devotion is an "earnest following after God," something that sweetens the cruel torments of life in this world.[58] "In short," he writes, "devotion is simply a spiritual activity and liveliness by means of which Divine Love works in us, and causes us to work briskly and lovingly."[59] Devotion, therefore, is one of the main ideals that he sets up for the reader to embrace and follow after.

This is because, as just mentioned, devotion is very much related to love. In fact, he asserts, "The difference between love and devotion is just that which exists between fire and flame—love being a spiritual fire which becomes devotion when it is fanned into a flame."[60] For de Sales, "love alone leads to perfection" and "love is the great healer of all ills."[61] Even more than this, he claims, "Foremost among the soul's affections is love. Love is the ruler of every motion of the heart; drawing all to itself, and making us like to that [which] we love."[62] It is because of this, that we

- 55. Ibid., xxxvii.
- 56. Ibid., 7.
- 57. Ibid., 91.
- 58. Ibid., 6, 42.
- 59. Ibid., 4.
- 60. Ibid., 4–5.
- 61. Ibid., 115, 53.
- 62. Ibid., 127.

Francis de Sales' Introduction

must seek after the love of God and others.[63] It is in our love for God, and Christ's love for us, that we can be united with God.[64] We must therefore seek after "good dispositions," as "purity is the lily among the virtues ... its special glory is in the spotless whiteness of soul and body."[65] It is, therefore, love, and the devotion which bursts forth from it, that is to be among our central quests in the personal spiritual life.

SPIRITUAL FORMATION APPROACHES

These ideals, according to his system, are to be nurtured in a diverse number of ways. As noted, de Sales' humanistic bent toward valuing the individual and cultivating one's own will in love is a central part of his approaches. It is up to each person to choose between heaven and hell, to choose the devout life, and to choose not to yield to temptations.[66] We are the ones who must carefully carry out our inspirations, seeking "to produce the intended results" of our growing life in God.[67] So for instance, he writes, "Strive when your meditation is ended to retain the thoughts and resolutions you have made as your earnest practice throughout the day" and then go and act on them.[68]

However, his humanistic emphasis is not a secular one that places all power and authority solely in the hands of the individual, but rather is one that turns to God for the strength and guidance to do this. "Resolve to do better," he asserts, with God's help and follow only after God.[69] He further admonishes his readers to rely on God and not on one's "own industry or efforts," encouraging them to aspire only for Heaven and God.[70] Hence, one of de Sales' primary spiritual formation approaches is for each person to exert their will, with the help of God, toward the things of God.

It therefore follows, and as was discussed above, that the intentional cultivation of the virtues holds a central place for his approaches. De Sales asserts that there are "universal virtues" that everyone must cultivate in their lives. Some of these universal virtues include gentleness, temperance,

63. Ibid., xxxix, xli, 4, 95, 98, 136, 52, 200, 207, 29.
64. Ibid., 82.
65. Ibid., 42, 117.
66. Ibid., 32–33, 34–35, 193.
67. Ibid., 75.
68. Ibid., 56; see also ibid., 59.
69. Ibid., 24, 38, 225, 41.
70. Ibid., 31, 202.

PART FIVE: Protestant Reformation

modesty, and humility, forbearance, cheerfulness, and poverty as well as chastity and obedience.[71] He claims that we need to cultivate them all because they fill the soul with "untold sweetness after being practiced" and move one toward perfection.[72]

While these virtues need to be nurtured by everyone, each vocation in life also has its own unique sets of virtues that need to be especially cultivated.[73] Also, as was mentioned above, certain vices require certain virtues to be nurtured in order to combat them. In light of this, de Sales spends some time discussing a few of the virtues that are more primary for him. Looking across this text, it is apparent that the most central virtue for him is humbleness, a virtue of literally and metaphorically prostrating ourselves before God.[74] For him, humility is "above all other virtues," it "makes our lives acceptable to God," and it "forbids us to aim at excelling or being preferred to others."[75] He also cautions his readers that all true humility is inward, that it is not found in outward manifestations of "humble acts" because such outward acts can actually foster "self-love, self-sufficiency, indolence, and evil tempers."[76] The intentional cultivation of humbleness is therefore a central virtue for his system.

Besides humbleness, there are a few other virtues that de Sales emphasizes as being necessary for the devotional life. One is supposed to embrace an impoverished disposition toward all material possessions, seeing all things as being in service to God, lest one become too attached to them.[77] We should also embrace gentleness, especially when angry.[78] We are to likewise nurture courage, patience, forbearance, and endurance by complaining as little as possible, enduring and rejoicing in anything that God sends our way, and not being "disheartened by our imperfections."[79] Purity should therefore ever be our goal as we reject all things that are contrary to God and are trifling.[80] Such purity should also be prevalent

71. Ibid., 85, 91, 115–16, 44.
72. Ibid., 105, 15–16, 235.
73. Ibid., 86.
74. Ibid., 17, 19, 23, 34, 36, 52, 59, 76, 98, 113, 214, 32.
75. Ibid., 96, 105, 108, 15.
76. Ibid., 99, 100.
77. Ibid., 122, 23–24, 25, 78.
78. Ibid., 110–11.
79. Ibid., 12, 92–93, 102, 77, 218, 42.
80. Ibid., 19, 32, 163.

in the holiness of all our speech and action.[81] We are also to be fair in all things, to "be careful and diligent in all [our] affairs," righting all evils when they occur, and seeking lives of service.[82] Along with humbleness, these are core virtues to be sought after and nurtured.

Somewhat related to the intentional cultivation of the virtues, de Sales also asserts some ascetical views and practices as a part of his approaches to personal transformation in this text. He advises his readers to reject their former worldly life of material indulgences and to "despise the world."[83] Do not voluntarily expose yourself to temptations, he asserts, but instead resist them all.[84] He writes, seek to "tear up the roots of sin from your heart, especially this and that individual sin which troubles you most" and come to abhor your sins.[85] In pursuit of this, we are encouraged to practice self-mortification, such as fasting, which helps "to keep the sensual appetites and the whole body subject to the law of the Spirit."[86] We are to be ready to endure even martyrdom for God, for the Enemy can use any number of ways, even friendships, through which to tempt and trick us.[87] While de Sales preaches moderation in all things—in ascetical practices as well as in recreational activities[88]—we are to use these practices in an effort to help guard ourselves from the vices and grow, instead, in the virtues.

With such an emphasis on being ever aware of vices and virtues, as well as with the Ignatian influences in his own life, it is no surprise that de Sales also repeatedly stresses the need for the regular examination of consciousness and for confession.[89] These important practices are "required to steady and fix the soul" giving us self-knowledge and thereby better enabling us to ever remember how unworthy we are so that we might ask for pardoning from God.[90] As he writes, "Be sure always to entertain a hearty sorrow for the sins you confess."[91] Such confessions should therefore not

81. Ibid., 149, 59.
82. Ibid., 104, 13, 51, 70, 215.
83. Ibid., 20, 22, 26, 189, 213.
84. Ibid., 196, 99.
85. Ibid., 24, 28, 38, 112.
86. Ibid., 140; see also ibid., 91.
87. Ibid., 135, 66.
88. Ibid., 141, 62.
89. Ibid., 13, 18, 23, 37, 60, 76, 200, 203, 13, 26–27.
90. Ibid., 14, 22, 24.
91. Ibid., 76.

PART FIVE: Protestant Reformation

be done out of mere routine, but rather should be plain, simple, and direct.[92] Much of this is done so that one can begin to address the desires for sin, and not just the forsaking of the sinful actions, so that we meditate on the consequences of all our sins in these self-examining practices.[93]

Another central set of personal spiritual formation approaches for de Sales is the frequent use of prayers and meditations. "Prayer," he claims, "opens the understanding to the brightness of Divine Light, and the will to the warmth of Heavenly Love—nothing can so effectually purify the mind from its many ignorances, or the will from its perverse affections."[94] Hence, there is a need for "earnest mental prayer." Throughout his text, de Sales makes use of various meditations and encourages his readers to engage in them as a means of nurturing their growing devotional life as "meditation excites good desires in the will, or sensitive part of the soul."[95] Encouraging us to engage in meditation and mental prayers for at least one hour per day, preferably in the morning, he invites us to meditate on death, hell, heaven, and especially on Christ's passion and crucifixion.[96] Such prayers should always, he asserts, be begun by "placing yourself in the Presence of God."[97] While he does have many guided meditations, he also invites his readers to be open to the leadings of the Spirit and to go wherever the heart might lead us. He writes, "If, while saying vocal prayers, your heart feels drawn to mental prayer, do not resist it, but calmly let your mind fall in to that channel," and go where you are led and fed when praying.[98] Such guided meditations and heart-led mental prayers are therefore a significant part of the personal transformation system of his that seeks to nurture one's dispositions toward the things of God.

In addition to these more formal approaches to prayer, de Sales also encourages one to generally look to and give thanks to God.[99] In doing so, we are to offer ourselves continually to God, ever seeking God's help, and ever recalling God's goodness.[100] It means that one is to keep God ever before themselves, striving to keep themselves ever in God's Pres-

92. Ibid., 76, 77.
93. Ibid., 15, 17.
94. Ibid., 47.
95. Ibid., 17–36, 54, 164–65, 224–26.
96. Ibid., 25, 29, 30, 47, 48, 53, 95, 107, 20, 87, 97, 200, 209, 36–37.
97. Ibid., 48, 50.
98. Ibid., 49, 54.
99. Ibid., 17, 26, 55, 59, 81.
100. Ibid., 18, 20, 21, 26, 55, 98, 202, 14, 24, 39.

ence throughout the day when possible, even praying if awakened in the middle of the night.[101] It means being ever watchful and on guard, praying spontaneously, called "ejaculatory prayer," throughout our day on "whatever springs forth from the love within [us], which is sure to supply [us] with all abundance," he asserts.[102] In short, we are to ask for help and guidance from God, Jesus, angels, and the Virgin Mary, especially in particularly dry times in our prayer life.[103] Such a life of continuous prayer and turning to God is therefore central for de Sales' system in this text.

Finally, he emphasizes the absolute centrality and need for community and mentoring in one's devotional life. For him, there is a necessity for the guidance of souls by spiritually mature elders.[104] They can help guard us against the snares of the Evil One and we should turn to them, as well as to our community, in difficult times laying "bare all the feelings, thoughts, and longings" that are within us before them.[105] We should then ever follow their advice and counsel.[106] We, too, should seek to be an example for others, just as we should seek the examples of the saints.[107] As a result of such communal encounters, de Sales asserts that true friendship is founded on mutual love.[108] We are to therefore seek only good and pure friendships in life "because it comes from God, because it tends to God, because God is the link that binds [us]," to seek God together.[109] Such friendships and spiritual community therefore "implies an interchange of what is good."[110] We can therefore see that spiritual formation at the close relationship level is also a part of de Sales' more holistic system.

On the other hand, regarding the evil societies in which we live, we are to "turn away, like the bee from a dunghill."[111] Instead, our churches and their liturgies can become our primary and supportive communities. For instance, Communion, "the very center point of our Christian religion, the heart of all devotion, the soul of piety," can and should be

101. Ibid., 20, 61, 63, 81, 115, 45, 48, 227.
102. Ibid., 63–64, 67, 133, 70.
103. Ibid., 33, 35, 55, 58, 71, 95, 114, 39, 205.
104. Ibid., xxxix–xl, 90, 117, 20, 214, 33, 41.
105. Ibid., 10, 206, 18.
106. Ibid., 24.
107. Ibid., 175, 235.
108. Ibid., 127.
109. Ibid., 130–31.
110. Ibid., 138.
111. Ibid., 144, 88.

PART FIVE: Protestant Reformation

attended every day, though it is not mandatory.[112] We should also help out with the liturgies as often as possible as well as with the Divine Offices.[113] Hence, community, especially our religious communities, should be a central part of our lives.

These, then, are the primary spiritual formation approaches that de Sales seems to address in this text. They are intended to vividly and directly address the dispositions of one's life thereby ever enabling us to gradually transition from worldly desires for vice toward a holy love of virtue in God. Taken collectively, they represent a full and holistic approach to spiritual formation at the individual level.

DISCERNMENT

As it relates to discernment, de Sales offers a few specific examples from which guidelines for engaging in these approaches may be extracted. For example, he asserts that we must be able to discern what the differences are between true and false, or empty, devotion.[114] Examples of false devotion include: fasting while the heart is full of bitterness, praying often but one is still often angry, and almsgiving without forgiveness.[115] When these things happen, he asserts, some people can come to believe that they have perfection "before they are [even] born."[116] True devotion, on the other hand, hinders nothing but rather perfects everything.[117] Knowing the difference between these therefore seems to be based on a "know them by their fruits" type of approach where we consciously reflect on the fruits of our life.

He also asserts that different kinds of devotional practices are required for different kinds of vocations and "such practice[s] must be modified according to the strength, the calling, and the duties of each individual."[118] So, for instance, there are other kinds of devotion, besides monastic contemplation, that are "well suited to lead those whose calling is secular along the paths of perfection."[119] Related to this, he additionally

112. Ibid., 68, 79.
113. Ibid., 70.
114. Ibid., 3, 7.
115. Ibid., 3.
116. Ibid., 12.
117. Ibid., 7.
118. Ibid.
119. Ibid., 8, 240.

Francis de Sales' Introduction

writes, "Every calling stands in special need of some special virtue . . . each should cultivate chiefly those which are important to the manner of life to which [she or he] is called."[120] In other words, while we should cultivate all the virtues, we should also focus specifically on the ones we most need for our unique lives and vocations.[121] For de Sales, then, it appears that discernment must also be based on the unique contextual considerations of what is being discerned.

Finally, as part of discussing relational spiritual formation, he also spends some time distinguishing between true and false friendships. True friendships are "sweeter to the taste than ordinary honey, owing to the aconite infused; and so worldly friendship is profuse in honeyed words, passionate endearments, commendations of beauty an sensual charms, while true friendship speaks a simple honest language, lauding naught save the Grace of God, its one only foundation."[122] He continues by asserting that a false friendship "upsets the mind, makes its victim to totter in the ways of purity and devotion, inducing affected, mincing looks, sensual caresses, inordinate sighing, petty complaints of not being loved," etc.[123] In essence, he seems to be embracing an Ignatian approach to discerning between these two different types of friendship. In other words, true friendships are essentially those that are genuinely and affectionately consoling, leading ever more toward God, while false friendships are more shallow, disordering, and self-centered.

Overall, then, the approach to discernment that de Sales seems to be embracing here is one is comprised of at least three parts. First, discernment is to be based upon the cognitive appraisals of the fruits that one is seeing in one's life as a result of their choices. If the results are reflective and manifesting of God, then, they are to be embraced. Secondly, discernment must be thoroughly immersed in the unique context that one finds one's self within. Each calling has its own requirements, each action its own needs, and we must ever be attentive to these particularities. Lastly, the final discerned choice must be affectively consoling to the individual, "sweeter to the taste than ordinary honey." It seems that de Sales would assert that based upon these three foundational aspects of discernment, one can effectively and continually progress in one's ever changing and growing spiritual life—both personal and relational.

120. Ibid., 86.
121. Ibid.
122. Ibid., 133.
123. Ibid., 134.

PART FIVE: Protestant Reformation

Evaluative Techniques

From all of the above, we can see that there are at least three evaluative techniques that are central for de Sales' personal transformation system. First, through the regular examination of consciousness, one is to use self-observations and reflections in the effort to know if and how one is progressing in the spiritual life. Second, through their connection to mentors and community, one is to also make use of the advice and observations of others in evaluating and guiding their devotional life. Similarly, comparing one's self with mentors, the expected virtues of religion, and the models of the faith that one has (such as with the lives of the saints), is yet another way that one can reflect on their personal spiritual life in de Sales' system. These three evaluative techniques seem to be among the primary ones found within this text.

Summary/Reflections

Overall, as we can see below, de Sales' personal transformation system is quite comprehensive and holistic. As we might expect, he appears to be very Ignatian with his emphases on disposition cultivation and the methods of discernment that he employs as well as his uses of imaginative meditations. Of particular interest are his discernment approaches: cognitive, affective, and contextual. Of all of the systems that we have considered thus far, these approaches are among the most clearly articulated. Generally, we can also see the Ignatian influences of de Sales' system in his focus on finding and cultivating the presence of God in one's affective self. He emphasizes devotion, love, virtues, and various practices and meditations that are intended to nurture the affective aspects of the individual. It seems clear that de Sales' system is one that is based on an anthro-cosmology aspect (i.e., affective formation) rather than a specific theological treatise, though God's omnipresence and immanence is also a core model for his system. Finally, we note that de Sales' text is especially intended for laypersons. This is very characteristic for the post Protestant Reformation time period and the systems of personal transformation that emerged thereafter. As we continue with our explorations, more and more of the systems we will be considering will be written for laity and often by laity.

Francis de Sales' Introduction

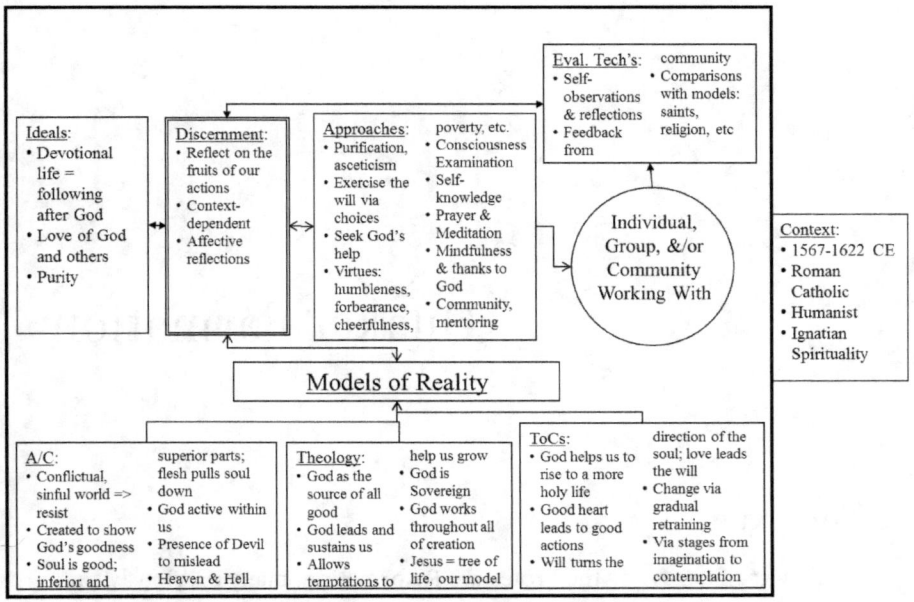

10

Quaker Formation

Context

IN THE AFTERMATH OF the Protestant Reformation, many previously suppressed sects emerged.[1] Many of these groups, such as the Puritans, saw themselves as the "true Catholics." Puritan-like groups splintered into two general directions: those that embraced a more orthodox and formal approach to Christianity, and those who embraced a "more rapturous and enthusiastic strain." The Quakers emerged from the latter strains of Puritanism. Quakerism took its distinguishable form in the 1640s and spread quickly thanks to such charismatic leaders as George Fox.

Fox condemned church history and, rather than preaching a return to scriptural roots as were many other Protestant sects, instead preached on the immediacy of Christ's Light within every person. It is because of the presence of this light, Fox asserted, that we must each look directly within to find it and therefore come to live a sinless life. Such teachings were considered dangerous by others and the early Quakers were therefore a persecuted group of people. Nevertheless, milder forms of Quakerism continued to spread both in England as well as in America thanks to such notable Quakers as: William Penn, "who founded the colony of Pennsylvania," John Woolman, known for his stand against slavery in America, and American philosopher Thomas Kelly.

The text I have chosen in order to more fully understand the Quaker approach to personal transformation is Douglas Steere's *Quaker*

---

1. All contextual notes herein come from Wakefield, "The Quakers."

*Spirituality: Selected Writings.*² This text not only contains a fairly good introduction and overview to Quaker spirituality and history, written by Steere, but it also contains selected essays and journal entries from the following Quakers : George Fox (1624–1691), Isaac Penington (1616–1679), John Woolman (1720–1772), Caroline Stephen (1834–1909), Rufus M. Jones (1863–1948), and Thomas R. Kelley (1893–1941). These writings therefore span from the Post-Reformation times right up into the Twentieth Century. As with texts like the *Conferences* and the *Philokalia,* we will be attempting to synthesize a unified system across various thinkers, so there will be limits to the statements made in this chapter. Nevertheless, it is to these writings that we now turn for a fairly systematic approach to Quaker spiritual formation at the individual level.

Models of Reality

Anthropological-Cosmological

While these writings do briefly mention that the world is something to be lived in but not of, and while they do mention the presence and oppressions of the devil, most of their anthro-cosmology seems to focus on the human person.³ For at least one of these authors, there are at least two layers within us: the "thinking, discussing, seeing, calculating" layer, and one that is deeper within, more profound, and "behind the scenes." One is the secular mind, which is fragmented, the other is the religious mind, which "involves the whole of [a person], embraces [her or his] relations with time within their true ground and setting in the Eternal Lover," and it is between these two layers we live and struggle.⁴ As a result, there is tension and intentional transformation that must happen.

As we shall see below, God acts directly within people, but such divine actions are tainted. As another writer asserts, "These leadings come to us by the route of our own psychological mechanisms and are capable, therefore, of blemish."⁵ Temptations, and the tensions that they can give rise to, are therefore very much a part of both inner and outer lives.⁶ As one writer puts it, "I fear are too [many people] clogged with the things of

2. Steere, *Quaker Spirituality.*
3. Ibid., 51, 133, 44.
4. Ibid., 291.
5. Ibid., 46.
6. Ibid., 63, 65, 75, 117, 66, 220.

this life and do not come forward bearing the Cross in such faithfulness as the Almighty calls for."[7] However, we are also persons who are intimately connected with one another because of the divine movements in our life[8] and it is towards such connections that we must strive to be transformed. Hence, the human person is one who, while intimately connected to both God and other people, is also caught between the deeper levels of the divine and the more superficial happenings of the world.

As mentioned, it is a core belief of these authors that the Presence of the divine is within each individual. In fact, this belief is the very heart of Quaker Spirituality and personal transformation. As Steere writes about George Fox, one of the pioneers of the Friends movement, "His own discovery of the living Christ within and his repeated experience of the inward tendering of the Holy Spirit which are movingly recorded in his *Journal* brought him in to a whole new relationship with his fellow creatures and with creation."[9] Fox's, and other Quaker's, chief revelation was that "Christ [is] the teacher of his people and their savior,"[10] and that this seed and teacher is within all people.[11] This view of humanity came to utterly transform how Friends saw their fellow beings. For example, Steere asserts, "As a Quaker, William Penn saw [a person] not as a depraved sinner but as child of God with the Seed of the Spirit within [her or him] to be drawn out and nurtured."[12] Because of this, Quakers believe that "all believers are priests," "liberty [is] the natural right of all [people] equally," and that the same spirit that gave the Scriptures lives in each one of us.[13] It is therefore the core of the Quaker anthro-cosmology that God dwells within every single one of God's children and that we must therefore treat them with the highest regard. As we shall see below, the entire spiritual formation system outlined below hinges almost entirely on this one insight and is the very essence of spirituality for Quakers according to these writings.

---

7. Ibid., 176.
8. Ibid., 18.
9. Ibid., 7.
10. Ibid., 80; see also ibid., 84, 120, 33–34, 40.
11. Ibid., 11, 63, 65, 67, 71, 73, 78, 79, 83, 97.
12. Ibid., 49.
13. Ibid., 31, 83, 132, 82, 310.

Theological

Theologically, God's Presence within humanity is most central for these writers. In this vain, it is asserted that only Christ can redeem and save us and help us with all our struggling situations and difficult conditions.[14] He is the one who opens us up, destroys the power of the devil, and came to "open up a new and living access to God."[15] This inward Presence can ever be with us preserving us and guiding us in every step, speaking and acting through us, even saving our lives when we are threatened, and healing us when we are hurt.[16] On this point, Steere claims, "One of the first things that the Quakers would accent is that revelation is still going on."[17] In other words, God is actively present in the world through each person and we must therefore ever attend to and follow this Presence. In Fox's own words, "God was come to teach his people by his spirit and to bring them off all their old ways."[18] For these authors, then, God's Presence within humanity is one that is dynamic and transformative, one that is the most integral and active part of our lives.

More generally, God's everywhere present nature is one that is steadfast and good. Regarding God's omnipresence, one author asserts that "by his breath the flame of life was kindled in all animal and sensitive creatures."[19] It is because of this potent Presence that we must never give up hope, for to be with God is to always be on the winning side of things.[20] God's nature is therefore seen as one that is everlasting, always unfolding, ever "pure and precious."[21] As one of the early Quakers, James Nayler, stated on his deathbed:

> There is a spirit which I feel that delights to do no evil, nor to revenge any wrong, but delights to endure all things, in hope to enjoy its own in the end . . . It sees to the end of all temptations. As it bears no evil in itself, so it conceives none in thoughts to any other. If it be betrayed, it bears it, for its ground and spring

---

14. Ibid., 66, 67, 70, 106, 67, 97.
15. Ibid., 29, 91, 144, 253.
16. Ibid., 9, 60, 64, 65, 71, 78, 79, 80, 82, 83, 92, 99, 114, 20, 50, 91, 94, 265, 68, 302.
17. Ibid., 5.
18. Ibid., 79.
19. Ibid., 165.
20. Ibid., 47.
21. Ibid., 86, 123, 45, 266.

PART FIVE: Protestant Reformation

is the mercies and forgiveness of God. Its crown is meekness, its life is everlasting love unfeigned."[22]

God, for many of these authors, is therefore one that enduringly resides in all things, especially humans, and is the Source of love, transformation, and hope.

Theories of Change

The primary theory of change that seems to emerge from these pages is that transformation gradually comes as one continues to intentionally dwell in the Presence of the God that is within one's self as well as in the community. As Steere claims, "This tendering power of the Spirit at work on the heart of a member in the meetings and in the close fellowship with one another that developed in the Quaker community was an inward baptism of the whole life of the participant, and again and again drew him or her to make the successive changes that were required."[23] It is therefore by one coming to again and again seek to dwell in Christ's Presence, "an ingrafting in to Christ," that holy transformation happens.[24] Articulated succinctly, "your growth in the Seed is in the silence, where ye may find a feeding of the bread of life . . . and there is innocence and simplicity of heart and spirit is lived in and the life is fed on."[25] Such a growth, which also occurs by tangibly acting in the world,[26] therefore comes by participating in the transforming life of God in one's soul as well as in one's community.

However, this change is not viewed as happening overnight. On the contrary, change is seen to start with small things and proceeds to great things later on in a step-by-step manner.[27] Comparing such gradual change with the growth of corn, one writer claims, "He hath changed, and doth change thy spirit daily; though it be as the shooting up of the corn, whose growth cannot be discerned at present by the most observing eye, but it is very manifest afterwards that it hath grown."[28] This is partly because wrong habits are often deeply rooted and only change "as one

22. Ibid., 96.
23. Ibid., 18; see also ibid., 29, 150.
24. Ibid., 148, 65.
25. Ibid., 132.
26. Ibid., 311.
27. Ibid., 144, 50, 54, 248, 92.
28. Ibid., 143; see also ibid., 46.

faithfully does his set tasks, and goes to work with an enthusiastic passion to help make other people good."[29] One of these writers, philosopher Thomas Kelley, views such change as progressing through at least three stages: a purifying stage; a stage of "habitual divine orientation"; and one where there is a "Greater [One] who prays in us."[30] Overall, then, the primary theory of change here seems to be one of a gradual progression that comes as a result of our intentional engagement with God in the silent inner recesses of our soul as well as in one's community. The personal spiritual formation approaches, discussed below, therefore have the purpose of enabling such holy encounters so that this change can come about.

Spiritual Formation Ideals & Goals

Regarding the ultimate ideal of the spirituality of the Friends, Steere writes, "Fox preached and described the transforming mercies of the interior Christ in the hearts of men and women and bid them to listen within for the 'Christ who has come to teach his people himself' and having listened and found, to obey him."[31] The Quaker goal is therefore to come to find Christ within themselves and others, for "nothing is more precious than the mind of Truth inwardly manifested," and to seek God's guidance in all things.[32] Doing so is therefore intended to lead one into "purity, perfection, and righteousness."[33] "To live the Sermon on the Mount," one author claims, "and in all things to listen for the living voice of the good Shepherd, watching constantly that no human tradition divert our attention from it,—this is our acknowledged aim and bond of union as a Society."[34]

Such devotion is then leads to an experiential feeling of God in one's life.[35] As another writer claims, "This is our religion; to feel that which God begets in our hearts preserved alive by God, to be taught by him to know him, to worship, and live to him, in the leadings and by the power of his Spirit."[36] Quakerism is therefore often conceived of as a mystical strand

---

29. Ibid., 271; see also ibid., 175.
30. Ibid., 292–94; see also ibid., 132, 49.
31. Ibid., 8; see also ibid., 24, 61, 66, 69, 155, 256.
32. Ibid., 12, 21, 188, 203.
33. Ibid., 73.
34. Ibid., 254.
35. Ibid., 143, 44.
36. Ibid., 157.

of Christianity, a direct experience of God.[37] With God's will and union being the heart of Quaker spirituality, "Life is meant to be lived from a Center, a divine Center."[38] The main goal and aim of the approaches to personal transformation below are therefore a direct and living relationship with the loving God who actively dwells within the depths of each and every individual.

Spiritual Formation Approaches

Quakers self-reportedly have a noted tension with formalized religion, and therefore spiritual formation approaches. On this, Steere writes,

> Quakers find it hard not to look with suspicion on talk about the interior life and about the practices that nurture it . . . [Nevertheless] they do possess testimonies that they seek to embody; they do have a deep faith in divine guidance and in the concerns that often spring from it; they do have practices that enhance discernment; they do have a unique form of corporate worship on the basis of silence and obedience; they do have a special form of vocal ministry and a unique way of conducting their meeting for business and of arriving at decisions.[39]

So while Quakers do have a guardedness toward the forms of religion, they do still possess such forms. This basic tension and guardedness arises from their core Models of Reality articulated above: if God acts directly on the soul of each individual, and we need only to look for God within us who "speaks to each one in a language that no other can hear,"[40] then why, therefore, do we need others to tell us how to live our life with God? Why do we need organized religion at all?

As a result, from the very beginning with Fox, there was a strong resistance and aversion to formalized versions of religion.[41] As one writer reflects, Friends want "the autonomy of the soul [to] be protected and safeguarded . . . We have here, then, a type of Christianity which begins with experience rather than with dogma."[42] This is also because doctrines

37. Ibid., 16, 247, 62, 306, 12.
38. Ibid., 38, 304.
39. Ibid., 5.
40. Ibid., 247; see also ibid., 154, 258.
41. Ibid., 11, 19, 275, 311.
42. Ibid., 277.

Quaker Formation

can be held without "cleansing, purifying, or transforming one's heart in the very least" and Quakers want to nurture a personal life with Christ, not doctrine.[43] They also assert that "the 'Word of God' is Christ, not the Bible," and while we should read the Bible, "no Creature can read the Scriptures to profit thereby, but who come to the light and Spirit that gave them forth."[44] As it relates to formalized approaches to spirituality, then, Quakers are careful in the practices and statements that they make about them.

Nevertheless, as noted by Steere, there a number of personal spiritual formation approaches that Quakers engage in to help foster the kinds of transformation that were discussed above. Central for every Quaker is that of community. On this, Steere asserts, "The corporate meeting for worship is the ground of Quaker spirituality that undergirds nearly all that Quakers do."[45] It is through community connections and relationships that the Quaker movement spreads as Quakers seek to take care of each other, make decisions as a unified body of holy listening, and watch over each other's prayerfulness and progress.[46] Such community is therefore an essential part of the Friend's approaches to personal transformation.

It is in such communities that the heart of their approaches, the "Meetings," takes place. While Quakers to sometimes engage in imaginative meditations,[47] their core prayer and worship practice is one of silent gatherings. From the very beginning, "[Fox] encouraged [women and men] as a corporate group to sit together in the silence, to open themselves to the gathering power of the spirit of Christ, to experience the power of the inward quickening that had marked the primitive Christian community."[48] The primary aim of these silent encounters, in which sometimes scripture is read or a "vocal ministry" is given, was "to assist each other in coming into the presence of Christ within, and where they might come to 'know each other in that which is eternal.'"[49]

Quakers therefore consider themselves to be a group through which the Holy Spirit moves, embodying the purest form of worship conceivable,

43. Ibid., 278, 311.
44. Ibid., 21, 247, 63, 66.
45. Ibid., 37.
46. Ibid., 10, 22, 41, 43–46, 114, 54, 245.
47. Ibid., 64, 219.
48. Ibid., 8; see also ibid., 13–14, 77, 130, 31, 211.
49. Ibid., 12; see also ibid., 24, 30–31, 85, 97, 193, 243, 312.

where all are joined together into one life according to these authors.[50] Comparing these Meetings to the Real Presence of Christ for Catholics in the eucharistic elements, Kelley writes of Quaker worship, "the Real Presence of the gathered meeting is an existential fact . . . The bond of union in divine fellowship is existential and real . . . It is the life of God himself, within whose life we live and move and have our being."[51] These sacredly impregnated Meetings are therefore the very heartbeat and core of the Quaker system of spiritual formation because they are directly intended to nurture the divinely oriented ideals articulated above. As we can also see, they are wholly in line with their theory of change wherein personal transformation occurs through prolonged and repeated personal encounters with the living God within.

As stated above, Fox, and other Quakers, wanted to "direct people to the Spirit that gave forth the Scriptures, by which they might be led into all Truth,"[52] to the secret and "precious things" written on the heart.[53] As a result, and related to the Meetings, another personal spiritual formation approach that Quakers are encouraged to participate in is waiting on God for guidance and direction.[54] They are to seek, trust, and follow God's directions for their life, so that God becomes Real to them in their daily lives.[55] Quakers are therefore encouraged seek God continuously, in all of life and throughout one's day, for "Now is the dwelling place of God himself."[56]

As we have already seen, for these authors, such contact with and seeking of God emerges out of silence, which they encourage us to live out of. This silence is described as "a deep quietness of heart and mind, a laying aside of all preoccupation with passing things—yes, even with the workings of our own minds; a resolute fixing of the heart upon that which is unchangeable and eternal."[57] It to this silence, the "inner sanctuary of the soul," that we must continually return to in order to personally experience "a holy place, a Divine Center, a speaking Voice."[58] In such silence,

50. Ibid., 15, 250, 309.
51. Ibid., 313.
52. Ibid., 69; see also ibid., 90, 99, 129, 52, 246, 55, 76, 82, 306, 15.
53. Ibid., 156, 241.
54. Ibid., 23, 99, 129, 43, 46, 55, 72, 246, 54, 308.
55. Ibid., 186, 217, 64–65, 308.
56. Ibid., 290, 98, 314, 300–301.
57. Ibid., 250; see also ibid., 98.
58. Ibid., 290.

Quaker Formation

not only can the voices of angels be heard, but also, as one author asserts, "nothing but silence can heal the wounds made by disputations in the region of the unseen."[59]

There are many diverse ways to enter into this deep silence and to deal with distractions. For some it is by simply abandoning the distractions completely, for others through prayer, and still for others by being ever patient and present to them.[60] Overall, however, the "when in doubt, wait" motto is given as a central guide.[61] Hence, ever seeking the guidance of God through the cultivation of a peace-filled silence is a fundamental personal transformation approach. As we can hear in the admonishments of Isaac Pennington: "let us retire, and dwell in the peace which God breathes, and lie down in the Lamb's patience and stillness, night and day, which nothing can wear out or disturb."[62]

While Quakers, according to these writings, have a tense relationship with formalized religion, and while their central focus on silence seems somewhat like an attempt to avoid such external structures, they do still encourage one another to engage in at least five other tangible practices and approaches. The first is related to their unwavering commitment to service and nonviolence to humanity. On this, Kelley writes, "Social concern is the dynamic Life of God at work in the world, made special and emphatic and unique, particularized in each individual or group who is sensitive and tender in the leading-strings of love."[63] Quakers must, once they are "open to the light," "not refuse the first small act God demands of [them]," but rather be "doers of the word," letting their "lives and conversation preach, that with a measure of the spirit of God [they] may reach to that of God in all."[64] Quakers must therefore treat all people the same for God is within them all, and they must take good care of one another, even sharing in one another's afflictions.[65] On this, John Woolman journals, "Desires were now renewed in me to embrace every opportunity of being inwardly acquainted with the hardships and difficulties of my fellow

---

59. Ibid., 234, 49.
60. Ibid., 27–28.
61. Ibid., 46, 134, 51.
62. Ibid., 153.
63. Ibid., 303; see also ibid., 309.
64. Ibid., 30, 129, 35.
65. Ibid., 69, 172, 213.

creatures and to labour in [her or his] love for the spreading of pure universal righteousness in the earth."[66]

Such empathy, love, and belief in the sacredness of each person must therefore lead one to a complete commitment to nonviolence.[67] It must lead one to where they will not carry or draw "any carnal sword against any," for it is asserted that "wars are inconsistent with the purity of the Christian religion."[68] We also need to work to end all violence and suffering and to stand against what we believe is wrong because violence toward others is violence toward the Seed within both them and ourselves.[69] It is based upon these views that Quakers, such as Woolman, took a strong stand against slavery.[70] Quakers also sought to reach out to others, such as Native Americans and miners, by trying to understand their ways of life and to have more compassion for them.[71] In short, "These [people] are the souls for whom Christ died,"[72] and Quakers therefore embraced a strong stance toward both nonviolence as well as service to all of humankind.

A second approach that is found in these writings, and is further related to their nonviolent convictions, is enduring persecutions. The early English Quakers endured scorn, imprisonments, and beatings for reasons such as not taking their hats off to people, not paying tithes to churches or the government, and for being nonviolent.[73] As Fox recalls in his journal, "[Persecutors] fell so upon Friends in many places that they could hardly pass the highways, stoning and beating and breaking their heads."[74] In the midst of such painful abuses, Quakers were encouraged to forsake the friendship of the world in order to follow God's will enduring the difficult and demanding lives that God calls them into.[75] Remaining steadfast under harsh challenges to one's faith is therefore another personal spiritual formation approach that is articulated in these pages.

Closely related to this is a third approach: the pursuing of a virtuous life. As Woolman writes, "Conduct is more convincing than language,"

66. Ibid., 227.
67. Ibid., 48, 50, 106, 25, 32, 281.
68. Ibid., 88, 187; see also ibid., 256.
69. Ibid., 93, 97, 98, 102, 108, 36, 63–64, 65, 76, 95, 98.
70. Ibid., 119, 69, 73, 89, 95.
71. Ibid., 119, 35, 204, 208, 34.
72. Ibid., 184.
73. Ibid., 69–70, 94, 100, 104, 108, 12, 24, 25, 35, 41.
74. Ibid., 82; see also ibid., 102.
75. Ibid., 178, 88, 227.

Quaker Formation

and Friends were people who were to be honest, not cheat anyone, and who could therefore be trusted in all things.[76] They are encouraged to put off unrighteousness and put on righteousness for "here the soul is new created in Christ Jesus."[77] Every part of life must exhibit God's love and peace by looking to the Light within rather than to toward sin, evil, and temptations, which only lead to greater "unquietness" and "malady."[78]

In these virtuous pursuits, for these authors, humility, or keeping "low," holds a central place. "All Friends be low," Fox exclaims, "and keep in the life of God to keep you low."[79] In such "lowness" we must surrender everything to God, dying to ourselves, our knowledge, our wisdom, our judgments, etc., so that we might "become truly integrated as a richer self" into the mercies and blessings of God.[80] Living the virtuous life, especially as it relates to humility, is therefore another central approach for Friends.

As one seeks to live the virtuous life, as tempted and conflicted humans, we must have some way of watching how well we are achieving this. A fourth practice that is found in this text is that of the examination of conscience, or what is termed "Queries." These queries, which are occasionally presented in Meetings, sometimes took the form of questions that were asked of the community to reflect on such as "Do I in all my proceedings keep to that use of things which is agreeable to universal righteousness ?"[81] One of the primary goals of these reflections is therefore to help the individual to see where they are living contrary to God so that they might better follow the leadings of the divine staying firm in what one's inner conscience tells them.[82] These queries are therefore another integral part of the Quaker approaches to spiritual formation.

A fifth and final additional approach is the use of teachers and mentoring. Quakers believe that God does send people "to instruct us in the way of God more perfectly."[83] For instance, as Rufus Jones found as a single parent after his wife died, sometimes these teachers are even little children who can help us to "become simple and childlike, gentle and loving,

---

76. Ibid., 85–86, 134, 80.
77. Ibid., 148; see also ibid., 295–96.
78. Ibid., 177, 96, 249, 85.
79. Ibid., 86; see also ibid., 130, 55, 65, 96, 99.
80. Ibid., 145, 47, 51, 304, 308.
81. Ibid., 22, 202, 16–17, 45.
82. Ibid., 146, 53, 75.
83. Ibid., 9, 81, 140.

PART FIVE: Protestant Reformation

confident and trustful."[84] While Quakers have no paid clergy, and some of these authors are skeptical of both them and clergy training institutions in general,[85] they do still hold a strong view of mentors and education in their close-knit communities.

For instance, as it related to the rearing and religious education of Quaker children, it is asserted that "personal example was the greatest force of all."[86] Fox himself established a school for boys and girls, and emphasized education of the young.[87] However, with all education one needs to be patient and let God work to take God's teachings to the hearts of the students.[88] Also, as it relates to youth, Steere claims that "Quakers have had to learn again and again that young people respond to situations where they are really needed and are actively involved in carrying out concerns."[89] These youth, through such means, need to be taught the ways of purity, health, morality, etc.[90] Education and mentoring is therefore another central spiritual formation approach at the individual level found in these writings.

These approaches each have the intention of nurturing the life in God that Quakers have come to pursue. It is a Life that is present within each and every individual and these practices therefore attempt to open one up to it; both in one's self and as it is experienced in others. These approaches impact not only one's inner life, as happens in the Meetings, but also one's concrete outer life in the world, as in their nonviolent and virtuous actions. It is through these various means, therefore, that the transforming Life of the divine is intended to take hold change our world one individual at a time.

Discernment

As it relates to discerning the status and direction of one's spiritual life, George Fox believed that "by bringing [others] to something that was of God in themselves, they might the better know and judge of [God] and

84. Ibid., 274.
85. Ibid., 13, 32–33, 33–34, 81.
86. Ibid., 25; see also ibid., 93, 263.
87. Ibid., 114, 99.
88. Ibid., 152.
89. Ibid., 25; see also ibid., 311.
90. Ibid., 63.

themselves."[91] The Quaker approach to discernment is therefore one that primarily emerges out of the silence that was so often discussed above. As another author admonishes, "wait to hear the voice of the Lord there; and waiting there, and keeping close to the Lord, a discerning will grow, that you distinguish the voice of the stranger when ye hear it."[92] It is out of such waiting that guidance, insights, and directions will come according to some of these authors.[93] Simply sitting and waiting, as we have already heard in the motto "When in doubt, wait,"[94] is therefore central to Quaker spiritual discernment.

While waiting, however, one is also to notice what is happening with one's inner life. As one author reports, "Mind what stirs in your hearts; what moves against sin, what moves towards sin. The one is the Son's life, the Son's grace, the Son's Spirit; the other is the spirit and nature which is contrary thereto."[95] It is through our noticing which movements are of God and which are not that we can come to know and commit ourselves to the will of God.[96] Such listening discernment must also be carried out at the communal level as well.[97] However, we must also know that it is not always clear what we should do in every situation and that God often works in unseen ways, such as when we sleep.[98]

Quaker discernment therefore seems to be one that is largely a matter of one coming to know the movements of God within themselves. As was noted above, God "speaks to each one in a language that no other can hear,"[99] and it is therefore up to each person to come to cultivate a recognition of and obedience to God's voice within their own hearts and lives. As this happens, the person can then live a life that is ever more fully rooted in God, a life that emerges out of the silence of their souls.

91. Ibid., 61.
92. Ibid., 129.
93. Ibid., 85, 167–68, 74.
94. Ibid., 38, 46, 134, 51, 269.
95. Ibid., 153.
96. Ibid., 206, 304.
97. Ibid., 38, 269.
98. Ibid., 222, 25.
99. Ibid., 247.

PART FIVE: Protestant Reformation

Evaluative Techniques

In light of all of this, it seems that there are a number of evaluative techniques that one can rely on as a Quaker to help them know if they are moving in a progressive direction or not. One technique is self-reflection through both the Queries that one engages as well as in relation to what is arising from deep within as they regularly sit in silence. Another technique might be the feedback that one's community gives them both in terms of what they are told by members of this community as well as in relation to what they see in their mentors as compared to themselves. Yet another, similar, technique might come from comparing themselves to the Scriptures and other educational sources on the spiritual life. One other way to evaluate one's life is by looking at the how they are tangibly living in their actions—Is it virtuous? Nonviolent? One of service? Is one enduring persecutions with lowness? Et cetera. Each of these can help to keep the individual on the path to an ever deepening relationship with the divine.

Summary/Reflections

Overall, the Quaker system of personal transformation articulated in this text is one that seems to center almost completely around their theological anthropology—the presence of God within each and every human being. In light of all of the other systems we have considered thus far, this is by no means a novel insight into human nature. However, what is quite extraordinary is how the Quakers have crafted a complete way of life that actually takes this claim to be literally true. This spirituality is therefore both a testimony to the workings of God in the world as well as a radical challenge and calling to all other religions on our planet.

Quaker Formation

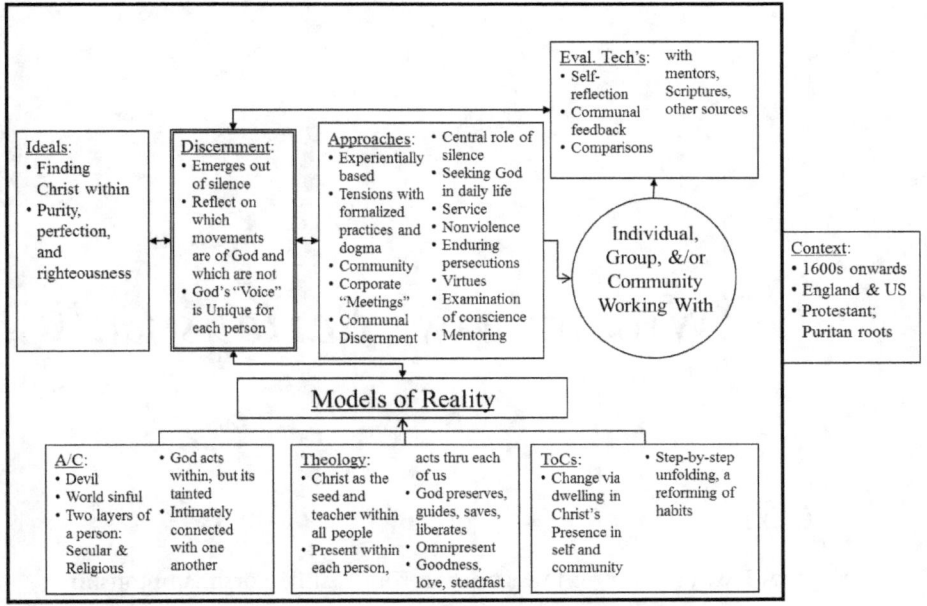

Also in light of the other systems we have considered, this system seems like a unique blend of the *Philokalia* and de Sales' Spiritualities. Not only does it stress the centrality of silence for one's spiritual life, but it also emphasizes the importance of one seriously attending to the inner affective movements that emerge out of that silence. This spirituality is definitely one of our seeking to become "Contemplatives in Action," something that is often sought in Ignatian Spirituality circles, of which de Sales text is sometimes considered to be central. Overall, then, the Quaker system of personal transformation depicted in these writings offers us yet another and increasingly diverse way to both view and approach spiritual formation at the individual level. As we move toward contemporary times, such diversity will continue to expand.

11

William Law's *Serious Call*

Context

WILLIAM LAW (1686–1761) was born in King's Cliff, Northhamptonshire and was educated at Emmanuel College in Cambridge, England.[1] Law was a "Nonjuror" and "represented the heart of Anglican spirituality as it developed during the sixteenth and seventeenth centuries."[2] The Nonjurors were a group of Anglicans who considered themselves the true and purer form of the Church of England and sought to revive devotion in England in their times.[3] Law similarly viewed the status of contemporary English church and society as being in need of reform.[4] He was influenced by the writings and spirituality of Madame Guyon, John Newton, Johann Tauler, Jan van Ruysbroek, Thomas a Kempis, the Greek Fathers, de Sales' *Introduction*, and, most importantly for him, Jacob Boehme.[5]

His *Serious Call* is therefore "a plea for reform and also a work of spiritual guidance describing the way to reform."[6] In this text, Law seeks to articulate a way to live the devout life with his intended audience being "idle rich" of his own day,[7] something that is apparent from the topics he discusses. This text was among one of the most popular devotional works

1. Law, "A Serious Call," 7.
2. Booty, "Preface," 1.
3. Grisbrooke, "The Nonjurors and William Law," 453.
4. Booty, "Preface," 1, 2.
5. Ibid., 1; Stanwood, "Foreward," 7; Warren, "William Law," 15.
6. Booty, "Preface," 1.
7. Ibid., 1, 2.

of his time, comparable to John Bunyan's *Pilgrim's Progress,* and went on to influence such people as John Wesley, Samuel Johnson, many Quakers, and Roman Catholic Cardinal John Henry Newman.[8] In order to gain a better sense of this unique and influential Anglican approach to spiritual formation in this time period, we will be learning from Law's *Serious Call*.

Models of Reality

Anthropological-Cosmological

Law's cosmology is one that views the world as a fallen one. The world, for him, is a sad state of affairs and suffering, seeming as if it is really only a dream, where "we are fallen into an age where the love not only of many, but of most, is waxed cold."[9] It is also one where the happiness of most people is empty.[10] As he writes, "the world is still under the curse of sin and certain marks of God's displeasure at it, such as famines, plagues, tempests, sickness, disease, and death."[11] As a result, we are called to renounce the spirit of the world and its pleasures and to not desire them.[12] Instead, the pleasures of the world are only things to be endured as we are to live above them and to see the world as a stranger.[13] Only those things that can be offered for the glory of God are to be pursued, everything else is to be renounced.[14] In support of these claims, Law points toward the New Testament and how it condemns the world's ways of life and he asserts that Christian life and worldly life don't mix.[15]

While the world and its ways are sinful, Law does not seem to consider evil as something that is complete substantive, though he does also mention the works of the devil as well as angels and Heaven. In reflecting on the nature of some evils, he claims, "Pride is only the disorder of the fallen world, it has no place amongst other being; it can only subsist where ignorance and sensuality, lies and false hood, lusts and impurity, reign."[16]

---

8. Ibid., 1; Stanwood, "Foreward," 7; Warren, "William Law," 15.
9. Law, "A Serious Call," 132; see also ibid., 72, 270.
10. Ibid., 174.
11. Ibid., 336.
12. Ibid., 51, 196, 243.
13. Ibid., 78–79, 103, 39.
14. Ibid., 154.
15. Ibid., 49, 55, 237, 40, 46, 86.
16. Ibid., 232.

PART FIVE: Protestant Reformation

He likewise asserts that envy comes from the desire for glory.[17] Comments such as these can suggest that his views of sin are that evil is the result of poor choices or distortions more than they result from the nature of things as we read in Cassian's *Conferences* and the *Philokalia*. As he asserts, "Nothing hurts us, nothing destroys us, but the ill use of that liberty with which God has entrusted us."[18] Nevertheless, Law does also talk briefly about the presence and workings of the Devil.[19] He also discusses the help and modeling that angels offer and he speaks of Heaven as the unimaginable place of eternity.[20] Overall, then, Law's views of the world are that it is a fallen world that must be forsaken even though evil is at least partly the result of distortions and willfulness.

In this scheme, as we have found in some of the others, humans seem to mirror and/or embody these realities. Humans, too, are fallen and their sinfulness is the result of our not choosing to pursue the glory of God in all things. For example, in exploring some of the reasons for why people swear, he writes, "the reason of common swearing is this: It is because men have not so much as the intention to please God in all their actions" and without this focused intention toward God, all folly arises.[21] It is because of these ill-intended distortions that both the world and our flesh are corrupt, and he finds the some of the Scriptural basis for this in Romans 8 (if we live of the flesh, then we shall die of it).[22] Much of the devotional life, as we shall find below, is therefore directed toward overcoming these distortions.

However, Law also holds a high view of humanity in terms its relationship to God. "Every man," he writes, "is to consider himself as a particular object of God's providence, under the same care and protection of God as if the world had been made for him alone."[23] For Law, God made us so we must therefore give and live with all glory going to God.[24] We are to be preparing for "another body, another world, and other enjoyments" than our "earthly desires and bodily indulgences."[25] Such progress leads to

17. Ibid., 252.
18. Ibid., 325.
19. Ibid., 236.
20. Ibid., 91, 100, 59, 88.
21. Ibid., 56, 62.
22. Ibid., 283.
23. Ibid., 322.
24. Ibid., 159.
25. Ibid., 193.

an ever heightening relationship with God. Law asserts, "All human spirits, therefore, the more exalted they are, the more they know their divine original; the nearer they come to heavenly spirits, by so much the more will they live to God in all their actions and make their whole life a state of devotion."[26] Humanity, while it struggles with the distortions of the sinful world, therefore nevertheless has a sacred aim and purpose.

One further anthropological view that Law briefly mentions is related to the relationship between the body and the soul. On this, he writes, "The union of soul and body is not a mixture of their substances as we see bodies united and mixed together but consists solely in the mutual power that they have of acting upon one another ... the substance of one cannot be mixed or united with the other, but they are held together in such a state of union that all the actions and sufferings of the one are at the same time the actions and sufferings of the other."[27] It is because of the nature of this relationship that we have both so little and so much power over ourselves, because of the way these two apparent different aspects of our reality act on one another.[28] Such views, along with the ones discussed above, therefore seem to assert that the human person is one who is enmeshed in this struggle between the pleasures and ways of the world and the higher callings of God and the soul.

Theological

Law holds a very high view of God/Christ and God's relation to creation. For him, all things are God's, for "there is but one God and Father of us all, whose glory gives light and life to everything that lives, whose presence fills all places, whose power supports all being, whose providence ruleth all events."[29] He further claims that God is the "reason and cause of all the powers and effects which you see in the world."[30] Because of this, God is the one who has made the rich become rich, is over all things including famine, wars, etc., puts "good motions into [our] hearts," and helps us to receive and live a devout life.[31] It is in light of these high views of God's omnipotence and presence that he asserts the core of devotion that his

26. Ibid., 348.
27. Ibid., 214–15.
28. Ibid., 215.
29. Ibid., 77; see also ibid., 76, 255, 317, 50.
30. Ibid., 215.
31. Ibid., 90, 129, 319.

system calls for: "the reasons of religion, the calls to piety, are so written and engraved upon everything . . . Let us but intend to see and hear, and then the whole world becomes a book of wisdom and instruction to us."[32] As we can see, Law holds a very high view of God's omnipresence and omnipotence.

In relation to these, Law also upholds God/Christ as being all loving. He asserts this to his readers when he writes, "God, my child, is all love and wisdom and goodness, and everything that He has made and every action that He does is the effect of them all."[33] This view of God then becomes the basis for distinguishing between good and evil. "If therefore God," he claims, "be our greatest good, if there can be no good but in His favor nor any evil but in departing from Him" then we must worship and adore this God.[34] If we do not, Law proposes, then God will not be pleased, for "nothing can please God but what is wise and reasonable and holy" and that we love with a "universal fervent love to all [humankind]."[35] While we must know that this loving God is merciful to our weaknesses and failings, God is not merciful to the slothful.[36] In fact, God will eventually judge the world, and those who do not do the works of service and goodness will be condemned because "these works of charity are necessary to salvation . . . through the whole course of life."[37] Law therefore views God as a loving, all-powerful, and omnipresent Deity who saves the merciful and condemns the unrighteous of the world. Such a theology forms much of the motivation for why we should pursue the devout life.

Theories of Change

With the human person being caught in between the allures of a fallen world and aims of a devotional life, Law articulates a theory of change that is primarily one of gradual conditioning. Before discussing his theory, however, we must first consider how intention is central to it and how it leads to changed action. On these intentions, or "holy love," he writes, "Now there is nothing that so much exalts our souls as this heavenly love. It cleanses and purifies like a holy fire and all ill tempers fall away before

32. Ibid., 176–77; see also ibid., 324.
33. Ibid., 256.
34. Ibid., 348.
35. Ibid., 58, 256, 88.
36. Ibid., 64, 67.
37. Ibid., 102; see also ibid., 100.

it. It makes room for all virtues, and carries them to their greatest height. Everything that is good and holy grows out of it and becomes a continual source of all holy desires and pious practices."[38] Such love and intentions made "primitive Christians such eminent instances of piety," makes it less likely for us to sin, and its absence is the reason why so many people do not make progress in the devout life.[39] Such intentions and holy love are therefore central for any measure of progress and transformation in the devout life.

Why is this? Why is such intention so necessary for change? It is such intention that utterly changes one's life because, he writes, "change is not in the outward state of things but in the inward state of our minds."[40] For Law, it seems, the heart is one of the primary things that guides actions. On this, he asserts, "Every state of the heart naturally puts the body into some state that is suitable to it."[41] Hence, these intentions are central because they are core part of directing the one's actions in the world.

With these foundational pieces in place, Law's theory of change is therefore one in which the intentions of a person are gradually conditioned toward the devotion of God. As was noted above, for him, there is nothing more pleasing than to experience the "true sense of God's presence."[42] Such discoveries then lead to our transformations: "the more we find out God in everything, the more we apply to Him in every place, the more we look up to Him in all our actions, the more we conform to His will, the so much more do we enjoy God, partake of the divine nature and heighten and increase all that is happy and comfortable in human life."[43] As a result, this searching, and the changes that naturally come with it, must be sought after with all diligence and effort for "it seems plain that our salvation depends upon the sincerity and perfection of our endeavors to obtain it."[44] We must therefore seek to uproot sinful habits for the practice of "piety and devotion are the common unchangeable means of saving all the souls in the world that shall be saved."[45]

---

38. Ibid., 292–93.
39. Ibid., 56–57, 61, 104.
40. Ibid., 194; see also ibid., 59.
41. Ibid., 212.
42. Ibid., 326.
43. Ibid., 148.
44. Ibid., 65–66.
45. Ibid., 281; see also ibid., 195.

PART FIVE: Protestant Reformation

Such conditioning, however, can work both ways: toward the strengthening of the devotional life, or toward its weakening. As it relates to strengthening, Law discusses at least three examples for how such positive change can come. The first is in our practicing of the virtues and rejecting the vices.[46] As we do this, he asserts, transformation will come as God enables it to happen.[47] A second way change toward devotion can be strengthened, is through the use of regular prayers.[48] Such prayers, he asserts, will "make you able by degrees to renounce other pleasures and tempers that war against the soul" because praying daily for change leads to either forsaking prayer or forsaking the ways of the world.[49] A third example of how change comes and devotion is strengthened is the use of outward acts.[50] On this, he claims that just "as the inward state of the mind produces outward actions suitable to it, so those outward actions have the like power of raising an inward state of mind suitable to them."[51] Such outward actions, he further asserts, "are necessary to support inward tempers, and therefore the outward act of joy is necessary to raise and support the inward joy of the mind."[52] We can see from each of these three examples that one's devotional life is strengthened through gradual, continuous, and intentional practices. As we shall see below, Law's spiritual formation approaches fully embody this theory of change.

Law also articulates his theory of change in his discussions of how one's devotional life may be weakened. There are at least two things that Law highlights as weakening people. The first is related to the lifestyle that might seem harmless on the surface, but actually is cultivating a life of disorder. "For high eating and drinking," he claims, "fine clothes and fine houses, state and equipage, gay pleasures and diversions, do all of them naturally hurt and disorder our hearts; they are the food and nourishments of all the folly and weakness of our nature, and are certain means to make us vain and worldly in our tempers."[53] People who engage in these lifestyles make no progress "because their hearts are constantly employed, perverted, and kept in a wrong state by indiscreet use of such things as

46. Ibid., 154, 91, 289.
47. Ibid., 67.
48. Ibid., 85.
49. Ibid., 196, 228, 303–4.
50. Ibid., 216.
51. Ibid., 214; see also ibid., 16.
52. Ibid., 217.
53. Ibid., 98; see also ibid., 149, 50, 53, 91.

are lawful to be used" but keeps them from "receiving the life and spirit of piety."[54]

A second way we are weakened, which is related to the first, is the environment into which we are acculturated. For example, he asserts, women are not naturally vain. Instead, their vanity is because of the way of life into which they have been formed.[55] Similarly, he claims that most of us were educated into a corrupt world.[56] In both of these cases, the remedy is the same: change their education and one can change their hearts toward a more natural holiness.[57] The cultures into which we are educated are therefore another way that one's devotional life may be weakened. Just as with the things that can strengthen our lives of devotion, these weakening factors work to condition one in the direction of greater worldly sensuality and distortions.

Overall, we can see that Law's core theory of change is therefore one of gradual conditioning. While he does briefly mention the possibility of spontaneous and dramatic change occurring,[58] most of his discussions focus on more of the slow and long-term transformation of people. Centered on nurturing one's intentions, which then leads to changes in the actions of one's life, Law's change theory asserts that the more we diligently engage in something, be it good or bad, the more we grow in that direction. Such a conditioning view of personal transformation comes to undergird the approaches to spiritual formation that he presents in this text.

Spiritual Formation Ideals & Goals

The most central ideal that Law discusses throughout this text, which is reflected in its title, is the aim of living a devout life; though he also discusses the necessity of our striving for virtues as well. For him, devotion is essentially a life in which every work and way is be according to God's will.[59] Put succinctly, he writes, "Devotion signifies a life given or devoted to God. He therefore is the devout [person] who lives no longer to his own will, or the way and spirit of the world, but to the sole will of God, who considers God in everything, who serves God in everything, who makes

---

54. Ibid., 104–5; see also ibid., 10, 23.
55. Ibid., 263.
56. Ibid., 248.
57. Ibid., 266.
58. Ibid., 268.
59. Ibid., 47, 76, 113, 218, 316, 26.

all the parts of his common life parts of piety by doing everything in the name of God and under such rules as are conformable to His glory."[60] We must therefore do "the utmost of [our] power [to] live a wise and holy and heavenly life," looking wholly unto God in our lives as our prayers for everything must be considered as being holy.[61]

Such devotion therefore has at least two central components that makes any person or action "devout." The first are the intentions and affections with which one engages their life and works. He claims that "devotion is nothing else but right apprehensions and right affections toward God," it is "a lively fervor of the soul" for "there is nothing that so powerfully governs the heart, that so strongly excites us to wise and reasonable actions, as a true sense of God's presence."[62] Devotion is therefore partly defined, asserts Law, by the intentions with which we engage in our activities and our lives.[63] Hence, we must "intend to please God in all the actions of our life, as the best and happiest thing in the world."[64]

As second element of devotion is that everything we are and do must be for the service and glory of God.[65] In order for something to be considered as "piety," it must be done for God.[66] As a result, he asserts, "It is absolutely certain that no Christian is to enter any further into business, nor for any other ends than such as he can in singleness of heart offer unto God as a reasonable service."[67] It is these ends, the glory and service of God, that are intended to utterly transform not only the things we do, but also how we go about doing them.[68]

This well-intentioned devotion in the glory and service of God is therefore to be the aim of all Christians.[69] On this, he writes, "Christianity supposes, intends, desires, and aims at nothing else but the raising fallen [humanity] to a divine life, to such habits of holiness, such degrees of devotion as may fit [her or him] to enter amongst the holy inhabitants

---

60. Ibid., 47; see also ibid., 75, 83, 321, 50.
61. Ibid., 48, 50, 75, 145.
62. Ibid., 192, 208, 326.
63. Ibid., 141, 43.
64. Ibid., 62; see also ibid., 89.
65. Ibid., 81, 86, 137, 39.
66. Ibid., 112.
67. Ibid., 82; see also ibid., 91, 96, 129.
68. Ibid., 124–25.
69. Ibid., 134, 287.

of the Kingdom of Heaven."[70] As a result, our common, daily life must be conformed to the ways of the Gospel for "all Christians are called to the same holiness of life."[71] This ideal of devotion therefore holds a central place for Law in this text.

In addition to devotion, Law also asserts the need for us to aspire to certain virtues. He claims that "it is the one only business of a Christian . . . to distinguish [herself or himself] by good works, to be eminent in the most sublime virtues of the gospel."[72] For him, the most important Christian virtues are humility and charity, with humility being the most central: "a humble state of soul is the very state of religion . . . humility is the life and soul of piety, the foundation and support of every virtue and good work, the best guard and security of all holy affections."[73] In addition to these, Law asserts, God desires us to be true, faithful, and honest "in all our actions and designs" and we are expected to love all of humankind just as Christ did.[74] These virtues, together with his many elaborations on devotion, comprise some of the central ideals that Law seems to be orienting his personal transformation system around. These aims, he claims, will lead to filling us "full of content and strong satisfactions,"[75] something toward which we should all aspire.

Spiritual Formation Approaches

Law's personal spiritual formation approaches are quite extensive and broadly encompassing, as is this text. I find eight fundamental approaches that he presents as being necessary for such a devotionally transformative journey as described above. These approaches are therefore intended to help each person to reorient their lives and intentions toward the service and glory of God, thereby overcoming the falleness of the world and achieving a devotion that is pleasing to God.

The first and most central approach that he discusses is prayer, and much of this text is organized around the different times he proposes for prayer to be engaged throughout one's day. For Law, "Prayer is the nearest approach to God and the highest enjoyment of Him that we are capable of

70. Ibid., 208; see also ibid., 41–47.
71. Ibid., 142; see also ibid., 50–51, 47.
72. Ibid., 144.
73. Ibid., 228; see also ibid., 64.
74. Ibid., 84, 85–86, 137, 289.
75. Ibid., 148, 62, 70.

in this life," and it "looses the bands of sin ... purifies the soul, reforms our heart, and draws down the aids of divine grace."[76] As a result, it is "the best antidote in the world to expel the venom of that poisonous passion."[77] The whole point of our prayers is for us to turn to God, for God is the center and focus of all our prayers. Expounding on this, he writes, "God alone is to be the rule and measure of our prayers, that in them we are to look wholly unto Him and act wholly for Him, that we are only to pray in such a manner for such things and such ends as are suitable to His glory."[78] It is because of this, Law goes on to assert, that we must therefore "beg of God to adorn [our soul] with every grace and perfection."[79] Prayer therefore brings us closer to God.

For Law, there are many different kinds of prayer. While he doesn't seek to prescribe any specific form of prayer, especially if "your heart is always ready to pray in its own language," he does assert that having specific forms at hand is very helpful, especially at times when praying is hard for us do.[80] For instance, he spends an entire chapter discussing some of the ways to go about praying: have a special, private, and regular place to pray; being on one's knees; silencing self and placing self in the presence of God; using diverse images and expressions of the attributes of God to cover the diverse forms God takes; giving thanks, praise, and oblation to God in every prayer; expressing self honestly, whatever is coming up pray with that to God; also having some devotional study time to better learn what devotion is; using one's imagination and seeing the heavens opening up as an "excellent means of raising the spirit of devotion within you"; and beginning all prayers with a Psalm, not with reading it, but with singing or chanting it.[81] These practices are intended to help raise one up into greater union with God as discussed above. He also discusses spontaneous prayers, intercessory prayers for others, and meditations "on the perfection of the divine attributes" as well as on sin and suffering.[82] For Law, then, while there are diverse forms of prayer unique to each individual, there are also some essential ingredients to prayer that he recommends.

76. Ibid., 190, 226.
77. Ibid., 309.
78. Ibid., 47.
79. Ibid., 91.
80. Ibid., 196–97.
81. Ibid., ch. 15; see also ibid., 209, 20–21.
82. Ibid., 174, 300–302, 10–11, 35–36.

William Law's Serious Call

However, in spite of the his claims that we shouldn't prescribe specific forms of prayer, he does recommend that one engage in prayer at regular, set times throughout one's day.[83] Regular prayer throughout one's day is "recommended to all people as the best, the happiest, and most perfect way of life" because "prayer is a duty that belongs to all states and conditions of [people]."[84] It is because God is everywhere present that we must all in Heaven and on Earth give praise to God, for "this is the common business of all persons in this world."[85]

Law therefore asserts that we should each prayer at five different times during our day, each with a theme that we should focus on. We are to rise up early in the morning to raise our "heart to God in acts of praise and adoration," and oblation.[86] We should pray again at 9:00 a.m. to "address [ourselves] again to the throne of grace" with humility being the focus of these prayers.[87] At 12:00 p.m., our focus is to be on the universal love of God and all creation and to love one another as Christ loves us.[88] Next, we should pray at 3:00 p.m. where we "are desired to consider the necessity of resignation and conformity to the will of God."[89] Finally, at the 6:00 p.m. prayer, we are to make an Examination of our day, a practice that will be discussed in greater detail below.[90] Such regular, daily prayers are intended to help further the long-term conditioned transformation of our lives. Hence, prayer is one of the most central personal transformation approaches in the system that Law articulates in this text.

A second approach is for each of us to focus on and practice the virtues, as described above. As baptized Christians, we must habitually exercise the virtues, following the regiments of religion and what it commands for that is what we are obliged to do.[91] Relating the practice of the virtues to God's love for us, he writes, "The measure of our love to God seems in justice to be the measure of our love of every virtue. We are to love and practice it with all our heart, with all our soul, with all our mind,

---

83. Ibid., 114, 40.
84. Ibid., 139, 280.
85. Ibid., 77; see also ibid., 139, 256.
86. Ibid., 189, 95, 219, 316.
87. Ibid., 225, 28.
88. Ibid., 287–88.
89. Ibid., 316.
90. Ibid., 328.
91. Ibid., 101, 35, 57–58.

PART FIVE: Protestant Reformation

and with all our strength."[92] We are to therefore practice all the virtues with right tempers, making "our labor or employment an acceptable service unto God."[93] As discussed above, Law describes the different virtues that we should intentionally cultivate such as humility, living a lifestyle devoted to the will of God, honesty, and love for our neighbors.[94] In short, he writes, "If our common life is not a common course of humility, self-denial, renunciation of the world, poverty of spirit, and heavenly affection, we don't live the lives of Christians."[95] In these virtues, such as humility, we must ever consider ourselves as learners.[96] Dedication to living and practicing a life of virtues is therefore another central practice for Law.

Related to the practice of the virtues, is a third approach of living a form of asceticism from the world. Law asserts, in accord with his anthro-cosmology, that we must renounce this world and all selfish motives.[97] Finding the Scriptures as a source for his view, he claims that Jesus and the Apostles "call us to renounce the world and differ in every temper and way of life from the spirit and way of the world," and we are to therefore live in a different world with different views.[98] We are to do penance, abstaining from all things that are not needed to help us in our devotion; though we are to do so in moderation.[99] Being, therefore, ever watchful,[100] such asceticism from the world is yet another approach that Law asserts for the growing devotional life.

A fourth personal spiritual formation endeavor that we are to engage in regularly is, as mentioned above, the examination of our lives. We are to examine our life according to the Scriptures, as well as according to the things of religion, by the leadings of the "Spirit of Christ."[101] Such examinations are intended to give direction to our lives and should be engaged in every day.[102] They can be done in conjunction with meditations and reflections on our own death, or on whether we did all that we could to

92. Ibid., 67.
93. Ibid., 77–78.
94. Ibid., 85–86, 91, 274, 96, 316, 20.
95. Ibid., 52.
96. Ibid., 236.
97. Ibid., 78, 219.
98. Ibid., 51, 53.
99. Ibid., 91, 112, 28.
100. Ibid., 306.
101. Ibid., 65, 73, 95, 116.
102. Ibid., 167, 73, 32.

pursue a perfect life, or in relation to the realization that "the greatness of those things which follow death makes all that goes before it sink into nothing."[103] We can also consider the world and how it lives and the consequences of its actions.[104] As with the ascetical ways and with the virtues, these examinations must help us to be ever watchful of even the smallest part of our lives so that we might continually guard against such vices as vanity.[105] These self-examination approaches are therefore yet another part of the system of spiritual conditioning that Law proposes.

In order to make such examinations, however, one must know what to compare their lives against. Hence, education also holds a central place in his personal transformation program. All such education should teach us to "learn the methods of God's providence over the world."[106] This is because, unless someone tells us about living the devout life, we will not know that the ways of the world are of the Devil since all of us have been educated into a corrupt world and "indevotion is founded in the most excessive ignorance."[107] Those who educate us, he asserts, therefore form us for good or bad.[108] Religion must therefore teach us how to live our lives, use our materiel, how to treat others, what the things of eternal life are, etc.[109] For Law, "The history of the gospel is chiefly the history of Christ's conquest over this spirit of the world" and we must therefore study Scriptures in order to live according to them thereby leading us into the devout life.[110] In addition to this, we must also study and learn the wise teachings of saints and holy persons, and this is especially needed for "youthful minds" so that they too are not corrupted by the education of the world.[111] Such education is therefore intended to help shape and guide our lives with God and is therefore another central approach for Law.

A sixth approach is related to education. As we come to learn more about the lives of Christ, the saints, and other holy persons in Scriptures and in other texts, as well as those that we personally know, we are called

103. Ibid., 71; see also ibid., 68, 339–40.
104. Ibid., 71.
105. Ibid., 112, 27.
106. Ibid., 258; see also ibid., 50.
107. Ibid., 49, 93, 248, 344.
108. Ibid., 262.
109. Ibid., 50, 127–28, 79, 84, 93, 240, 300.
110. Ibid., 91, 115, 21, 206, 10, 37.
111. Ibid., 249, 69.

PART FIVE: Protestant Reformation

to imitate them.[112] Just as God is holy, so should we likewise be holy and these holy persons, and even the angels, are to be models for us in this.[113] Law recognizes that such imitation is to be of their intentions and not their particular embodiments. On this, he writes, "It is their spirit, therefore, their piety, their love of God, that you are to imitate, and not the particular form of their life."[114] Embodying this approach himself, Law shares many stories of devout people he knows who are models of the kind of devotion that he discusses.[115] He also considers the disordered lives of others, and their poor examples, for us to reflect on and learn from as well.[116] Such imitation and modeling is therefore to be an integral part of our lives and encompasses the need for one being connected to a community as well as the Christian religious tradition.

In the lives of many of these saints and holy ones do we find lives of service to God and creation. As a result, we too are called to imitate this by doing good works by helping others with the things that we have.[117] We need to view all that we have as God's gifts, using them for good and making a careful use of our time and talents.[118] As we learned from Law's understanding and ideals of what true devotion is, we must do all things together for the service of God.[119] Such service is therefore another necessary approach that is needed to answer Law's "serious call."

A final spiritual formation approach that I find in Law's text, is the use of reason. For Law, "Reason is our universal law that obliges us in all places and at all times; and no actions have any honor but so far as they are instances of our obedience to reason."[120] We are therefore to use reason to guide our life and know that living the religious life everywhere and at all times is necessary and we need to use our reason for good.[121] He further claims that we are "obliged to live according to reason and order," for it is God's will that we use it.[122] However, he also warns, use of it can also lead

112. Ibid., 90, 95, 121, 93, 225, 87–88, 344.
113. Ibid., 91, 232, 50, 90.
114. Ibid., 125.
115. Ibid., 113–20, 253–60, 68–74, 303–5.
116. Ibid., 152, 63, 66–67, 71, 204–5, 32, 64, 314–15.
117. Ibid., 91, 115, 17, 272.
118. Ibid., 77, 97, 126.
119. Ibid., 76.
120. Ibid., 351.
121. Ibid., 92–93, 95, 345.
122. Ibid., 137.

to "disorders of the soul," such as "pride, sensuality, and covetousness."[123] Hence, the wrong use of reason is a fearful and dangerous thing.[124] Nevertheless, the use of reason in one's growing spiritual life is a necessary approach.

These eight spiritual formation approaches are ones that can be found in Law's text. They are quite broad and diverse, covering inner learning and growth as well as outer practices and lifestyles. They also include communal and historical approaches in terms of the connections and support that one needs for their prayers and modeling and in the education that is required for their guidance. These practices are also mostly in accordance with his anthro-cosmologies and theory of change. Through these approaches, one is supposed to achieve liberation from the sinful world via the gradual conditioning that they intentionally nurture. All in all, Law offers a fairly well-rounded system of personal transformation with these approaches.

Discernment

As it relates to discerning the path of one's spiritual life, Law does not seem to have too much to explicitly say. He does mention the need for it because there are many who go through the motions of church and religion, but still live as the world does.[125] He also claims that just "as the essence of stupidity consists in the entire want of judgment in an ignorance of the value of things, so on the other hand, the essence of wisdom and knowledge must consist in the excellency of our judgment or in the knowledge of the worth and value of things."[126] Discernment is therefore a central part of the growing personal spiritual life for Law.

But how do we go about engaging in such discernment? There are at least three aspects of Law's discernment process, all of which are related to his spiritual formation approaches. The first is by using the Scriptures to examine and compare our life with.[127] On this, he writes, "Every exhortation in scripture to be wise and reasonable, satisfying only such wants as God would have satisfied; every exhortation to be spiritual and heavenly, pressing after a glorious change of our nature; every exhortation to love

123. Ibid., 137, 345.
124. Ibid., 135.
125. Ibid., 48, 52.
126. Ibid., 347.
127. Ibid., 65.

our neighbor as ourselves, to love all [humankind] as God has loved them, is a command to be strictly religious in the use of our money," all these are taught everywhere in the New Testament and are to be pursued by us.[128] His discernment is therefore one that makes use of the Scriptures, as well as the lives of those we seek to imitate, in order to know what the devout life consists of so that we might better nurture and attune to it.

Related to this is the use of reason to know what, how, and when to use our lives and the things that we have.[129] Such reason, as was discussed above, is given by God and is therefore to be used to further our lives with God. A third aspect of his discernment process is related to our reflecting on what the truer and deeper intentions and essences of our actions are. For instance, Law asserts that one who intends to be "thankful in every part and accident of his life because it comes from God" actually engages in a truer form of prayer than one simply has "has some set time for singing of Psalms."[130] In our discerning whether something is devout or not, we must consider not just the actions themselves, but also the intentions with which we engage them. As Law asserts, "You must not consider the thing barely in itself but what it proceeds from, what virtues it shows to be wonting, what vices it naturally strengthens. For every habit of this kind discovers the state of the soul and plainly shows the whole turn of your mind."[131]

The discernment process that Law seems to be articulating, then, is one that is both external and internal. Externally, we are to compare the status and direction of our devotional lives against those presented in Scriptures and in the lives of holy persons. Internally, we are to use reason and reflect on the underlying intentions of our actions. Taken together, Law's approach to discernment is one that seeks to be aware of and to guide our intentions through the use of both reason and external comparisons. In short, it seems to be a further expression of his overall system where intentions are at the heart and we are seeking to gradually reshape and guide them through the use of both internal and external approaches and processes.

---

128. Ibid., 99.
129. Ibid., 93, 97.
130. Ibid., 139.
131. Ibid., 192–93.

Evaluative Techniques

Reflecting back over the elaborate system that Law articulates in this text, we can see that they are a number of evaluative techniques. Clearly, one is to make use of the self-examinations that Law daily recommends in order to help them to every stay upon the growing devotional path. These examinations can be based on two other evaluative techniques: reason and models. One can, as we have heard, use reason to help them know if they are progressing in their journeys. One is to also use the models found in Scripture, as well as in the lives of others, to evaluate their lives against. One is also, as we just read, to ever reflect on the intentions with which they are performing their actions, for such intentions are the defining foundation of what makes something devout. Finally, one can also make use of their community's feedback to them in order to help them further evaluate the progress and direction of their lives. All of these techniques make for a robust approach to evaluating one's personal devotional life.

Summary/Reflections

Overall, Law's system seems to be one that primarily seeks to attend to the intentions of one's life. These intentions, when oriented toward the glory and service of God, are what makes one "devout." Law's theory of change then seems to be centered on the gradual conditioning of these intentions for they are what lead to holy actions. Each of the personal spiritual formation approaches that then follow are intended toward this gradual reshaping of one's distorted intentions, which come from this fallen world into which we have all been acculturated, through their regular and rigorous engagement. For Law, then, personal transformation appears to primarily a task of reshaping the heart of God's children.

PART FIVE: Protestant Reformation

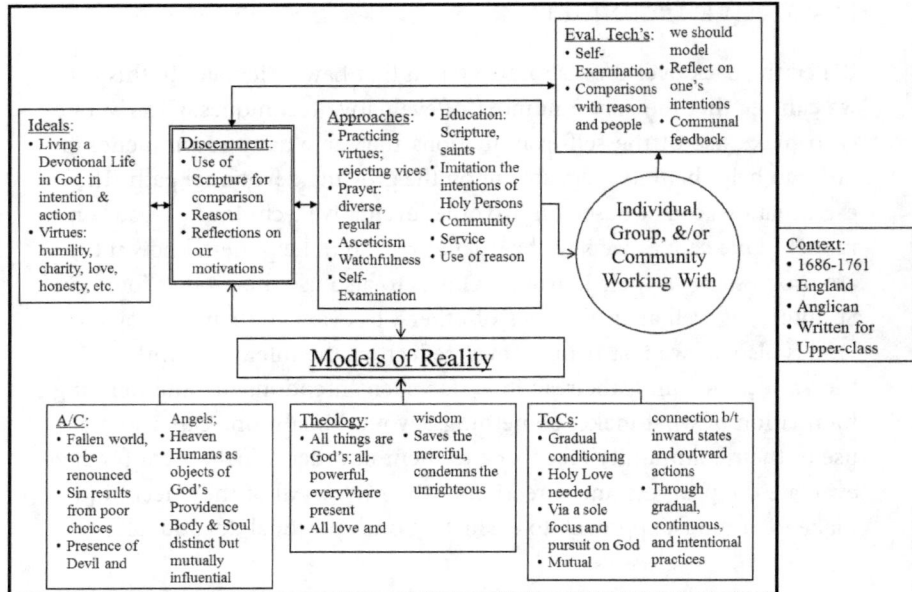

Also of particular interest is how he adapted the regular hours of prayer for laity and the themes that he tied to each one. There are many Roman Catholic and Anglican monastic religious orders that follow a very similar schedule both then and today. However, Law is not articulating this for them but rather for laypersons who may be living busy lives. Law's text is therefore another example of the personal transformation texts that began to emerge in this post-Protestant Reformation time period.

PART SIX

Contemporary Movements

WHEN THE TWENTIETH CENTURY dawned upon the pages of this planet, our world was to witness transformations that it had never before seen in its history to extent that it did. The Industrial Revolution continued to gain momentum as technological breakthroughs occurred at an increasing rate.[1] New machines, medicines, and electronics emerged that have and continue to reshape contemporary life.[2] Violent confrontations increased in devastation with world wars, genocides, and as weapons of mass destruction, such as the atom bomb, were developed and capable of inflicting destruction in ways never before seen on our globe.[3] Societal changes continued to sweep through parts of our world as governments came and went and new political systems, such as communism and socialism, were implemented.[4] Empowerment of women and minorities also rose during this time period in the West as social justice movements spread.[5] The world's population, which originally did not crest one billion people until the 1800s, has topped more than seven billion in only the

---

1. Holt, "Spiritualities of the Twenieth Century," 307; Sheldrake, *Brief History of Spirituality*, 172; Woods, *Christian Spirituality*, 261.

2. Chidester, *Christianity*, 542; Holt, "Spiritualities of the Twenieth Century," 307, 64; Sheldrake, *Brief History of Spirituality*, 173; Woods, *Christian Spirituality*, 261.

3. Chidester, *Christianity*, 495, 515, 32; Holt, "Spiritualities of the Twenieth Century," 307, 65; Sheldrake, *Brief History of Spirituality*, 173; Woods, *Christian Spirituality*, 244, 61.

4. Chidester, *Christianity*, 489; Holt, "Spiritualities of the Twenieth Century," 310; Sheldrake, *Brief History of Spirituality*, 173; Woods, *Christian Spirituality*, 243.

5. Chidester, *Christianity*, 486, 523, 24–25; Holt, "Spiritualities of the Twenieth Century," 307, 27, 39, 43, 57, 58, 65; Sheldrake, *Brief History of Spirituality*, 173, 75, 83–84, 87, 91; Woods, *Christian Spirituality*, 245, 49–50, 65.

last couple of years.⁶ Furthermore, ecological spiritualities have flourished as questions of global warming, pollution, and other environmental concerns have been raised.⁷

Amongst such broad and sweeping changes, two major developments have worked to alter the current course of religion in the West. First, modern scientific, secular, and consumerism narratives have continued to displace traditional religious paradigms for understanding how the world works.⁸ Secular worldviews now dominate many areas of contemporary culture from schools, to government and non-government agencies, to mainstream media in the United States.⁹ As we shall see in this section, contemporary spiritual formation authors have sought to recast, or even fundamentally redefine, classical formation in accordance with, or in avoidance of, scientific findings.¹⁰ In tandem with these developments, however, many have also sought to reconnect with classical Western Christian sources.¹¹

Secondly, globalization has brought our world together in ways never before witnessed historically.¹² Via the Internet and other technologies, we now have the capacity to communicate with peoples and cultures in many, and previously "remote," parts of the world.¹³ The combination of communication technologies, relatively fast transportation, migration, and the rapid increase in world population is creating a climate of cultural

6. Allan, "Population Growth over Human History"; Bureau, "U.S. & World Population Clocks."

7. Holt, "Spiritualities of the Twenieth Century," 359–60; Sheldrake, *Brief History of Spirituality*, 207; Woods, *Christian Spirituality*, 258–60, 72.

8. Chidester, *Christianity*, 539, 46; Holt, "Spiritualities of the Twenieth Century," 309, 51; Sheldrake, *Brief History of Spirituality*, 172, 204; Woods, *Christian Spirituality*, 243.

9. Woods, *Christian Spirituality*, 255, 57.

10. Chidester, *Christianity*, 428; Holt, "Spiritualities of the Twenieth Century," 331, 48–49; Sheldrake, *Brief History of Spirituality*, 176, 94, 208–9; Woods, *Christian Spirituality*, 252, 56.

11. Chidester, *Christianity*, 520; Holt, "Spiritualities of the Twenieth Century," 324, 27, 32, 38; Sheldrake, *Brief History of Spirituality*, 176, 79, 85; Woods, *Christian Spirituality*, 243–44, 52, 63.

12. Chidester, *Christianity*, 538; Holt, "Spiritualities of the Twenieth Century," 346, 64; Sheldrake, *Brief History of Spirituality*, 173; Woods, *Christian Spirituality*, 267.

13. Chidester, *Christianity*, 538–39, 43; Holt, "Spiritualities of the Twenieth Century," 364; Sheldrake, *Brief History of Spirituality*, 173; Woods, *Christian Spirituality*, 267. A colleague of mine regularly meets online in a synchronous fashion with fellow researchers who are living in the Americas, Europe, and Africa.

PART SIX: Contemporary Movements

intermixing on massive scales.[14] While various religious traditions have always been present in the West,[15] more genuine and mutual ecumenical and interreligious dialogue and interaction has progressed throughout this time period.[16] Throughout previous eras, Western Christian missionaries helped to spread this tradition to many parts of the world and the communities they established continue to spread throughout to today.[17] In conjunction with these efforts, Westerners have continued to struggle with the fine line that exists between evangelization and enculturation as many new strands of Christian spirituality have emerged around the world.[18] As a result, it is increasingly important for spiritual formators to have some basic knowledge of transformation as it is conceived of and approached by other religious traditions and in different cultures,[19] and we will be looking at one such system in this section.

Within this increasingly complex and every changing context, we will explore four different texts/communities and their approaches to personal transformation. We will begin by visiting with an author from the Evangelical Protestant Christian tradition, Dallas Willard and his book, *Renovation of the Heart*. Providing a systematic view of the human person, Willard provides a comprehensive way to work with an individual's growing life with Christ. From here, we will next take a look at personal transformation from a liberal perspective. Based on my personal experiences of the formation program that was offered at the Claremont School of Theology in Los Angeles, California, we will gain insights into how Christian personal transformation is being conceived of in light of both modern science and other religious traditions.

---

14. Chidester, *Christianity*, 540; Holt, "Spiritualities of the Twenieth Century," 364, 65; Sheldrake, *Brief History of Spirituality*, 206; Woods, *Christian Spirituality*, 246, 67, 72.

15. Chidester, *Christianity*, 344–50.

16. Chidester, *Christianity*, 540, 54–55; Holt, "Spiritualities of the Twenieth Century," 307, 308, 11, 15, 28, 46–47; Sheldrake, *Brief History of Spirituality*, 174, 77, 81, 85, 95, 97; Woods, *Christian Spirituality*, 247, 62.

17. Chidester, *Christianity*, 413, 15, 537; Holt, "Spiritualities of the Twenieth Century," 316; Sheldrake, *Brief History of Spirituality*, 174; Woods, *Christian Spirituality*, 251, 64.

18. Chidester, *Christianity*, 436, 52–53, 551, 57; Holt, "Spiritualities of the Twenieth Century," 317, 20–21, 46, 65; Sheldrake, *Brief History of Spirituality*, 208; Woods, *Christian Spirituality*, 244–45, 54–55, 64.

19. Holt, "Spiritualities of the Twenieth Century," 346–47; Sheldrake, *Brief History of Spirituality*, 206–7; Woods, *Christian Spirituality*, 274.

PART SIX: Contemporary Movements

Next, we will learn from psychiatrist Gerald May and his book, *Will & Spirit*. In addition to this being an alternative way to conceive of an approach personal spiritual formation, May will provide us with further insights into how contemporary authors are reconceiving classical Western Christian views in light of modern science, particularly the field of psychology. Finally, we will round out our historical journey by looking at a system, developed by members of Yale University's psychiatry department, that seeks to blend modern cognitive schema theory with elements found in Buddhism. This will be our one venture into beginning to understand how practitioners from other religious traditions are conceiving of personal transformation in this increasingly multicultural context.

12

Dallas Willard's Renovating Heart

Context

DALLAS WILLARD IS A professor of philosophy at the University of Southern California. He writes his book, *Renovation of the Heart*, in order to help Christians to live the life that is depicted in the New Testament and to be ever more fully transformed into the Christlikeness that they desire.[1] Willard writes from a more conservative and evangelical Protestant perspective, as these biblically-focused comments suggest. His book has been endorsed by a Biola University professor as well as by Richard Foster, which suggests to me that it is to the evangelical community that he is writing this text for more specifically.

In his own words, this book "aims to help those who are 'seeking the kingdom of God and His righteousness' to find them and to fully live in them."[2] Its primary focus is on empowering people to be better disciples of Jesus as his life is depicted in the pages of the Bible. His goal is to therefore articulate more of a systematic approach to individual Christian spiritual formation. It is therefore to this text that we will now be turning in order to gain a better understanding of the contemporary evangelical approach to Western Christian personal transformation.

---

1. Willard, *Renovation of the Heart*, 10.
2. Ibid., 25–26.

PART SIX: Contemporary Movements

MODELS OF REALITY

Anthropological-Cosmological

As it relates to his views of the world, Willard asserts, "In today's world, famine, war, and epidemic are almost totally the outcome of human choices, which are expressions of the human spirit."[3] He goes on to also claim, "Our human world as we find it is not like God, though it was intended to be . . . Love is not natural in our world, though desire or lust certainly is."[4] For Willard, then, the world is one that is not the way that it was intended to be, there is too much sin and distortion that results from the poor choices of humans. Following these assertions, Willard's anthrocosmology primarily focuses on two central topics: the nature of humans, and the nature of evil.

Anthropologically, Willard asserts that there are "six basic aspects in our lives as human beings."[5] The first are the thoughts that we have. They are the images and beliefs that we hold.[6] Second, we all have feelings. While feelings and thoughts always go together, "feelings move us," "they change the overall tone of our life and our world."[7] Thirdly, all humans have a "will, decision, [or] character."[8] This is "the capacity of the person to originate things and events that would not otherwise be or occur."[9] Willard asserts that while the will is dependent on thoughts and feelings, it also influences them.[10] He also claims, in his system, "that 'heart,' 'spirit,' and 'will' (or their equivalents) are words that refer to one and the same thing, the same fundamental component of the person."[11] While they may each have their individual nuances, heart/will/spirit basically refer to the same underlying core of an individual that is an intimate part of guiding one's life.[12] Clearly, this part of the person is central for Willard's framework.

---

3. Ibid., 13.
4. Ibid., 131.
5. Ibid., 30.
6. Ibid., 31.
7. Ibid., 33, 121, 24, 39.
8. Ibid., 30.
9. Ibid., 33.
10. Ibid., 142.
11. Ibid., 29.
12. Ibid., 13, 16–17, 18, 24, 29, 30, 34, 35, 95.

A fourth aspect of the human person is the body. This aspect is basically related to "action, interaction with the physical world."[13] "The body," Willard writes, "lies right at the center of the spiritual life" and is primarily intended for good, for God's kingdom.[14] The fifth aspect is related to our social context. For him, "the human self requires rootedness in others."[15] However, Willard also asserts, the true circle of community is the Trinitarian circle.[16] Finally, the soul makes up the sixth aspect of his anthropology. The soul is "the factor that integrates all of the above to form one life."[17] "Our soul," he claims, "is like an inner stream of water, which gives strength, direction, and harmony to every other element of our life" and it "is the most basic level of life in the individual, and one that is by nature rooted in God."[18]

Willard views these six aspects as concentric circles with spirit being the most central part and the environment being the most outer part. From inside to out, these concentric circles are: spirit (heart/will), mind (thought/feelings), body, social, soul, and infinite environment.[19] All actions then come from the interplay of all of these various aspects.[20] Taken collectively, then, these six aspects can be considered to comprise one's character. On this, he writes, "Our character is that internal, overall structure of the self that is revealed by our long-run patterns of behavior and from which our actions more or less automatically rise."[21] However, one must also recognize the need for God in the transformation of these, for God is the "fundamental 'other'" and the only one who can sustain our existence.[22] It is precisely because of God that restoration of the human being in the midst of a distorted world is possible.[23] These six aspects of the human person therefore not only comprise his holistic anthropology, they also come to be the framework upon which his entire personal transformation system is founded, as we shall see more clearly below.

13. Ibid., 30.
14. Ibid., 159, 60–61, 69.
15. Ibid., 36; see also ibid., 179.
16. Ibid., 180.
17. Ibid., 30; see also ibid., 37, 199.
18. Ibid., 204, 207.
19. Ibid., 38.
20. Ibid., 39.
21. Ibid., 142.
22. Ibid., 18, 36.
23. Ibid., 63.

PART SIX: Contemporary Movements

In addition to unpacking his model of the humans, Willard also expends some effort discussing the nature of evil and its role in both people and the world. Since this text is primarily focused on the transformation of the individual rather than society, his discussions on evil center mostly on its relation to humans.[24] However, he does mention the presence of evil in the world, and that Satan uses the things of this world to "defeat God's purposes."[25] However, for Willard, many societal evils are the direct result of the choices and actions of human hearts.[26] As a result, he claims, "Profound transformation [in the inner life] is the only thing that can definitively conquer outward evil."[27] Hence, most of the evil in the world results from the evil that is operative in the hearts of individual people.

As it relates to individuals, Willard proclaims that "choice is where sin dwells."[28] He further asserts that "sin, through desire and pride, alienates the life in us (the soul) from the life that is in God and leaves us in the turmoil of a soul struggling with life on its own."[29] Every person must therefore acknowledge, as a first step in the redemption of such evil, the "ruined condition" of their soul.[30] However, he notes, "Sin does not make [a human being] worthless, but only lost" and this "lostness is a factual condition of the self, of the ruined soul."[31] For Willard, to be lost is to be apart from the life and ways that God wants us to live and it is to be disconnected from the inner "living stream" of one' soul.[32] This lostness is dangerous because it can ultimately lead one to a deadness of soul, a state wherein a person can no longer desire God or the things of God and can only wait to fall apart.[33] In the presence of our continually distorted world, then, we must ever be cautious because "we are never out of danger."[34]

Willard's cosmology is therefore one that is filled with evil. This evil, for him, primarily results from the choices and inclinations that come

24. Ibid., 24.
25. Ibid., 14, 100.
26. Ibid., 55.
27. Ibid., 24.
28. Ibid., 46.
29. Ibid., 211.
30. Ibid., 45, 52, 59, 60.
31. Ibid., 46, 58.
32. Ibid., 55–56, 57, 206.
33. Ibid., 58, 125, 47.
34. Ibid., 81.

from the distorted and "ruined" souls of individuals. It is in this difficult context that the six aspects of anthropology are therefore located. Working formatively with each one of these, in light of his cosmology, will be central to his system.

Theological

Theologically, Willard's discussions primarily focus on Jesus and God, though he does talk about the Trinity in relation to social aspects.[35] For him, "[Jesus] is the power and the wisdom of God," the one through whom God comes to us.[36] Jesus started a world revolution, "one that is still in process and will continue until God's will is done on earth as it is in heaven."[37] He further asserts, "From the person of Christ there uniquely came into the world the energy and knowledge by which human beings could be delivered from evil and enabled to live life as it ought to be lived."[38] Jesus, then, is viewed by Willard as the transforming agent in the world, one who is seeking not only to bring God to people, but also people to God. Willard's system, as will be discussed in more detail below, is therefore one that is centered almost exclusively on the person of Christ.

Like Jesus, though he seems to use these terms interchangeably, God is dynamically active in the world in the form of love, gentleness, and searching. On the love of God, Willard writes, "The constant love of God is extended to every human being who ever lives, sometimes in places and postures that God himself would not prefer, but still with some good effect," for God is fundamentally relational.[39] In God's omnipresence, God is ever looking for people who are seeking God "as the highest being of all," for people who respond to God in their hearts.[40] While Willard does assert that God "periodically moves upon his people and in their surrounding culture to achieve his everlasting purposes,"[41] God never does so forcefully. On this, he writes, "Certainly the will of a spiritual being is the one thing in creation that God chooses not to override and force to take

---

35. Ibid., 184.
36. Ibid., 14, 131, 249.
37. Ibid., 14.
38. Ibid., 229.
39. Ibid., 19, 184, 94.
40. Ibid., 148–49.
41. Ibid., 21.

on a specific character. He allows it to go its way or ways."[42] Both God and Jesus are therefore conceived by Willard to be loving, dynamic, and gentle forces in the world who are ever striving for the transformation of our lives and our world.

Theories of Change

Of all the parts of the framework, Willard seems to spend the most time discussing this element. He begins by offering a definition of "spiritual" as simply being "nonphysical," that which is hidden and it can therefore be good or bad.[43] From here, he then proposes a generic definition of spiritual formation, one that differs markedly from other authors we have explored: "the process by which the human spirit or will is given a definite 'form' or character. It is a process that happens to everyone . . . Terrorists as well as saints are the outcome of spiritual formation."[44] Given his thoroughly Christian location, he then takes a final step toward articulating what spiritual formation is in this religious tradition. On this, he writes, "We can say, in a preliminary manner, that spiritual formation for the Christian basically refers to the Spirit-driven process of forming the inner world of the human self in such a way that it becomes like the inner being of Christ himself . . . Christian spiritual formation is focused entirely on Jesus."[45] As we can see, this is an understanding that Willard comes back to again and again throughout his text.

Given these conceptions, we can therefore ask how these transformations into such Christlikeness come about. We can already see that the heart/will/spirit is central for such formation in Willard's system, just as it was for Law. In fact, he asserts, "the greatest need you and I have—the greatest need of collective humanity—is renovation of our heart."[46] This is because, for Jesus and God, "the heart is what matters, and everything else will then come along."[47] The heart/will/spirit, then, is what spearheads the changes that God's grace is ever seeking to manifest in our lives.[48] As Willard asserts, "By standing in the correct relation to God through our

42. Ibid., 146.
43. Ibid., 17.
44. Ibid., 19; see also ibid., 45.
45. Ibid., 22; see also ibid., 31, 77, 143, 59, 226.
46. Ibid., 14; see also ibid., 16.
47. Ibid., 86.
48. Ibid., 14.

will we can receive grace that will properly reorder the soul along with the other five components."[49] However, we must also address and seek to intentionally transform each of the other aspects of our lives as well.[50] Hence, the heart/will/spirit is a central part of his theory of change because it is what primarily leads the other aspects to be reformed into Christlikeness.

Such transformation, as we have heard now so often in the other authors above, does not come quickly, but only incrementally over the long-term because of the environments in which we have already been wrongly formed. As it relates to the influence of one's environment on their personal transformation, Willard writes, "The human spirit is an inescapable, fundamental aspect of every human being; and it takes on whichever character it has from the experiences and the choices that we have lived through or made in our past. That is what it means for it to be 'formed.'"[51] Every soul, by the very nature of its existence, has already been formed by the life that it has experienced.[52] Due to the distorted nature of the world in which we live, many people are "enslaved" by the bodily desires that our culture has encouraged them to follow after rather than God.[53] All is not lost, Willard goes on to claim, for "if we—through well-directed and unrelenting action—effectually receive the grace of God in salvation and transformation, we certainly will be incrementally changed toward inward Christlikeness."[54] Our individual Christian spiritual formation, though it may not be fully completed in this lifetime, will incrementally bring us ever more fully into Christlikeness.[55]

As it relates to the various aspects of the person, Willard offers a few examples of how such incremental change will happen. For our thoughts, "The needed transformation is very largely a matter of replacing in ourselves those idea systems of evil (and their corresponding cultures) with the idea system that Jesus Christ embodied and taught and with a culture of the kingdom of God."[56] For one's feelings, "The proper course of action is to replace destructive feelings with others that are good, or to subordinate them—anger and sexual desire, for example—in a way that makes them

49. Ibid., 40.
50. Ibid., 42, 222.
51. Ibid., 13.
52. Ibid., 201.
53. Ibid., 71, 200–201.
54. Ibid., 82.
55. Ibid., 152.
56. Ibid., 98; see also ibid., 101.

constructive and transforms their effects."[57] Finally, for our bodies, they "must increasingly be poised to do what is good and refrain from what is evil. The inclinations to wrongdoing that literally inhabit its parts must be eliminated."[58] In each one of these aspects, personal transformation is viewed to come about only gradually via intentional effort for each of the anthropological aspects. We therefore can see how Willard's primary theory of change is one that is intentionally incremental in nature; that is, it comes about incrementally by our intentional efforts.

With intentionality being at the heart of his theory of change, Willard further elaborates on what patterns are needed in order to pursue such incremental growth. While he does claim that "there are no formulas—not definitive how-to's—for growth in the inner character of Jesus," he also asserts the need for having "a path of clear intention and decision, with appropriate spiritual disciplines and accompanying grace."[59] To help his readers to better know what is needed as a general pattern of personal spiritual growth, he asserts that there three elements to it. The first is that one must have a vision that explains why we are doing what we are doing.[60] Such a vision should illuminate the path that we are embarking upon.[61] Secondly, one needs to have intention because "projects of personal transformation rarely if ever succeed by accident, drift, or imposition."[62] "Everyone," he asserts, "must be active in the process of their salvation and transformation to Christlikeness. This is an inescapable fact."[63] Finally, one must have the means to carry out the transformation that they are seeking.[64] Such means can be as elaborate as are found in many churches today, but they really only need to be "ordinary people who are [Jesus'] apprentices, gathered in the name of Jesus and immersed in his presence, and taking steps of inward transformation as they put on the character of Christ."[65] These three elements are therefore intended to help orient and keep a disciple on the path of continual transformation.

57. Ibid., 123; 28.
58. Ibid., 159.
59. Ibid., 94, 112, 56.
60. Ibid., 83.
61. Ibid., 49.
62. Ibid., 83.
63. Ibid., 82.
64. Ibid., 84.
65. Ibid., 251.

Dallas Willard's Renovating Heart

However, as we have already heard, such transformation is not possible without direct, divine intervention. Relating this assertion to Jesus, Willard writes, "his is a revolution of character, which proceeds by changing people from the inside though ongoing personal relationship to God in Christ and to one another. It is one that changes their ideas, beliefs, feelings, and habits of choice, as well as their bodily tendencies and social relations. It penetrates to the deepest layers of their soul. External, social arrangements may be useful to this end, but they are not the end, nor are they a fundamental part of the means."[66] For Willard, we can see, Christ is the whole of our spiritual formation journey. Christ moves through our depths and provides us with all of our needs.[67] Ultimately, our transformation "is an inescapable human problem with no human solution" and we do not have control of it, for "it is, finally, a gift of grace."[68] We must therefore turn to God in Christ because "God has made provision for achieving this aim [of the kingdom]. To 'grow in grace' means to utilize more and more grace to live by, until everything we do is assisted by grace."[69] Hence, God/Christ is the central element in Willard's theory of change.

His theory is therefore one that looks to the working of Christ in one's heart that then leads to a transformation of the whole of one's life. With the goal being Christlikeness, Willard views our journey of growth as one that happens incrementally. Our steps into greater goodness and righteousness are not haphazard, however. They will only come about by the visions, intentions, and means that we engage in. Overall, then, his theory of change is one of an intentional participation with Christ via the well-planned, thoroughly envisioned, and systematic use of the individual spiritual formation approaches that one utilizes.

Spiritual Formation Ideals & Goals

As it relates to the ideals that Willard sets up, in addition to and a part of achieving Christlikeness, there are three that he seems to place at the center of his system. The first is the doing of the will of God, which, for him, is the establishment of the kin-dom of God. He asserts, "[Christian Spiritual formation's] aim is to bring every element in our being, working

---

66. Ibid., 15; see also ibid., 18.
67. Ibid., 16, 19.
68. Ibid., 20, 23, 41–42, 90, 189, 210.
69. Ibid., 93; see also ibid., 70, 91.

from inside out, into harmony with the will of God and the kingdom of God."[70]

The second goal that Willard considers is working toward goodness and righteousness. We are to be transformed into "thoroughly good and godly persons, yet purged of arrogance, insensitivity, and self-sufficiency" because people who are truly dead to self, "are free to focus their efforts on the service of God and others and the furthering of good generally."[71] In relation to such goodness, Willard offers his definition of sanctification as "a condition of the human soul established in imparted (not just imputed) righteousness."[72] Goodness and righteousness, as well as the doing of the will of God, is therefore another central ideal for him.

A third goal that he discusses at length, is that of unifying the individual and all of their various aspects. Willard claims, "Experienced-based confidence in God's loving care allows all six dimensions of the human self progressively to come into harmony with each other and enables us to be generous in every respect to those around us."[73] While he does discuss the centrality of the heart in such transformations, it is really the whole self that he seems to be seeking to unify in God.[74]

In addition to and as a part of Christlikeness, these three ideals therefore comprise the ends toward which Willard's approaches to personal Christian spiritual formation tend. Not only do they address every aspect of his anthropology, they also seem to be formulated in such a way as to directly combat the presence of evil that he identifies. We can also see that his theology is also a central part of these ideals, thereby making for a fairly philosophically consistent set of ideals.

Spiritual Formation Approaches

There are numerous approaches to personal transformation that Willard addresses. In addition to these, he also clarifies how churches should work with disciples who are at different stages of their Christian journey. In discussing these steps, by which churches should nurture new disciples, he asserts that there are at least three stages. First, is for them to come to

70. Ibid., 93; see also ibid., 86, 143.
71. Ibid., 25, 72.
72. Ibid., 224.
73. Ibid., 70.
74. Ibid., 20, 30, 31, 40–41, 43, 148, 94, 218–21.

see themselves as apprentices of Jesus, trusting everything to him.[75] Second, is the immersion of the individual into the Trinitarian Life of God in the community.[76] Finally, the disciple should implement the means of transformation that the community engages in.[77] While we have already discussed the centrality of Christ in this process,[78] it was also noted that we, as individuals as communities in Christ, have an intentional part to play in this. On this, Willard asserts, "Concretely, we intend to live in the kingdom of God by intending to obey the precise example and teachings of Jesus."[79]

A central part of such intending, for him, is the need for self-abandon in this process of transformation from the very beginning. Because of our "pre-formation" in this world and the "ruined" state of our soul, we must begin by striving to relinquish what we currently are and have become to date.[80] On this, Willard writes, "Christian spiritual formation rests on this indispensable foundation of death to self and cannot proceed except insofar as that foundation is being firmly laid and sustained."[81] Such a death involves the abandoning of our false beliefs, all our defensiveness in relationships, and all that we have and want.[82] We must have remorse, seeking the lower places rather than the higher, for "humility is the framework within which all virtues live."[83] Only when we have done this, will we have a free life in God, to "want the good and be able to do it, the only true human freedom."[84] Such self-abandon is therefore a central part of one's spiritually growing life for Willard.

Willard then proceeds to discuss some of the means of personal transformation for each of the six aspects of his anthropology that were discussed above. As it relates to transforming one's thoughts and thinking, he highlights at least three basic approaches for its shaping. First, education and learning are key. "Without correct information," he asserts similarly to Law, "our ability to think has nothing to work on . . . Failure

75. Ibid., 241–42.
76. Ibid., 245, 47.
77. Ibid., 248.
78. Ibid., 23, 133, 35, 96, 254.
79. Ibid., 87.
80. Ibid., 60, 64, 71.
81. Ibid., 64; see also ibid., 75.
82. Ibid., 65, 66, 68, 195.
83. Ibid., 209; see also ibid., 60, 73.
84. Ibid., 65.

to know what God is really like and what his law requires destroys the soul, ruins society, and leaves people to eternal ruin."[85] We must therefore know what God's laws are for that is what Jesus initially shared when he started his earth ministry.[86] Secondly, we must guard and watch over the images and thoughts that enter our minds and we must ever keep God and scripture on our minds.[87] In speaking of Paul of Tarsus, he writes, "There remained in him a spark of evil that could be fanned into a flame were he not watchful or if God did not continuously direct and uphold him in every dimension of his nature."[88] Finally, Willard, not surprisingly being a philosopher, asserts the importance of right and critical thinking.[89] "What is thinking?," he rhetorically asks, "It is the activity of searching out what must be true, or cannot be true, in the light of given facts or assumptions."[90] We must therefore "think well," which means that in order "to serve God well we must think straight."[91] For Willard, this means that our thinking must "conform to the truths of scriptural revelation" wherein we "take that Word in, dwell on it, ponder its meaning, explore its implications—especially as it relates to our own lives."[92] Such thinking, watchfulness, and education are therefore some of the means that he identifies for continually reshaping our thoughts.

Willard then discusses what the spiritual formation of our feelings and desires entails. For him, "feelings and emotions are fostered and sustained by ideas and images, though social and bodily conditions also factor in."[93] As a result, one must learn to use their ideas and images to thereby nurture self-control in their lives, which is "the steady capacity to direct yourself to accomplish what you have chosen or decided to do and be, even though you 'don't feel like it.'"[94] For people who are holy, "their strategy is not one of resisting [their injurious or wrong feelings] in the moment of choice but of living in such a way that they do not have such feelings at all, or at least do not have them in a degree that make it hard to

85. Ibid., 103; see also ibid., 90, 211.
86. Ibid., 103, 215.
87. Ibid., 111, 12, 13, 218.
88. Ibid., 80.
89. Ibid., 111, 248.
90. Ibid., 104.
91. Ibid., 106.
92. Ibid., 104, 109.
93. Ibid., 127.
94. Ibid.

decide against them when appropriate."[95] Ideally, then, the goal is to have feelings that lead us away from sin as a part of the incremental changes that come into our life via personal transformation in Christ.[96] Willard then sets up peace, joy, and love, as well as hope and faith,[97] as the ideal feelings to be nurtured. For him, love is the will to good, joy "is a pervasive sense . . . of well-being," and "peace is the rest of will that results from assurance about 'how things will turn out.'"[98] By working toward these, through self-control, changing our thoughts and images, and by other means, our feelings will gradually come to be oriented in Jesus.

As we have already seen, the formation of the will/heart/spirit is a central focus for his system. As I have already discussed this aspect at length above, the comments here will be brief. At its core, spiritual formation of this aspect is almost entirely directed toward surrendering our wills to God as we must come to "consent to his supremacy in all things."[99] We must come to have "intelligent, energetic participation in accomplishing God's will in our world," and we must really be "devoted to doing what is good and right."[100] To help with such transformations, Willard suggests the practices of solitude, fasting, worship, and service.[101] All of these are intended to help root out the "duplicity and malice" that is buried deep within us thereby better freeing us for the will of God in our lives.[102] Such, then, is partly how Christian spiritual formation of our will/heart/spirit can come.

Willard also discusses the absolute need of our working with our own bodies in spiritual formation. He points out that Jesus came in the flesh "in order that he might bring redemption and deliverance to our bodies."[103] We must therefore use our bodies for righteousness, releasing it to God.[104] We must avoid using it sinfully, for self-gratification or to dominate others nor must we idolize it.[105] Rather, we are called to care for

95. Ibid., 119.
96. Ibid.
97. Ibid., 129, 219.
98. Ibid., 131, 32, 34.
99. Ibid., 150–51.
100. Ibid., 151, 219.
101. Ibid., 155.
102. Ibid., 155–56.
103. Ibid., 162.
104. Ibid., 165, 68, 70, 72, 220.
105. Ibid., 173.

PART SIX: Contemporary Movements

it, to "nourish, exercise, and rest it."[106] The body is therefore an aspect that we must intentionally seek to nurture and care for according to God's will and ways.

As it relates to the social dimension of our being, Willard asserts, "Spiritual formation, good or bad, is always profoundly social."[107] As a result, he claims, one must "seek out others in your community who are pursuing the renovation of the heart" and this includes people we actually know as well as saints and holy people of the past and present.[108] Such community is to be, at its core, loving and nurturing. On this, Willard writes, "Love is not a feeling, or a special way of feeling, but the divine way of relating to others and oneself that moves through every dimension of our being and restructures our world for good."[109] It is communities, then, that are the basis of divine love and transformation. Even small communities, such as marriages, are called to be encounters of self-giving and support.[110] The social aspect of our lives is therefore another key part of the spiritual formation system that Willard emphasizes.

The final aspect of Willard's anthropology, and therefore a primary focus for his approaches, is the soul. The soul, perhaps even more centrally than the will/heart/spirit, is what each disciple must attend to. "The very first thing that we must do," he claims, "is to be mindful of our soul, to acknowledge it. In spiritual formation and transformation it is necessary to take the soul seriously and deal with it regularly and intelligently."[111] Whether we do or not, he further asserts, our soul will eventually find a way to emerge within our lives and bring guidance and restoration. On this, Willard writes, "Soul will always reassert itself as a reality, if only by the shambles left behind when it departs."[112] It is therefore the enduring and life-giving part of our world, and even God has a soul.[113] To help form it, as already mentioned, we simply need to "acknowledge its reality and importance, understand scriptural teachings about it, and take it into the yoke of Jesus, learning from him humility and the abandonment of

---

106. Ibid., 174.
107. Ibid., 182.
108. Ibid., 114.
109. Ibid., 183; see also ibid., 220.
110. Ibid., 190, 93.
111. Ibid., 207; see also ibid., 21.
112. Ibid., 204.
113. Ibid., 205.

'outcomes' to God."[114] Transformation of the soul is therefore intimately linked to the spiritual formation of each of the other aspects discussed above.

In addition to discussing the spiritual formation of each of these six aspects, Willard also mentions a few other approaches throughout this text. As noted, he briefly mentions the need for ascetical practices such as fasting.[115] He also discusses the need for "giving and forgiving."[116] In giving, we share our love, joy, peace, and our service with others, and we offer our churches up as spiritual "hospitals."[117] In forgiving, we must release our hurts to God for healing in order for them to not infect our lives.[118] Finally, he discusses the supremacy of worship above all other approaches. On this, Willard asserts, "To think of God as he is, one cannot but lapse into worship; and worship is the single most powerful force in completing and sustaining restoration in the whole person."[119] These additional approaches are intended to further help one to intentionally partner with Christ in their spiritually formative journeys.

Willard's approaches to personal transformation are therefore primarily organized according to his six anthropological aspects of the human person. For him, each one of these aspects is to be intentionally engaged so that each may come to conform ever more fully to the likeness of Christ. With self-abandon being necessary, and with additional approaches being available for use in their transformation, each one of these aspects will incrementally come to attain the ideals that Willard upholds for his sacred system.

Discernment

Willard does not seem to directly address this as a topic in this text. He does, at various points throughout the text, discuss what some of the differences between how a true Christian and a person of the world behaves.[120] In each of these cases, he seems to be trying to embody his personal spiritual formation approach of education discussed above by

114. Ibid., 215.
115. Ibid., 155.
116. Ibid., 69.
117. Ibid., 137, 55, 231, 34.
118. Ibid., 137.
119. Ibid., 107; see also ibid., 55.
120. Ibid., 57–58, 118–19, 47, 88–89, 200, 27.

comparing what we know to be right against what we know to be wrong. Part of his discernment therefore seems to be based on learning what is right and wrong and then reflecting on one's life in light of this knowledge. It is one that is therefore thoroughly rooted in the kind of critical thinking that he highlighted previously.

Such an approach therefore seems consistent with his heavy emphasis on one having a systematic and intentional approach to their personal transformation. One must do the learning and planning for their growth in God and then continually reflect on each one of the aspects of their lives in order to ascertain how it is going and to where they should go next. While one may, and I think Willard would say "definitely should," do so in consultation with mentors, the spiritual formation plan for each anthropological aspect seems to be a primary basis for his approach to discernment. Unlike with de Sales' spirituality, where one seeks to reflect on how God is moving in creation (especially in one's affective states), Willard's approach seems to be more of comparing each part to external and predetermined models or laws, especially those that are given by Scripture. We might therefore characterize his approach to discernment as more of a moralistic/ethical approach, where one compares their own progress with predetermined standards.

Evaluative Techniques

For Willard's system, how might one evaluate the progress, or non-progress, of their development ? Clearly, each one of the six aspects can be a basis for such evaluations: Are my thoughts and thinking pure? Do my feelings draw me away from sin and toward the things of God ? Is my will/heart/spirit in tune with God's will for my life and the life of the world? Et cetera. While Willard again does not explicitly address this area, it seems that these are the techniques that are embodied in this text. Each of these anthropological aspects is therefore an element to be intentionally cultivated and watched with carefulness, intentionality, and direction.

Another source of feedback can come from one's community and the observations they make of us. Still another source of spiritual evaluation might come from comparing one's self to the world as it currently is. For Willard, as was noted several times above, we are to be distinctly different from the world's distortions in many ways. As a result, such comparisons might also help one to know how they are progressing and where to go next.

SUMMARY/REFLECTIONS

Overall, Willard's text seems to be more of a philosophical or theoretically oriented work, meaning that he seems to focus more on the theories and models that he unpacks than on the practices and approaches of personal transformation. As a result, and knowing that he has a close relationship with Richard Foster, I think this text would be very powerful for people if it were read in tandem with Foster's *Celebration of Discipline*. Nevertheless, Willard's text is quite systematic and holistic in and of itself as the above is a testimony to.

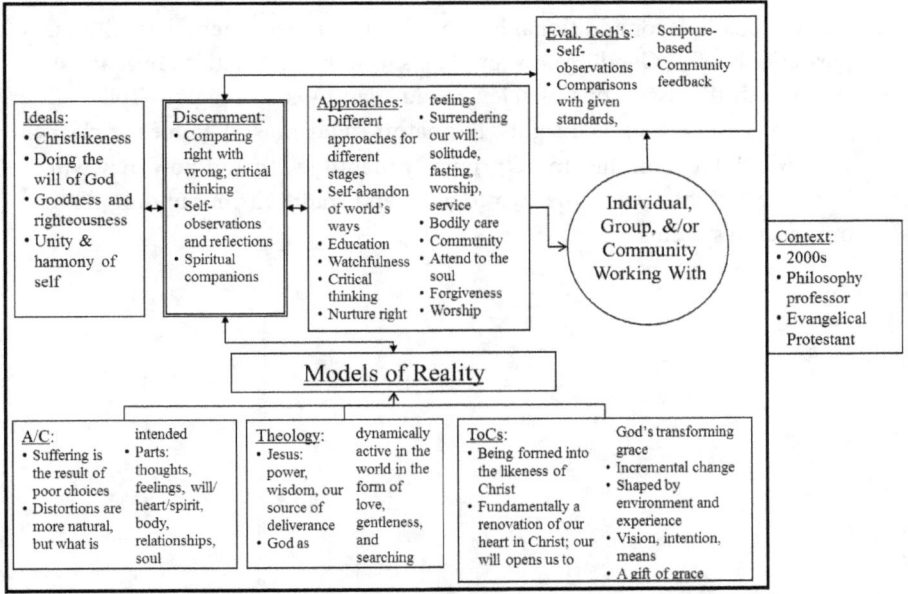

It generally seems to have a central focus of our coming to conform every aspect of our life to the image of Christ. Such an image is primarily given, for Willard, in the pages of the Bible, but also through the lives of the mentors, saints, and communities that we immerse ourselves in. His stated focus is on the individual's heart, hence the title of his book. Because of the image of Christ that he alludes to throughout this text as being one who comes into our lives and enacts transformation, we might categorize his system as a "Deity" spirituality. This would be one that is focused on nurturing a personal relationship with a God who is understood to have ontology (i.e., a being, will, intention, action, etc.) and is therefore primarily viewed as a separate Deity within and apart from creation. However,

PART SIX: Contemporary Movements

we also note that Willard's theology has strong incarnational aspects to it as well.

We can also note how, for each of the six aspects of the person, Willard addresses themes that are common in contemporary sciences, particularly the field of psychology: positive thinking, taking care of the body, listening to one's emotions, building healthy relationships, etc. As we shall increasingly see as we continue through this era, this contemporary author looks to some of the findings of the modern sciences as a partial basis for his systematic formulations. In contrast with some of the other contemporary systems, however, Willard's approach to building these systematic views is one of starting with the Christian tradition and looking to modern sciences for additional insights. In the sacred system that follows, particularly with Gerald May's and Yale's 3-S, the alternative approach is begin with the assertions of science and then look to religious/spiritual traditions for additional insights. Formators today must therefore be clear as to which location they more primarily identify with and how they will integrate insights from other worldviews and traditions in building their own sacred systems.

13

Personal Transformation at a Liberal Christian Seminary

Context

MOVING NOW FROM EVANGELICAL Protestant to a more liberal and pluralistic environment, we next turn to a predominantly Christian seminary. The Claremont School of Theology (CST), now a part of the interreligious Claremont Lincoln University, is located near Los Angeles, California. Being the seminary that I attended and graduated from, this chapter will focus on articulating how personal transformation is conceived according to course lectures as well as spiritual formation programs that were offered on campus from the beginning of the spring of 2008 until the end of the spring of 2009.[1] As an active participant in this program, this chapter is therefore a summary of what I experienced at CST from both educational and experiential perspectives. While each of the other sacred systems we have explored in this book have been literature-based research projects, this is more reminiscent—though not in a rigorous sense—of ethnographic methods. One of the hopes of this chapter is therefore to

---

1. The four classes were: Rogers, "RE 437—Advanced Seminar"; Dreitcer and Rogers, "RE 451—Personal and Relational Vitality"; Dreitcer, "IS 201—Spiritual Growth Group"; Dreitcer and Rogers, "RE 453—Compassionate Social Engagement." The dates refer to the days that the notes were recorded on and are of the format: Month/Day/Year. Please note, as with all ethnographic data, that these class notes are the ones that I have personally taken and are therefore at least partly imbued with personal interpretations. They might also include reflections that the class as a whole made collectively rather than being only those offered by the instructor.

demonstrate the need for more of these kinds of methodologies in the study of how spiritual formation is embodied in Christian communities around the globe.

As far as the context goes, there are a number of contextual factors that are necessary in order to more deeply understand this personal spiritual formation system. One is related to the contextually related factors that seem to influence the development and implementation of this sacred system. There seem to be two primary contextual factors that influence this system in this way. The first is modern psychology, particularly depth psychology. As we shall see, this system is heavily rooted in Jungian psychology[2] and other depth psychological frameworks such as Internal Family Systems, which has been pioneered in part by Richard Schwartz and furthered by Tom Holmes.[3] It also relies on Robert Kegan's *Evolving Self*[4] for its personal and relational dynamics theory.[5] Hence, modern psychological insights have played a major role for this system, something that will also be noted for Gerald May's framework in the forthcoming chapter.

A second contextual factor that seems to under gird this system is CST's interreligious community and commitment.[6] As it was asserted in one of the classes, it is asserted that one doesn't necessarily need to have a formal, traditional religion in order to have a spirituality; we only need to nurture a life in the Spirit.[7] Both of these contextual factors seem to influence not only what this system is comprised of, but also how this system is articulated and implemented. It could be asserted that modern psychology is a part of the internal structure of this system, while the interreligious commitment forms the living flesh that enables it to effectively touch the lives of its current participants. Both therefore seem essential to CST's personal transformation system in this context.

Another set of contextual factors to consider for this system and these reported observations, is for whom the system is being offered to, who its audience is. Clearly, much of the audience was interreligious, as was noted. The spiritual growth groups, however, were also observed to be predominantly female in make-up at the time, about 60 percent.[8] It

2. 2/29/08; 3/7/08; 10/9/08; 11/7/08; 11/14/08; 2/13/09.
3. Schwartz, *Internal Family Systems Therapy*; Holmes, *Parts Work*.
4. Kegan, *Evolving Self*.
5. 9/12/08.
6. Theology, "About CST—21st Century Theological Studies."
7. 2/22/08.
8. Personal Observation. This means that they are reflections and observations

was also noted, being at a theological institution, that the audience was primarily middle class and mostly Caucasian.[9] Such observations are important, because audience does influence what material is presented as well as how one goes about presenting it.

In addition to these, I think I should also note the location of the professors and directors of this spiritual program at the time: Frank Rogers Jr. and Andrew Dreitcer. Both are white Western males, coming from a distinctively Christian perspective in both personal practice (Catholic and Presbyterian, respectively) as well as in vocation (Religious Education and Spirituality, respectively), and both were educated at two prestigious universities (Princeton and GTU-Berkeley, respectively). It was also noted that Rogers' personal experiences as a sexually abused child, and his subsequent processes of healing, heavily influenced the development of this system, as well as its presentation. These are therefore some of the ethnographically-oriented contextual factors that seemed to play either a direct role in this system's development and implementation and/or as more of a seed bed for it.

This system is also an example of the views of and approaches to personal transformation from a more liberal, pluralistic Christian perspective. Most of the contemporary resources on spiritual formation are dominated by an Evangelical worldview, such as Willard's. There is therefore a need for personal transformation to be articulated more systematically from alternative Christian perspectives, namely: Mainline Protestant, Roman Catholic, and Eastern Orthodox perspectives. This chapter is therefore also an attempt to present such alternative perspectives.

Models of Reality

Anthropological-Cosmological

As was noted above, depth psychology had a major influence on the development of this sacred system. As a result, its anthro-cosmology is more primarily focused on the anthropological aspects than on the cosmological ones. As it relates to human nature, this system asserts that each and every single person is "radiant," that each of us is unique.[10] Referring to

---

that were made by me either at the time of the class notes being taken or as I look back and reflect while writing this book.

9. Personal observation.

10. 9/19/08.

PART SIX: Contemporary Movements

Merton's framework, this system asserts that humans have both a true and a false or distorted self. The true self is on that is grace, spiritual, holiness, Christ-centered, integration, of the Spirit, Whole. The distorted self, on the other hand, is one that is sinful, carnal, distorted, ego-centered, fragmented, of the flesh, dis-eased.[11] It is therefore the view of this system that while, at our core, we are good, we must also contend between two aspects of our self: one that is true, and one that is distorted.

This system then spends much time articulating the inner dynamics of such tensions. It discusses the inner turmoil and disorder that is within us all, the role of emotions and yearnings, the presence and functions of our "Shadow" side (the Jungian understanding of it), and the presence of God within each of us. Each of these characterizes the inner life of every person. As it relates to the inner turmoil and disorder that we all experience, there are two ways of being in the world: enveloped by one of our ego-states, or from our deeper center.[12] At the surface of our consciousness, there is lots of noise and distractions[13] and these can distract us from seeing the beauty of others.[14] Part of these surface level stirrings stem from internal response mechanisms of either a fight or flight response, which are often triggered by an external event.[15] Or they sometimes come from, referring to Schwartz's and Holmes' work, inner parts within us that fight and vie for our attention.[16]

As a result, we don't always experience our true selves,[17] and it is difficult to settle down into the wordless Presence of God because of these superficial thoughts. Instead, our temptations are to go along with these various distractions and distortions rather than to settle down into a deeper place.[18] Being radically inclusive is therefore tremendously difficult for us as is showing and sharing kindness with others; especially with those we have personal issues and struggles with.[19] This is because these distortions distract us from being more fully present and open to others. Nevertheless, as we can experience when praying for our enemies

11. 9/26/08.
12. 2/6/09.
13. 10/16/08; 11/20/08.
14. 10/24/08.
15. 2/29/08.
16. 10/9/08; 9/26/08; 2/6/09.
17. 9/19/08.
18. 2/15/08.
19. 3/28/08; 4/18/08; 10/24/08.

for example, there seem to be tensions between our longings for reconciliation and the resistances, bitterness, anger and other more superficial feelings toward them.[20] In other words, this system asserts, there is a deep center and source within us and we have to get below the surface stuff in order to really hear what our souls are saying.[21] This system therefore has an anthropology that articulates at least two aspects of the human person: a more superficial and surface level side, and a deeper, more centered and sacred Self.

In the inner descent to our deeper aspect, emotions and yearnings have a central role. Fundamentally, such inner stirrings are invitations to listen to what they are saying, for they can be invitations to greater life, harmony, etc., leading to greater hope and healing within ourselves and our world.[22] For instance, this system asserts that when we've hit our center and core, we just know it,[23] and when we get to the root of a problem or wound within us, we just somehow know it, it resonates deeply within us.[24] The primary claim, then, is that our deepest affective sense is our inner barometer of how things are going and where we should go next.[25]

In light of this, this system claims, we all long for the Spirit to breathe through all of our material lives,[26] and our deepest longing is to connect with God[27] as we all ache for better ways of living our lives.[28] We also all have twin yearnings for relationship both with ourselves as well as with others, for "we are wired for relationships."[29] These twin longings, however, are often in tension with one another within us.[30] We can therefore see that this system holds inner affective yearnings and stirrings to be a central part of the human person and their relationship with ourselves, others, and the Divine.

However, one's inner world below the surface is not always a place of centeredness and sacredness. This system upholds the Internal Family

20. 4/25/08.
21. 3/27/09.
22. 2/29/08; 9/12/08.
23. 2/15/08.
24. 11/7/08; PO.
25. 11/21/08.
26. 2/1/08.
27. 9/19/08.
28. 10/31/08; 1/23/09.
29. 10/31/08.
30. 9/12/08.

Systems theories of Schwartz and Holmes, which asserts that there are multiple parts and personalities ever vying for attention and aching for their needs to be addressed.[31] While each of these parts are good in their essence, and we do have a centered Self of compassion, calm, clarity, confidence, courage, connection, and creativity,[32] some of these parts can also be misguided and distorted, even exiled by other parts. In Jungian terms, the exiled parts would be collectively referred to as the "Shadow," and this Shadow plays a central part of this system's anthropology.

The Shadow is basically the sum of our "Prodigal Son" parts[33] that have been repressed and pushed down within us. We must note that not all of our Shadow is negative, or "Dark," for some parts of its parts are positive aspects that we have ignored or repressed such as longings, yearnings, special gifts, and passions and these are collectively referred to as our "Golden Shadow" in this system.[34] One of the core dynamics in this anthropology, then, is that when we repress parts of our self, they can begin to take on a life and almost demonic-like force of their own, and impact how we view and engage life, such as when we project things onto others.[35] In this system, projecting is basically a psychological dynamic of throwing parts of our inner world, like our Shadow, out onto the world like a mirror.[36] From this perspective, then, our "enemies" can therefore be gifts in that they can help us to see which parts of ourselves we are repressing.[37] This Shadow is therefore one of the major reasons that we are unable to access our deeper selves, and this system therefore seeks to work directly with our Shadow as a major part of its approaches as we shall see below.

Despite our Shadow side, as was noted above, there is also a deeper and more centered place within us to which we are all called; a place where God dwells within our souls. This system therefore has, what it refers to as, a "spiritual anthropology."[38] This is because it asserts that we have a "deep interior" where God dwells, and this place is our "true self."[39] There is something about us that makes a relationship with God directly possible

31. 2/6/09.
32. 2/13/09.
33. 10/10/08.
34. 3/7/08.
35. 3/7/08; 10/17/08; 10/31/08; 11/7/08.
36. 3/7/08.
37. 4/18/08; 4/25/08.
38. 2/15/08.
39. 9/19/08.

and it is available to everyone.[40] Citing the well-known German mystic Meister Eckhart, this system claims that "God is closer to us than our own heartbeat/breath."[41] Every person is therefore "spiritual," though some are more in touch with the Ultimate than others.[42] We must therefore all come to see that God is in all people, even our enemies,[43] and that we're all already held in deep grace and compassion.[44] Ultimately, it is asserted, there are no distinctions between us and God for we are co-creators;[45] we are both created and creative.[46]

Relating this to our affective states, God is understood to lead us through our emotions[47] and it is noted that some mystics have asserted that emotions are avenues to the Sacred.[48] Self-transcendence is therefore conceived of as transcending our animal desires for survival as well as our ego tendencies[49] in order to descend to a place where we can hear the whispers of God within us and can come to live in harmony with the Spirit that is deep within,[50] not unlike the Quaker system we explored previously. God's Presence therefore has a profound effect on us for God nurtures life and love and ever calls us into ordered and harmonious living through our souls.[51] This system's anthropology is one that therefore sees God as being a central and active part of the various inner dynamics that comprise part of the lived experience of humanity.

With this extensive anthropology in place, this system also discusses two cosmological aspects. The first is related to the role and effect of the world on people. Fundamentally, this system holds that we live in a world of brokenness.[52] It is asserted to be one that is very dualistic and

---

40. 2/15/08; 3/7/08; 9/19/08.
41. 2/15/08, 10/16/08.
42. 2/1/08.
43. 4/18/08.
44. 3/7/08; 1/30/09.
45. 3/14/08.
46. 4/4/08.
47. 5/2/08.
48. 2/29/08.
49. 2/1/08.
50. 1/25/08.
51. 2/8/08; 2/29/08; 11/21/08.
52. 4/18/08.

PART SIX: Contemporary Movements

dichotomized,[53] with a great deal of violence and hatred.[54] It is noted, for instance, that many social justice movements have too much violence in them,[55] and that even religious/spiritual communities have a Shadow side to them that must be transformed.[56] As a result, the world is often experienced by people as being "disconnected" and apart from the Sacred that is the ultimate Source of all of creation.[57]

As an example of one of the influences of this broken world, it is observed by this system that many of us have been taught that our emotions are sinful and that we need to repress, project, and/or act-out on them rather than to listen to the Sacred invitations that lie deep within them.[58] Such teachings can therefore lead us to experience self-loathing, among many other things.[59] Our world is also viewed as squashing creativity[60] and its understandings of such concepts as peace, love, forgiveness, etc., are very superficial and repressive of our own inner feelings.[61] This system therefore views the world as contributing to a life of continued superficiality and thereby avoids connecting to the deeper Source that is within us all.

A second cosmological factor that this system addresses is the notion of sin. Unlike some of the other frameworks we have considered in this project, such as with the Desert Monks (Cassian's *Conferences* and the *Philokalia*), that views sin as a substantive reality to be guarded and battled against, this system views sin as a distortion of reality. Sin is viewed essentially as that which is disharmonious and out of attunement with the sacred Source.[62] As we shall see below when we discuss the theology of this system, the ground of creation is considered to be fundamentally good,[63] and sin is therefore viewed as being a deviation from this inherent goodness. As it relates to humans, this system likewise declares the goodness

---

53. 2/13/09.
54. 1/23/09.
55. 4/18/08.
56. 5/2/08.
57. 3/7/08.
58. 2/29/08.
59. 2/29/08; 3/14/08.
60. 3/28/08.
61. 4/4/08.
62. 2/29/08.
63. 3/7/08.

of every person,[64] for our creative abilities directly contradicts the claim that humans are inherently sinful.[65] Personal sin is therefore asserted to manifest when our emotions are off-center,[66] or when some of our parts are not being heard and they begin to get out of control in an effort to gain our attention.[67] Destructive desires are therefore honest desires that have gotten way out of control, and have been distorted because of the wounds and pains that we have suffered.[68] Hence, there is no evil so deep that it cannot be held and transformed,[69] for "God holds everything."[70] Sin is therefore seen as being the result of some part of our lives, or creation, that has been distorted and is "off-center" from its more fundamental and sacred Source.

This is the anthro-cosmology that this system seems to centrally hold. It is one that more primarily focused on the intrapersonal and inner dynamics of the human person. Drawing primarily from depth psychology, this system underscores the inner Shadow and affective movements of a person's life in the midst of a broken world. As we shall see below, much of this system's personal transformation approaches are directed toward addressing these complex inner dynamics. Also, since sin is viewed as being nothing more than a distortion of the truer and deeper realities of life, there is no place in creation, or within ourselves, that cannot be redeemed by the Sacred. It is to this system's views of the Sacred that we will next turn to.

Theological

As was already noted, the fundamental ground of creation is grace, love, and compassion[71] for God holds everything.[72] As a result, everything can be seen as an invitation from God[73] for God is in everything[74] and

64. 9/26/08.
65. 4/4/08.
66. 2/29/08.
67. 2/6/09.
68. 2/13/09.
69. 2/13/09.
70. 10/17/08.
71. 3/7/08.
72. 10/17/08.
73. 3/14/08; 9/12/08; 10/16/08.
74. 9/4/08.

therefore comes in many different forms.[75] For instance, it is asserted, God manifests God's self through our imagination,[76] talks to us through our emotions,[77] and is in everything that stirs within us.[78] We can therefore look into creation and see the presence and movements of a "Spirit"; one that dances and plays music at the heart of creation and ever invites us to live in rhythm and harmony with it.[79] This Spirit is an indescribable element,[80] an energy,[81] and a creative power[82] that can be experienced as a "Presence" that we feel, but it can also be experienced as an absence in the silences of life too.[83]

But if God is so everywhere present and active, we can ask, how can we know its truer movements from the more distorting ones of the world? One of the fundamental theological assumptions of this system is that God is immanent and wants to be known[84] and that God has passion and is moved by creation.[85] As a result, the Sacred is viewed as not being neutral, but rather it is experienced as compassion, grace, etc., as has already been asserted.[86] For example, "grace" is defined as being when we hold a painful and/or distorted part of us and feel a Sacred Presence come into it.[87] God's presence is therefore one that brings new life and vitality,[88] it is about nurturing and sustaining the fullness of life,[89] and it brings wisdom and healing to the distorted parts of our lives and world when we open up to it.[90] God is therefore conceived of as having a disposition and will for

75. 11/14/08.
76. 11/6/08.
77. 5/2/08.
78. 10/17/08, 12/11/08.
79. 1/25/08; 2/29/08; 4/25/08; 9/4/08.
80. 1/25/08.
81. 11/14/08.
82. 12/5/08.
83. 2/1/08.
84. 2/8/08.
85. 2/8/08.
86. 2/8/08.
87. 10/17/08.
88. 2/8/08.
89. 2/8/08.
90. 9/25/08.

creation for God is "Pregnant with Compassion,"[91] loving everyone,[92] and working for the redemption of all of creation.

In order to help further know the essence and stirrings of God in creation, this system asserts that there are three fundamental movements of the Spirit: a contemplative movement; a creative one; and a socially engaged one.[93] Each of these movements is intended to capture a different aspect of the nature of God in the world and this system's spiritual formation approaches are primarily organized around them. The contemplative movement of the Spirit, this system asserts, is one that is primarily concerned with inwardly connecting with the Source; it is a grounding movement, a deepening and centering one.[94] It therefore seeks to ground and root us in the compassionate presence of God,[95] centering us in real experience[96] so that we might take "a long loving look at the real."[97] This movement of God in creation is therefore a deepening and inwardly downward movement.[98]

The creative movement is one that is primarily focused on personal and relational vitality.[99] It is one of emboldening, empowering, lifting us, making us whole and vital and full of power and is therefore more of an upward movement.[100] This movement of God seeks to nurtures us to the fullness of life,[101] exalting us into the glory of what it is to be alive.[102] Such fullness and exaltation happens for us individually, addressing our personal power, gifts, holiness, vocation, etc.,[103] as well as relationally, where we are seen, heard, felt, and delighted in by one another.[104] This creative movement of the Spirit is therefore one of empowerment and lifting us all upwards.

91. 2/8/08.
92. 11/7/08.
93. 1/25/08; 2/8/08; 9/4/08; 1/30/09.
94. 1/25/08; 10/16/08; 1/30/09.
95. 2/8/08; 3/7/08; 9/4/08.
96. 2/8/08.
97. 10/16/08.
98. 2/8/08.
99. 3/14/08; 9/4/08; 9/12/08.
100. 1/25/08; 3/7/08; 3/14/08; 1/30/09.
101. 2/8/08; 9/4/08.
102. 2/8/08; 3/14/08.
103. 3/14/08.
104. 3/28/08; 10/24/08.

Finally, the socially engaged movement of God is one that invites us to become agents of healing and transformation in the world, going out into the world in love.[105] This movement stirs us to be moved by the suffering of the world[106] because we live in a world of brokenness and this is asserted to be the way of Jesus; one of bringing God's compassion to the world.[107] This socially engaged movement of the Spirit is therefore one that calls us outwards into the world.

Overall, each movement feeds and nourishes one another[108] and they comprise a rhythm of the spiritual life, not unlike a heartbeat.[109] It is through these three different movements of the Divine that we can not only come to recognize God's presence in creation, but we can also be nurtured in them via our spiritual forming personal and social lives. These three movements can therefore be used as a basis for a spiritual formation program, which is exactly what this system seeks to do.

Theories of Change

Regarding transformation, this system asserts that it takes years of cultivating an attention to one's emotional life in order to get to a place where it becomes a more natural part of our daily lives.[110] It is, therefore, a life-long pathway of change.[111] This is because this work is very difficult work,[112] and such change comes via only baby steps.[113] Articulating a specific theory of change for emotions, this system asserts that it is by working with embedded emotional patterns that we are either born with or adopted from our care-givers, that we can change how we react to our emotions and thereby begin to change the shape and actions of these inner dynamics.[114] As an example of this kind of emotional unfolding, it is noted that the process of forgiveness comes only via a process that has its own life and unfolding.[115]

105. 1/25/08; 9/4/08; 1/23/09; 1/30/09.
106. 2/8/08.
107. 4/18/08.
108. 2/8/08.
109. 2/8/08; 1/30/09.
110. 2/29/08.
111. 4/25/08; 11/14/08.
112. 4/18/08; 11/14/08.
113. 10/31/08.
114. 10/31/08.
115. 3/6/09. The following resource was noted by the instructors as being

Overall, then, the primary theory of change seems to be one where transformation comes via its own pathways and unfolding, one that is led by the Spirit. While such change requires our intentional and long-term attention to it, it has a life of its own. Ours, then, is to simply be present to this unfolding life of the Spirit as it leads us and utterly alters the directions, reactions, and course of our entire life. It seems, then, that the inner affective side (the inner True Self) of the person is so central to this system's anthropology because it is the compass by which one is to live and change their life; a compass that must be trusted and followed with non-judgmental compassion, for it is the truer Source of God's Life within us.

SPIRITUAL FORMATION IDEALS & GOALS

"Spiritual formation" is defined in this system as being formed by the Spirit, or letting the Spirit form us in our lives, toward healing, reconciliation, etc.[116] It is concerned with an internal experience of the Ultimate, a deep immediate knowing of God, a personal experience rather than just simply knowing about God.[117] Knowing that this Spirit is embodied in the world—for spiritual and material are seen as distinct but intimately intertwined as Spirit breathes thru the material and therefore every aspect of our lives—there can therefore be, this system asserts, a "spirituality" of almost anything such as eating, working, parenting, etc.[118] While we don't necessarily need to have a formal, traditional religion in order to have a spirituality, it is claimed, we do need to intentionally nurture a life in the Spirit.[119] One of the primary aims of this system, then, is to help people to come to be formed in such a spiritual life; a life with the Spirit.

But what does such a life look like more tangibly? What are some of its more salient characteristics that we are to be working toward? Drawing primarily on the asserted characteristics of the Kin-dom of God [120] (but also on the characteristics of a "Spirituality"[121] and the characteristics of the Contemplative Life[122]), there are at least six ideals that this system up-

---

foundational for this claim: Linn et al., *Don't Forgive Too Soon*.

116. 2/1/08; 1/23/09.
117. 2/1/08; 11/7/08.
118. 2/1/08.
119. 2/22/08.
120. 1/30/09.
121. 2/1/08.
122. 2/22/08.

holds. First, we are to seek to be radically inclusive. We must always grow in the direction of love, for every religious tradition holds this as central and we are to be embodiments and agents of love in everything that we are and do.[123] This therefore means that we live life in non-judgmental, flexible, and unattached ways.[124] Next, we are to be embody radical reconciliation where we are called to love everyone, including our enemies.[125] One of the goals here is to bring all the various elements of our lives together around a center.[126] Thirdly, we should work to have lives that are radically flourishing. We should be concerned with vitality and the life that is ever breathing through our experiences,[127] waking up to the compassion we're already held within[128] in ever expanding ways.[129] We are to then work toward radical mutuality and equality where there is inner harmony, peace, etc.,[130] as we nurture the compassionate loving Presence between and within us.[131] Closely related to this is the radical social bond that we have amongst us all. Finally, we are to nurture a radical hope, which is one is one of a deep sense of joyful peace.[132] Taken collectively, these six "radical" ideals that this system seeks to work toward.

In addition to these, this system highlights again and again the need for one to be compassionately non-judgmental in their stance toward all of life. Seeming to stem directly from their theology of immanence and the view that sin is merely a distortion of the truer nature of reality, it is about being contemplatively present to each moment and continually deepening our capacity for the Real, Genuine, and Ultimate Life that is within life itself.[133] It is primarily about being where we currently are, where we are, and journeying with the Spirit who leads us.[134] Such compassionate dispositions are not just toward life, however, but also toward ourselves. Quoting Jack Kornfield, it is asserted that "the most important thing in the

123. 2/1/08.
124. 2/22/08.
125. 11/7/08.
126. 10/9/08.
127. 2/1/08.
128. 1/30/09.
129. 2/22/08.
130. 10/9/08.
131. 2/22/08.
132. 2/22/08.
133. 2/29/08; 12/11/08.
134. 3/7/08; 4/25/08.

spiritual life is to learn to love ourselves, in fact, it may be the only thing."[135] We must therefore hold ourselves as well as others with nonjudgmental compassion,[136] including our enemies;[137] i.e., to love as God loves.[138] As it relates to our inner affective lives, which are so central to this system, we need to practice being nonjudgmental toward our own emotions and inner movements, as well as the defenses that arise with them.[139] Instead of judging our inner parts, we should contemplatively explore what they are, what is underneath them, until we find the God within them; i.e., we need to "Pray it to the Source."[140] Ultimately, this system claims, we need to trust our own souls and whatever it wants to bring up in each moment of our life, for the soul is God's life within us.[141] Such nonjudgmental compassion is therefore a central ideal that this system seeks to work toward in addition to the radical ideals discussed above for one's growing life in the Spirit.

Spiritual Formation Approaches

As it relates to the approaches by which such personal transformations are to happen, this system fundamentally embraces a praxis oriented approach: to participate in it, learning about it, practicing it, and then reflecting on it.[142] With the two fundamental starting points for spirituality being intention and longing,[143] such motivations are to lead one to engaging in a set of spiritual practices. These practices stir the Spirit, or open us up to its movements, energies, et cetera and they help us to ever be more attentive to its invitations.[144] They also cultivate a way of life[145] and can help us to ultimately settle down into the wordless Presence of God.[146] In an effort to nurture such a praxis life in the Spirit, this system divides its

135. 3/7/08.
136. 3/7/08; 4/18/08.
137. 11/7/08.
138. 4/18/08.
139. 3/7/08.
140. 2/29/08; 4/25/08; 10/17/08; 2/13/09.
141. 10/16/08; 11/13/08; 11/20/08.
142. 1/25/08; 2/1/08; 2/8/08.
143. 4/11/08.
144. 2/1/08.
145. 2/1/08; 10/30/08.
146. 2/15/08.

PART SIX: Contemporary Movements

spiritual approaches according to the three movements described above: Contemplative, Creative, and Socially Engaged.[147]

Regarding the Contemplative Path, these approaches emphasize being present to what comes, without judgment.[148] It is asserted that everyone needs to take time for these practices,[149] and they can take many forms as some emphasize the interior life, others the exterior; some the kataphatic, others the apophatic, etc.[150] In general, they should take us out of the everydayness, put us in touch with our center, focus our attention on what really is with compassion, and help bring us to a wordless communion.[151] The practices that are recommended for this path in this program are the following:

- Beholding, Praying Contemplatively with another person[152]
- Centering Prayer [153]
- Compassion Practice, or Praying With Your Emotions[154]
- Prayer for an Enemy[155]
- Focusing/Body Prayer[156]
- Ignatian Contemplation[157]
- Jungian Active Imagination[158]
- Labyrinth[159]
- Lectio Divina[160]

147. 4/25/08.
148. 2/22/08; 11/20/08; 12/4/08.
149. 1/25/08.
150. 2/29/08.
151. 2/1/08; 2/13/09; 2/22/08; 3/7/08; 4/4/08; 4/18/08; 9/1/08; 9/4/08; 10/16/08; 10/24/08.
152. 3/14/08; 10/24/08; 3/27/09.
153. 2/15/08.
154. 2/29/08; 4/18/08; 9/4/08; 9/25/08; 10/16/08; 10/17/08; 11/13/08; 11/14/08; 12/4/08.
155. 4/18/08; 4/25/08; 11/7/08; 11/14/08; 11/20/08; 11/21/08; 3/6/09.
156. 9/1/08.
157. 10/30/08.
158. 11/6/08.
159. 4/11/08.
160. 2/1/08.

- Parts Work Prayer[161]
- Praying with our Shadow[162]
- Praying with a Sacred Moment[163]
- Welcoming Prayer[164]

For the Creative Path, imagination is a key to this way.[165] Its core convictions are: The glory of God, referencing Irenaeus, is humanity fully alive; How we flourish is utterly unique to each person; God aches for us to flourish in every part of our lives; and God is everywhere.[166] As a result, this path seeks to intentionally nurture a "Spirituality of Vocation," in which one's gifts and passions, one's deepest self, is shared in service to the world.[167] However, it is also known that every relationship can stir things up, so this path is also about doing both the intra-soul work within ourselves as well as cultivating compassion for other people.[168] Ultimately, then, this path of personal and relational vitality is about loving ourselves and others and it forms the basis for the third and final movement, which is sharing our Source of love with others in tangible ways.[169] Some of the practices for this path, in addition to many of the contemplative ones listed above, include:

- Doing an unconditional loving act toward someone[170]
- Through art: using it to explore the experience of lovingly contemplating ourselves through it[171]
- Reflecting on and doing the compassion practice with many of the different things that we've done in our lives that have given us great joy, like when we contributed to the common good, or of things that we have longed to do. Given all of this, we can then ask: What was so right about them? Why am I so energized by these? What might all

161. 9/26/08; 10/9/08; 10/10/08; 2/6/09.
162. 3/7/08; 10/31/08; 11/7/08.
163. 1/30/09.
164. 2/22/08.
165. 4/4/08.
166. 9/4/08; 10/31/08; 12/5/08.
167. 11/21/08; 12/5/08.
168. 11/14/08.
169. 4/4/08.
170. 3/28/08.
171. 4/4/08.

PART SIX: Contemporary Movements

of this say about my vocation? The goal here is vocational exploration and expression.[172]

Finally, the Socially Engaged Path is one that seeks to intentionally bring peace with justice through nonviolent means.[173] While they are often considered as separate dimensions of life, this system asserts that personal spirituality and social justice work go hand-in-hand; that we need both movements together.[174] The task of this path, then, is to learn how to live in the midst of evil without becoming evil ourselves or without being stepped on and dominated by it, but rather working with the Spirit to transform it.[175] The true measure of nonviolence is therefore taken to be the love with which we hold our enemies.[176] In other words, between utter passivity and total violence, referencing the work of Walter Wink, there is a "Third Way" of nonviolence.[177] Such nonviolent living is therefore the way of life that this final movement embodies and we are to seek to do so in four spheres of our life: self, relationships, community, and world.[178] In addition to the practices already mentioned, this path additionally utilizes the following practices:

- Who is someone who has embodied living in the world in a radical way? Reflect on their lives and the meaningfulness of it for our own[179]
- Simple acts of kindness can cultivate a sacredness in our daily lives through and through, therefore regularly do these simple acts[180]
- Nonviolent Communication = Center self, Articulate your true self, Receive the truth of the other person, Agree on a common ground[181]
- Discerning, planning, and engaging in a concrete nonviolent action in one's life[182]

---

172. 11/21/08.
173. 4/18/08; 1/23/09.
174. 4/18/08; 1/23/09.
175. 4/18/08.
176. 2/13/09.
177. 4/25/08; 3/6/09; 3/27/09.
178. 1/23/09.
179. 1/23/09.
180. 3/28/08.
181. 3/27/09.
182. Spring 2009.

In addition to these numerous approaches, there are three other spiritual formation approaches that this system utilizes in the quest to help its participants to grow in their life of the Spirit. The first is through the use of community. Each semester, we met in small groups where we were encouraged to share our experiential engagements with each of these three paths.[183] In addition, this system teaches that communities are invited to be places of Spirit, where healing and wholeness is nurtured, often via enculturation.[184] The role of leaders is basically to help such communities to follow God's movements in their midst and thereby enable the group as a whole to continue on in their growing life in God.[185] We must also remember and seek out mentors to lead and guide us through our ever changing spiritual lives.[186] Community is therefore another central spiritual formation approach of this system.

Another important approach is the use of journaling and reflection practices.[187] Each week, participants were led through contemplative practices. At the end of many of these experiences, they were then encouraged to journal the results of their experiences.[188] Such journaling is intended to help nurture the practice of reflecting on our personal spiritual life and all that the Divine is doing with it.[189] Hence, journaling is still another important approach.

Last, participants in this program were encouraged to craft a "Rule," in the tradition of monastic Rules such as Benedict of Nursia or Augustine of Hippo, for their lives.[190] The goal of this Rule is to create invitations of practice and intentional structure that are meant to meet the deepest yearnings of our lives and to foster life and vitality in the Spirit.[191] They are "patterns or structures that help us to be present with what currently is in our lives"; they are therefore intended to nurture the Spirit in our lives.[192] Following the questions that were provided, participants created a Rule that was intended to center them, help them to access their gifts,

183. 1/25/08; 9/4/08; PO.
184. 5/2/08.
185. 5/9/08.
186. 1/23/09.
187. 1/25/08; 2/1/08; 4/11/08; 5/9/08.
188. PO.
189. 2/1/08.
190. 4/25/08.
191. 4/25/08; 5/2/08.
192. 5/2/08.

PART SIX: Contemporary Movements

connect and harmonize them with others, and compassionately engage in the world.[193] We were then invited to live by this Rule and reflect on how it went. Crafting a Rule was therefore another central approach of this system.

These, then, are the primary spiritual practices that this sacred system utilizes to nurture the spiritually forming lives of its participants. Following the theological paradigm of the three movements of the Spirit, these approaches are categorized according to the contemplative, creative, and socially engaged paths of personal and relational transformation. Seen as necessary rhythms of one's life,[194] participants are to seek to nurture each one of these three movements via the many practices that are available. By doing so over the long-term, change will inevitably come as the deeper well-spring of Life within is ever more fully uncovered and subsequently becomes the dominant guide in one's life. With community for support, journaling to help with reflections, and a Rule to follow, this system asserts that such a life in the Spirit lies compassionately and non-judgmentally within all of creation.

DISCERNMENT

As it relates to questions of how do we know if we are really experienced the Spirit, this system asserts that we know it based on at least five reasons: There is a "knowingness" to it; it proves itself to eventually be true (i.e., things eventually happen); based upon community affirmation and discernment; it is empowering and fulfilling; it is faith and hope building; and there is a Silence, Stillness, Presence, Groundedness, and Realness to it.[195] In addition to these claims, regarding the presence of God in our emotions, this system asserts that we must discern the disharmoniousness of any situation and our reactions/emotions to them in their contexts, and we must pray with them to discern their deeper Source.[196] In other words, we must ever be aware of the movements that lead us to the Source as well as what blocks us from it.[197]

Discernment for this system, then, seems to largely be a matter of our learning from our own attentiveness, as well as the attentiveness of

193. 4/25/08.
194. 2/8/08; 1/30/09.
195. 2/8/08; 4/25/08.
196. 2/29/08.
197. 4/4/08.

others, to the spiritual journey.[198] By reflecting on what is stirring with us, and the effects that it is having on our lives, we can come to know what the movements of God in our own life are. In a sense, such a discernment process is sort of a "praxis" approach to discernment: We learn what the movements of God might look like; We then look for these movements in our own lives; Next, we go and act upon these discerned movements; and Finally, we reflect on what happened as a result. Through this iterative process, we can come to personally and experientially know what the Spirit's Life in our own lives is.

However, as it was noted, such discernment is not solely a solitary task, for mentors and our community can also provide continual and necessary feedback. I also noted for this system, not surprisingly given all that we have seen thus far, that an emphasis is given on the affective movements of one's inner life, as this "inner barometer" is to be a central basis for how harmonious or disharmonious any movement or action seems to be to us. This praxis approach, with its affective emphasis, therefore seems to be the primary approach to discernment that this system upholds, one that will lead to an ever growing life in the Spirit through our praxis-based engagement with it.

Evaluative Techniques

The primary technique that one has at their disposal in this system for evaluation is personal reflection on the status of their affective inner life; i.e., their soul. As was noted above, one is to also turn to one's community for feedback. One can also look to the mentors, Sacred texts, and religious/spiritual education that one receives for guidance in what their personal spiritual life might look like and how it is going and might next proceed. The three movements and paths of the Spirit are yet another central evaluative technique, for one can use these to assess how holistically and to what extent they are engaging their spiritual formation and how it is or is not progressing. These are the primary evaluative techniques that I see operative in this system.

---

198. 4/25/08.

PART SIX: Contemporary Movements

Summary/Reflections

Overall, this system seems to be one that is almost entirely focused around the anthropological model that it embraces, though with a likewise heavy emphasis on an incarnational theology. It is one that sees life, both inner and outer, as having at least two levels of reality: a more surface and superficial level; and one that is more deeply rooted in the Center and Source of creation. Personal transformation, then, is a matter of compassionately and nonjudgmentally engaging with all that is so that this inner Life within life can be accessed and manifested. The Contemplative Path is about such an inner deepening life, the Creative Movement seems to be about uncovering this vital life with both ourselves and with others, and the Socially Engaged Path is about our working to get beyond the distorted superficialities of our broken world so that this deep well-spring can emerge across our globe. All three movements therefore seem to be focused on accessing this deeper and more centered Life within life.

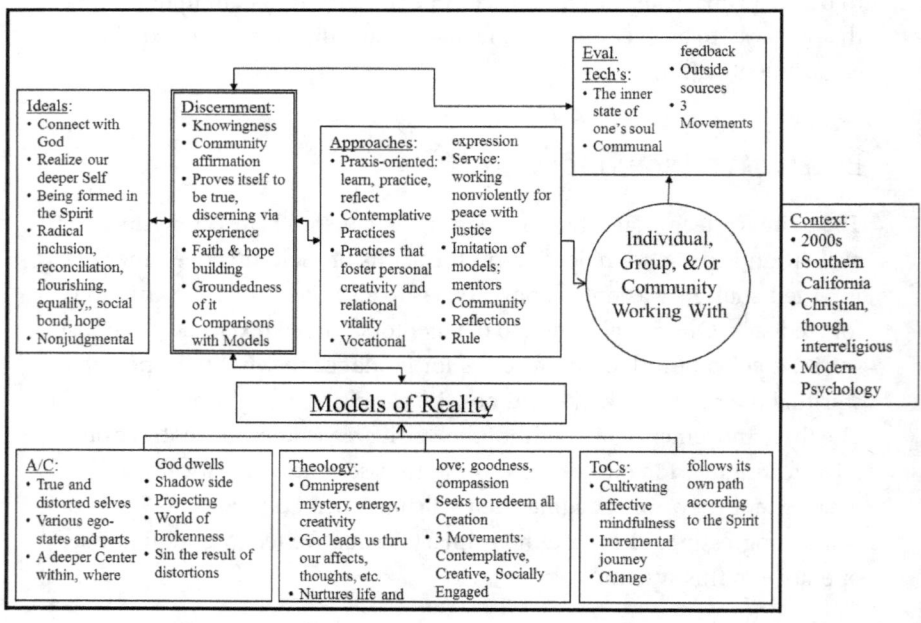

We can also note the extensive intrapersonal emphasis that this system has, specifically as it relates to the affective life of the individual. All three movements are seen as expressions of this inner life of emotions, pain, Shadows, yearnings, etc. These three movements themselves are even described in terms of feeling-concepts: Downwards/Deepening, Upwards/Lifting, and Outwards/Expanding. Discernment too, it was noted, seems to also have its core roots in the harmonious or disharmonious stirrings of one's soul. As this system therefore seeks to primarily focus on this aspect of the human person, we might therefore categorize it as an intrapersonal-affective spiritual formation system. Again, its theology is profoundly immanent, rivaling the Quaker system in terms of its emphasis on the presence of God within each person. Nevertheless, this system is nevertheless, as with each of the systems we have explored, extremely well-rounded and holistic in terms of the lifestyle that it seeks to cultivate. Finally, as we continue with our contemporary explorations, we again note the integration of modern scientific models, in this case depth psychology, into the Models of Reality of this sacred system. In our next chapter, we will find this be increasingly the case as we consider the Contemplative Psychology of psychiatrist Gerald May.

14

Gerald May's Willing Spirit

Context

MAY'S BOOK IS CONTEXTUALLY located in the U.S. secular, science-based, society of the late 1970s, early 1980s. In Chapter 1, he expends some time addressing this context as it relates to his own field of psychology. He seeks to ultimately topple the contemporary views of the time that science can know and control the human psyche.[1] He then spends some time reviewing contemporary psychological approaches and points out their inherent limitations. Ultimately, May concludes that "psychology, by its nature, is simply not big enough to include or even adequately address our deepest spiritual longings."[2]

While May stands in opposition to psychology as a cure-all for all people and longings, he does (as will be discussed below) utilize many of the findings and mappings of psychology. As May claims, he is seeking to integrate psychology and religion, "science and mystery."[3] Finally, May's purported audience is the field of psychology, but also for lay-persons, Christian and non-Christian, both in the English speaking world and beyond.[4] It is from this context that May sets out to develop his contemplative psychology for contemporary readers.

---

1. May, *Will & Spirit*, 7.
2. Ibid., 21.
3. Ibid., 10.
4. Ibid., vii–viii.

Models of Reality

Anthropological-Cosmological

May discusses these aspects at length throughout his book. Focusing on psychodynamics, his reflections center more on the anthropological side, but cosmology is there to some degree as well. As discussed above, May asserts that mystery is an inherent part of reality.[5] May highlights Eastern notions that the universe is fundamentally composed of energy.[6] For May, all of creation is therefore unified as One in this energy.[7] However, the dualistic mind of humans divides this unity up into conceptions of good and evil, light and dark, etc.[8] Human will is therefore, according to May, an inherent part of our existence.[9] From self-will comes true sin,[10] though May asserts that evil in creation is really nothing special,[11] and self-images are a key to understanding humans.[12]

May also provides complex models of intrapersonal, specifically psychological, dynamics. He differentiates between mind and consciousness, attention and awareness, and discusses three different personality styles.[13] He discusses some of the deep longings and needs of humans such as the need for something deeper,[14] for acceptance,[15] love,[16] and to just be.[17] For May, however, the ultimate longing is to forget ourselves and surrendering to something greater.[18] Fulfilling these needs, May claims, is not easy because of the many and various repression mechanisms that we have as well as our fears of self-sacrifice.[19] But May asserts that it is love, three different

---

5. Ibid., 29–30, 306, 309, 11, 14.
6. Ibid., 174.
7. Ibid., 249.
8. Ibid., 67–68, 249, 52, 61.
9. Ibid., 35–37.
10. Ibid., 233, 58, 66.
11. Ibid., 247.
12. Ibid., 100, 230.
13. Ibid., 39, 46, 75–76.
14. Ibid., 70.
15. Ibid., 73, 83–85.
16. Ibid., 85.
17. Ibid., 87.
18. Ibid., 1, 89.
19. Ibid., 93, 103, 107, 12, 14, 64.

kinds of love,[20] that overcome these fears and repressions as we work with our emotions and they unfold through the various stages that he defines.[21] It is these detailed anthropological-cosmological dynamics, which focus mostly on intrapersonal aspects, that May bases his approaches to personal transformation on.

Theological

Though he is partially writing to his own secular field of psychology, May's framework makes his theology quite explicit. From the outset, and throughout the book, he proposes a concept of Spirit as an active energy that is the underlying dynamic life force which continually works to connect all of creation into the unity he asserted in his anthro-cosmo model.[22] Just as May's view of creation is couched primarily in terms of energy as the basis of reality, so too are his views of the Divine and its relationship to creation. May goes on to assert that there are two ways to interact with this deeper level of reality: willingly and willfully.[23] Favoring the contemplative way of surrender and willingness, he claims that the only way to the realization of Divine love is by going beyond the confines of what the human will can achieve on its own.[24] Such an achievement is, for May, a solitary journey that becomes increasingly difficult as we go.[25]

Theories of Change

Having an energy-based view of creation as well as God, May's theories of change are therefore centered on working with and transforming the energies of one's life. Offering a detailed view of how energies originate and take shape within us,[26] he asserts that much of the personal spiritual life involves working with, transmuting, and more effectively differentiating these energies.[27] May asserts that ultimately we cannot willfully control

20. Ibid., 130.
21. Ibid., 135, 79–80, 201, 25, 33.
22. Ibid., 3, 32, 172, 74, 204, 209, 309, 19.
23. Ibid., 5–6.
24. Ibid., 168, 71, 209, 42, 67, 75, 88, 317.
25. Ibid., 299, 319.
26. Ibid., 179–80.
27. Ibid., 185, 97, 202, 204, 205.

these energies, only to be present to them.[28] While self-perpetuating cycles are difficult to change, May states that it is by willingly opening ourselves up to God's immanent influences, that change finally comes about.[29] His core theory of change is therefore primarily concerned with one becoming aware of these various energies, of which the Spirit is the Source, and willingly working with them as they eventually move one toward the unity that is the fundamental nature of reality and the primary goal of May's approach to spiritual formation as we shall next see.

Spiritual Formation Ideals & Goals

In May's book, he sets up wholeness, and the balancing of willfulness and willingness, as a central goals in the spiritual life.[30] He claims that each person is to work for connection and unity, and we must always seek ways of life that are open and alert to the realities of God in life.[31] Such dispositions, which are accompanied by surrender and willingness,[32] should also lead one in selfless service to others.[33]

It is also what he terms, the "unitive experience," that May sets as the center of his framework for this book. So central is this concept that he dedicates an entire chapter to describing some of the dynamics of this experience. Unitive experiences, for May, are a way of living willingly and have various unique characteristics about them. For instance, May emphasizes the importance of a loss of self-definition in them and in life.[34] Such experiences also have a quality of individuals being at one with creation, where focused attention is lost as a sense of timelessness sets in.[35] In such moments, people have an assurance of the existence of the Divine, and feel at home in creation.[36] Finally, May asserts that such unitive experiences have qualities of integrativeness and creativity about them, and they foster an experience of Divine love as well as a sense of wonder and awe.[37]

28. Ibid., 212, 13.
29. Ibid., 77, 194.
30. Ibid., vi.
31. Ibid., 3, 219, 60, 317.
32. Ibid., 319.
33. Ibid., 298.
34. Ibid., 53, 60, 92, 97, 105.
35. Ibid., 59, 61, 69.
36. Ibid., 69, 91.
37. Ibid., 62, 120, 35.

PART SIX: Contemporary Movements

Overall, May seems to set a life of willingness, which leads to ever increasing "unitive" living, as a central goal for his approaches to personal spiritual formation. As will be discussed below, he seeks to unpack how such a willing/unitive life is and comes about, what some of the pitfalls are, and how to begin to go about nurturing such an integrated life. It is this willing/unitive life that is, therefore, one of May's central ideals & goals.

Spiritual Formation Approaches

May's book, as the subtitle depicts, is primarily concerned with contributing to a "contemplative psychology."[38] He therefore does not seek to explicitly or systematically address contemplative practices. Nevertheless, he does suggest a few various practices throughout this book.

May discusses three ways to engage spirituality: affectively/experientially; metaphysically, which talks about spirituality; and contemplatively, which is primarily concerned with the source of spirituality and integrates all ways of knowing.[39] He also discusses growth groups and their limits, as well as kataphatic and apophatic approaches to spirituality.[40] From these discussions, it is clear that May favors contemplative apophatic approaches, or approaches that cultivate stillness, because they are more holistic and conducive to the cultivation of the unitive experiences that are so central for May.[41]

He also asserts that contemplative practices are necessary for evaluating emotional/energetic states and nurturing the kind of non-attachment that is necessary for the unitive journey.[42] He goes on to claim that beginners in the spiritual journey must not tamper with what emotionally/energetically is, but rather they must learn to be open and present to them.[43] And May asserts that evil may be overcome by practicing one not focusing on them.[44] Finally, he also discusses some specific contemplative

---

38. Ibid., vii.
39. Ibid., 23–24.
40. Ibid., 79–80, 109.
41. Ibid., 26, 109.
42. Ibid., 183, 84, 88, 213.
43. Ibid., 198.
44. Ibid., 247, 73, 79–80.

practices, such as meditation,[45] silence,[46] and the prayer of quiet,[47] and he stresses the need for individuals to root themselves in specific and long-standing religious/spiritual traditions.[48]

Discernment

While May does not seem to address his methods of discernment in any sort of explicit or systematic way, similar to many of our previous authors, he does demonstrate his approaches by helping the reader to discern specific issues. For example, he discusses William James' psycho-dynamic characteristics of "once-born" individuals,[49] how spiritual narcissism can become a diversion ploy of ego,[50] how people can confuse love for God,[51] eroticism for agape,[52] and escapism for union.[53] He discusses how to be aware of attachments,[54] ways to discriminate between good and evil,[55] and the dangers of imposing unitive views on dualistic realities.[56] He also distinguishes between true surrender and group surrender,[57] religion and magic,[58] and he asserts the necessity of having a spiritual director or friend for one's journey.[59]

May's discernment therefore primarily seems to be a combination of approaches. Much of his work references and works through complex psychological maps, but he also references contemplative traditions and insights throughout his work. May also seems to rely on the trial and error of one's own unique journeys in consultation with these other sources. May's general approach to discernment therefore appears to be one where

45. Ibid., 311.
46. Ibid., 314.
47. Ibid., 316.
48. Ibid., 320.
49. Ibid., 144.
50. Ibid., 144–45.
51. Ibid., 136–37.
52. Ibid., 152.
53. Ibid., 155, 58.
54. Ibid., 242, 83.
55. Ibid., chapters 9 and 10.
56. Ibid., 249–50.
57. Ibid., 275, 301–8.
58. Ibid., 286.
59. Ibid., 291–96.

each person reflects on their own experiences in light of the experiences and teachings of others and therefore discerns, in consultation with one's community, what one's unique responses should be. May's approach, then, is very contemplative in nature where each individual must be attentive to the moment-by-moment movements of their life and discerningly proceed along with the help of others.

Evaluative Techniques

As discussed above, May is not seeking to outline a systematic approach to personal spiritual formation. Hence, he does not directly address this issue of how to evaluate an individual's progress in the spiritual life. However, he does allude to what seem to be some of his own preferred methods.

As his concerns are with further unpacking a "contemplative psychology," and as was just discussed, many of his references appear to be related to self-observations. For instance, he considers his psychology to have, as its "laboratory," the "stillness of the human mind in silence."[60] He also makes references to making self-observations during meditation.[61] In addition, throughout his book, he relies on interviews and autobiographical statements to inform his psychology.[62] And he also, as was stated previously, encourages the use of spiritual direction. Each of these techniques seem to emphasize the centrality of self-observations and the observations that others provide to us as the basis for his evaluative techniques. This seems consistent because he is primarily concerned with an intrapersonal approach to spiritual formation, or more specifically, with an apophatic contemplative way of life.

Summary/Reflections

May's system of personal transformation is therefore one that seeks to foster the willing unitive experiences that are so central for him. By continually working with one's own psychological repressions, fears, dualisms, etc., all of which prevent a unitive way of life, one can come to ever more fully allow the energetic Spirit to fill, transform, and guide them. Contemplative practices, particularly apophatic ones, are therefore logically

---

60. Ibid., 27.
61. Ibid., 44, 48–50.
62. Ibid., 94, 162, 86–87, 203, 206.

Gerald May's Willing Spirit

consistent with his system for they seek to foster the kinds of willing silence that are central to May's understanding of unitive experiences.

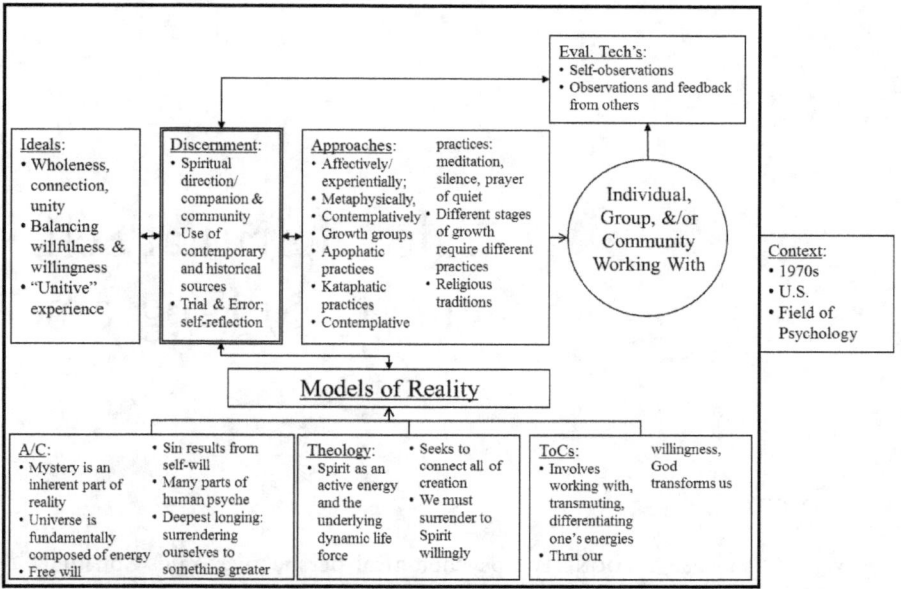

In this contemporary era, where modern science has come to be the dominate worldview in the West, we find May's system to be a helpful one as well as one that contrasts with Willard's. Not only has May sought to embrace some of the longstanding contemplative assertions and practices of the East and West, but he has striven to do so in light of some of the contemporary psychological findings and models of his day. As we are coming toward the end of our explorative journey in this final part of this book, we are finding more and more contemporary personal transformation systems to be doing this: seeking to cast longstanding views of and approaches to individual spiritual formation in light of the findings and models of modern scientific endeavors. However, in contrast with Willard's, May's system is an alternative of one who has sought to recast modern psychology in light of contemplative traditions, rather than the other way around. In our final sacred system next, we will see another example of this, but one that comes from more of an Eastern and distinctively Buddhist perspective.

15

Yale's Spiritual Self Schema (3-S) Program

Context

WRITING FROM A COGNITIVE psychological perspective, Yale's Spiritual Self Schema (3-S) Program seeks to help people to overcome the negative and distorting "schemas" that are operative in one's life.[1] By combining cognitive-behavioral therapy approaches with practices from various religious traditions, this system strives to help people to find their "spiritual nature," their "true self."[2] These authors seek to intentionally write from an interreligious perspective, one that tries to acknowledge and honor the many diverse religious/spiritual paths that are available and therefore intentionally seeks to not define certain things for people, such as how one defines their "spiritual nature."[3]

However, they do refer to Buddhism and its tenets in various portions of the text, even basing part of their program on its "3 Trainings," which are ethics, meditation, and wisdom.[4] Also, their bibliography and recommended readings are also overwhelmingly Buddhist in nature.[5] One

---

1. Avants and Margolin, *Spiritual Self Schema*, 7. Available at: http://info.med.yale.edu/psych/3s/training.html [last accessed on 12 September 2012].
2. Avants and Margolin, *Spiritual Self Schema*, 7–8.
3. Ibid., 10, 11.
4. Ibid., 21, 27, 28, 39–46, 63–66.
5. Ibid., 71–77. Out of eighty references total there are twenty-one Buddhist texts, as compared to only eight Christian texts and two Jewish texts (the rest are cognitively and psychologically related texts).

of their goals is to create a spiritual transformation system that is accessible by people of all faiths.[6] In some ways, then, this system seems to be written from the location of a more recent movement wherein American Buddhism is seeking to make inroads into Western secular culture by claiming that it is a distinctively non-theistic and even, as this text asserts, a non-Religious approach to transformation. As this text claims,[7] authors in this movement assert that it is therefore available for use by people of all faiths.[8] Coming from this location, this system seeks to transform the schemas that shape and define one's life. We will therefore be turning to this text in an effort to gain a better understanding of what personal trans-

6. Ibid., 12.
7. Ibid., 27.
8. For instance, see the following resources for claims that non-theistic meditative and contemplative practices are for people of all faiths and are therefore okay to be used in public school settings, see Hart, "Opening the Contemplative Mind"; Hill et al., "Contemplative Practices: Educating for Peace and Tolerance"; O'Reilley, *Radical Presence*, 13.

This view is succinctly summed up by Ed Sarath, Director Of University of Michigan's Program in Creativity and Consciousness Studies, who writes, "The main idea here is that the extrication of contemplative practices from tradition-specific spiritual contexts allows the construction of a spiritual identity that is rooted, first and foremost, in an interior experience, rather than shaped by exterior, institutional, or denominational influences. This trans-traditional identity is thus naturally more disposed toward acknowledging common ground among traditions because it is grounded in the transpersonal, contemplative core where all traditions intersect, even if their pathways differ" (Sarath, "Meditation in Higher Education: The Next Wave?," 229).

However, one may ask, what if one's "spiritual identity" is fundamentally and inseparably rooted in one's personal relationship with Theistic notions of the divine? Are we really finding "common ground" as Sarath asserts? Or are we merely asserting our own view of what such an identity is based on our own, or in this case Sarath's, theological anthropology? Could it be that Sarath is embracing Buddhist notions of the "No-Self" in making such claims? One of the potential challenges to claims like this is that some of these authors do not seem to be transparent about their own location. Instead, it could be argued, they are claiming "universality" when, in fact, their systems may not be.

For instance, I, as a Christian, do not find non-theistic meditation and contemplative practices to be as nourishing or meaningful or transformative as I do ones that are intentionally Theistic. I think attempting to pull these practices out of the original cultural and religious contexts that they were developed within and to then try and offer them as universal practices "for people of all faiths" is a potentially misleading thing to do. Or, at the very least, greater care and thought needs to be given to how one goes about doing this. Nevertheless, this is the claim that these other authors have and continue make as they seek to integrate contemplative practices into such secular arenas as public education and healthcare.

formation looks like from this more secular cognitive-behavioral psychotherapy, but primarily Buddhist location.

Models of Reality

Anthropological-Cosmological

As it relates to anthro-cosmologies, this program primarily focuses on two key concepts: the inherent ignorance and false self of humans, and something they call "schemas" and their relation to our lives. Both of these concepts come to under gird the nature and direction of their personal transformation program. These authors embrace the Buddhist notion that most humans are inherently ignorant of their true nature, one which lies beneath a false and illusory self.[9] They further assert that this false self must therefore be abandoned in order for us to reach our spiritual and religious goals. On this, they write, "As in a number of religious traditions which speak of the spiritual journey as culminating in an ultimate Union in which self merges or is abandoned, in Buddhist philosophy, through wisdom (panna) one understands not only that 'self' as a construct is no longer needed, but that it serves to keep us ignorant of our true nature."[10] Until we do this, they assert, we will be ever caught in the endless cravings and desires of this superficial and false self.[11]

This false self, for them, is fundamentally made up of "old habitual patterns of craving and aversion that lead to dissatisfaction."[12] Related to this, they discuss the operation of habitual patterns in our life, called "schemas." Essentially, "schema is used to describe a mental process for efficiently processing and organizing incoming information."[13] For instance, a driver of a car will have numerous memories, emotional dynamics, and behavioral responses that will be activated as they drive.[14] It is these "specific cognitive, verbal, and behavioral action sequences" that are called "schemas."[15] Continuously throughout our lives, we are creating,

---

9. Avants and Margolin, *Spiritual Self Schema*, 46.
10. Ibid.
11. Ibid.
12. Ibid.
13. Ibid., 3; see also ibid., 9.
14. Ibid., 3, 4.
15. Ibid., 5.

accessing, and modifying such schemas.[16] In short, these schemas "help us make rapid decisions and to behave efficiently and appropriately in different situations and with different people."[17] They are triggered by both internal and external cues, and multiple ones can be triggered in any given moment.[18]

As they relates to the construction of one's self, these schemas play a central role. On this, these authors assert, "habitual patterns of thinking, feeling, reacting, and behaving that characterize how we experience and express our "self" in daily life."[19] We also use these schemas to think about who we are as a person because "our brains store in memory feedback concerning our attributes and capacities that we get from various sources throughout our lifetime."[20] It is through these processes that "we create 'the world' of our personal experience believing that this is 'Me;' this is my 'Self.'"[21] It is this constructed and false self, as well as these habitual patterns, called schemas, that this program seeks to work with directly.

They seek to address these schemas because there a number of problems associated with their influence in our lives. For instance, they assert, "Typically, we are unaware of the discrete moments in our life because our daydreams, cognitive scripts, and behavioral action sequences allow us to go on automatic pilot."[22] Since these schemas are automatically activated by either internal or external cues, we often do not notice their effects on us and our behaviors.[23] They can also cause a great deal of suffering, especially if our constructed self is composed of negative concepts. For instance, they write, "Self-schemas that usually develop in childhood, like 'I'm bad, worthless, or unlovable' or 'I'm stupid or incompetent' set into motion extremely negative emotions and harmful behaviors throughout the individual's life."[24] We must therefore recognize that such self-constructions are merely "cognitive constructs" and are not our "true nature."[25]

---

16. Ibid., 4, 5.
17. Ibid., 5.
18. Ibid., 4.
19. Ibid., 14.
20. Ibid., 3.
21. Ibid., 9.
22. Ibid., 17.
23. Ibid., 10, 14, 48.
24. Ibid., 6.
25. Ibid., 5, 7, 14.

In fact, they go on, these "habitual self-schemas" can actually keep us from our accessing our spiritual resources and remaining on our spiritually transforming path.[26]

However, these schemas are not all bad, for they have significant implications for the cultivation of our "spiritual nature." While, as noted above, these authors do not attempt define what one's spiritual nature is, as such conceptions vary widely, they do assert that "our Spiritual nature is, at the very least, a source of compassion and insight that can provide each of us with a comfort, strength, and peace in our daily lives."[27] Schemas can therefore be used as a resource for cultivating our intentional and continuous access to our spiritual nature. On this, they write, "In the 3-S program, a Spiritual self-schema (i.e., the individual's Spiritual path) is viewed as a cognitive structure which, when carefully and elaborately constructed and maintained, provides the individual access to the experience and expression of what will be referred to in the 3-S program as, Spiritual nature."[28] In other words, they can be used to nurture our own personal spiritual growth.

This system's anthro-cosmology is therefore one that views the human person as being fundamentally comprised of schemas. These schemas are ever operative in our lives and they can either continue to keep us imprisoned in our "false selves" or they can be intentionally utilized to help our "spiritual nature" to emerge. This program therefore seeks to do the latter, as we shall see below.

Theological

In their own words, as it relates to one's spiritual nature, "The 3-S program makes no attempt to define Spiritual nature for the individual. Qualities and characteristics attributed to it, such as a sense of interconnection with all living things and/or with a Supreme Being or Higher Power, will vary widely."[29] Throughout this text, then, these authors do not seem to make any explicit statement regarding the nature or role of the divine in their framework.

Theoretically speaking, then, this is where our discussions of their theology might end. However, as my detailed discussions in the footnotes

26. Ibid., 7, 10.
27. Ibid., 7; see also ibid., 10.
28. Ibid., 10.
29. Ibid.

alluded to, I believe that all statements and practices are inherently theological; even allegedly secular ones. For this system, I find their views to be primarily of a secular humanistic flavor.[30] As we shall see below, personal transformation and development is placed almost completely in the hands of the individual. Their claim is that humans are fully capable of attaining their spiritual nature via the intentional, rigorous, and well-planned efforts that they put forth. All progress, they assert, will therefore come via one remaining focused on the goal of achieving one's own spiritual nature. "If you act 'as if' you are such a person," they write, "both in your imagery and in your daily activities, you will soon no longer be acting, but will actually become such a person."[31]

Based on this, I could see categorizing their theology as either being a-Theistic, or non-theistic, which is what we might expect from an American Buddhist-based system. In other words, the theology that seems to be embodied in this text is the claim that either there is no God and it is therefore completely up to humans to achieve their own progress or that there may be a God but we do not need to or cannot turn to this God for help. I think it would be much more helpful for these authors clearly state what their underlying theological assumptions and framework is (or range of frameworks), and forego their attempts to be all things to all people of all faiths, which I do not believe is really possible.

Given this position of mine, I also think it would have been better for them to develop specific Buddhist, Christian, Jewish, et cetera versions of their program, rather than to try and universalize it by creating one system that they claim works for all faith positions, which it may very well not. Nevertheless, these authors have chosen to remain silent on such theological issues altogether, it seems, based on the assumption that to not make any theological statements at all is the same thing as being totally neutral and non-located in their theology. Yet, as I have argued here, their system is not theologically neutral, but is rather one that is distinctively non-theistic.

Theories of Change

The theory of change that this system seems to embody might best be summarized in the phrase, "practice makes perfect." In accordance with

30. One that holds the values and efforts of the individual human to be supreme above all else.
31. Ibid., 52.

this, this program highlights the need for commitment and outlines three phases that we must pass through in our journey to nurture our spiritual nature. With such a high emphasis on the efforts of the individual, this program asserts the absolute necessity of commitment and vigilance. Working with the schemas of one's life requires working with our minds, and working with our minds requires intentional effort. On this, they write, "Anyone who has ever tried to control the flow or content of his or her thoughts, knows that it takes enormous effort to focus the mind."[32] Such an effort therefore requires commitment, a commitment "to taking back the power you have given to the wandering monkey mind."[33] This commitment to the efforts of the mind is necessary because what we are essentially trying to do in this program is to become aware of the schemas that are currently active in our lives.[34] We are trying to awakening to them, to turn off the habitual responses that we have from them, and to redirect our efforts toward cultivating spiritual self-schemas as discussed above.[35] As a result, vigilance and commitment are essential to these transforming processes.

As mentioned above, such changes are not viewed by these authors as happening immediately. As a result, there are three phases that they seek to intentionally lead their participants through. Each one of these phases, which are quite complex and well-structured, and are intended to walk an individual through the necessary steps of recognizing and changing their existing schemas into those that work to nurture one's truer spiritual nature. Phase One of the program, which has seven steps to it, strives to help one "to become aware of the readily accessed, high-speed path (or highway) one typically takes (the habitual self-schema) that defines how one experiences and expresses one's "Self" in the normal course of daily life, and to determine the compatibility of its automated pattern of thought, feeling, and behavior with the attainment of one's personal Spiritual ideals."[36] Each of the seven steps therefore helps the individual to gradually become aware of where habitual schemas are at work in their lives and to reflect on whether or not these schemas are nurturing or not of their spiritual nature. This first phase is therefore a phase of awakening and awareness.

32. Ibid., 40.
33. Ibid., 15, 25, 43, 45.
34. Ibid., 12–13.
35. Ibid., 7.
36. Ibid., 11; see also ibid., 14–16.

Yale's Spiritual Self Schema (3-S) Program

Phase Two of the program, which has four major sections (each of which have a number of steps or strategies to them) and comprises the bulk of this program, is intended to then help the individual to begin constructing, or modifying, and implementing schemas that do foster the expression of their spiritual nature.[37] In Section A of this Phase, participants create "a "blue-print" for the design of the new Path" that clearly identifies the end goal, creates the cognitive scripts and support systems to get there, and prepares one to deal with distractions and obstacles along the way.[38] In Section B, individuals are guided to ensure that they have the needed skills and tools to make the journey.[39] Relying on Buddhism's "3 Trainings" as the primary model, participants are encouraged to develop a core set of ethics, meditative practices, and wisdom ("Developing insight into one's true nature").[40] Next, in Section C of this Phase, students will be "reducing the automaticity of any habitually-activated self-schemas that are incompatible with your Spiritual path."[41] For this Section, the author's propose five strategies (use of internal dialogue, thought stopping, purposeful interjection, being aware of the choices that each moment brings, and being mindful of the objects of one's daily life) to help guide the participant in doing this.[42] Lastly, in Section D, the student "will begin construction by actual use of [her or his] new cues-to-action and by enactment of new cognitive scripts and behavioral action sequences in [their] daily life."[43] In other words, students will be implementing the spiritual schemas more fully into their daily lives. As we can see, Phase Two is primarily concerned with nurturing the schemas in one's life that encourage the expression of their spiritual nature.

Finally, in Phase Three, the goal is "to transform one's Spiritual self-schema into one's predominant or "habitual" self-schema."[44] The primary method utilized here is helping the student to gradually increase the number of difficult contexts where their spiritual self-schemas are activated and for them to continuously assess the successfulness of such efforts.[45] Having

---

37. Ibid., 11, 26.
38. Ibid., 26, 28, 29, 34, 35, 36.
39. Ibid., 27.
40. Ibid., 39, 40, 44.
41. Ibid., 27; see also ibid., 47.
42. Ibid., 48–50.
43. Ibid., 27.
44. Ibid., 11; see also ibid., 55.
45. Ibid., 56, 59, 60.

PART SIX: Contemporary Movements

only three steps to it, this Phase has the goal of helping the participant to continue increasing and growing in the life of their true "spiritual" self.

These three Phases, then, are the ones by which these authors seek to lead their readers through. We can see that the theory of change that emerges from it is one where the individual systematically brings about the changes they desire through their intentional and daily efforts to reshape the schemas that are operative in their lives. As stated above, their theory of change is primarily one of "practice makes perfect" and this is further supported by other statements on the nature of change that they make throughout this text. For instance, they make the following claims:

- "Through self-reflection and mindfulness training, individuals become increasingly aware of those habitually activated self-schemas that prevent them from experiencing and expressing their Spiritual nature, and by developing and rehearsing new cognitive scripts and behavioral action sequences they construct a Spiritual self-schema (a personal Spiritual Path) that will provide ready access to the experience and expression of their Spirituality throughout daily life"[46]

- "Your Spiritual path will never become as readily accessible as the other paths you take habitually in daily life unless it has as many points of access, and unless these points of access are used as frequently"[47]

- "Reaching the moment-by-moment destinations of your Spiritual path requires not only strong effort, and mindfulness, but also excellent concentration skills because you will need to remain fully aware of each moment as it arises and passes away"[48]

- Regarding situations that are difficult for one access their spiritual nature in, "you will need to discipline yourself to take back control of your thoughts, feelings, and behaviors, rather than allowing yourself to be controlled by your automatic pilot's habitual reactions to perceived obstacles"[49]

In each one of these statements, we can hear the decided emphasis that is placed on intentionality and repetition.[50] Unless we are fully mindful in each moment of our day, they assert, we run the risk of older and less spiritual schemas automatically taking over the operation of our lives

46. Ibid., 12.
47. Ibid., 35.
48. Ibid., 41.
49. Ibid., 56.
50. Ibid., 13.

thereby preventing us from fully living from our spiritual nature.[51] In their own words, "All that is required is that you shut down the automatic pilot of your habitual self-schema and change direction."[52] As we begin to do this, they claim, the diversions and illusions of the "false self" will begin to fall away and our true nature will finally emerge.[53]

Hence, we can see from all of these discussions that change comes about through the commitment that one makes to the intentional and repetitive processes outlined in the three Phases found in this text. Change is therefore viewed as being fully in the hands of the individual and how much effortful mindfulness they bring to their daily lives. This change, they assert, will eventually come through practice,[54] and their theory of change is therefore compatible with the "practice makes perfect" motto.

Spiritual Formation Ideals & Goals

In their own succinct words, "The goal of the 3-S program is therefore to construct a personal Spiritual path—a Spiritual self-schema—that will rapidly and efficiently provide access to our true Spiritual nature throughout daily life."[55] Unpacking what this means more broadly, it is their hopes that this system will help individuals "to discover their own Spiritual path that leads to compassion for self and others and to relief from suffering; to make their unique Spiritual path increasingly accessible in their daily lives; to use their Spiritual path to cope with adversity and to change behaviors that cause harm to self or others."[56] As we have already seen, their primary focus is on working with the schemas in one's life so that they become a part of one's spiritual nature emerging ever more fully and tangibly in one's life. In an effort to help individuals to know what their spiritual nature is, they turn to Buddhism's "10 Perfections," which are: Generosity, Morality, Renunciation, Wisdom, Effort, Tolerance, Truth, Strong Determination, Loving Kindness, Equanimity.[57] One of the central goals of the program is to therefore nurture these qualities.

---

51. Ibid., 29, 41–42, 43, 47.
52. Ibid., 50.
53. Ibid., 46, 52.
54. Ibid., 52.
55. Ibid., 7.
56. Ibid., 11.
57. Ibid., 21, 81.

PART SIX: Contemporary Movements

Spiritual Formation Approaches

As it relates to the approaches that are outlined in this text, the authors write, "To accomplish these goals, the 3-S program integrates cognitive-behavioral psychotherapy (CBT) with meditative practices common to a number of the major religious traditions into a non-sectarian, self-help program suitable for individuals of all faiths."[58] Based on these, there are three primary approaches that these authors explicitly utilize again and again throughout this text and for each of the three Phases. The first is the intentional use of reflection, which "includes both cognitive self-reflection and behavioral self-observation."[59] In Phase One of the program, such reflections center on the various schemas that are active in our lives in the forms of daydreams, internal dialogues, general life directions, our actions, et cetera in relation to our desired spiritual nature.[60] In Phase Two, these reflections then turn toward one's "ultimate destination," the spiritual schemas one already has, self-affirmations, where one is derailed from their spiritual path, the markers and entry points their desired path has, one's morality, the tools one has at their disposal, etc.[61] In Phase Three, such reflections next center "on those people, places, situations, and activities that are part of your daily life and that have been incompatible with you being able to experience and express your Spiritual nature."[62] These reflections are therefore intended to help the participant become more aware of the events and directions of their lives and how various habitual and intentionally chosen schemas influence them.

The second primary approach found in this text is that of rehearsing. This "involves mental rehearsal, using meditation and guided visualization, as well as behavioral practice (acting as if you are on your Spiritual path during the course of your usual daily activities)."[63] In Phase One, students are encouraged to step back from their daily life by picturing the events of their life as a TV show where actors play the parts of them and others in their life.[64] Then, as one watches the show unfold, they are encouraged to visualize such things as "what daydreams, scripts and behavioral action

58. Ibid., 12.
59. Ibid., 13.
60. Ibid., 14–15, 16, 17, 19, 20, 23, 24.
61. Ibid., 28, 29, 30, 31, 32, 35–36, 37, 39, 52.
62. Ibid., 56.
63. Ibid., 13.
64. Ibid., 16.

sequences are typically activated in your daily life that the actor would need to memorize," what the effects of these behaviors are on their lives and on others, as well as what their spiritual nature might look like if it were acted out.[65] In Phase Two, these rehearsal visualizations continue, but now the participant focuses more on what their spiritual nature looks like, what support is needed for it, and how to deal with diversions from its expression.[66] Students are also encouraged to practice breath meditation, becoming more aware of their mind's chatter in daily life, and other guided visualizations.[67] Finally, in Phase Three, the visualizing rehearsals lastly turn toward further identifying obstacles to one's spiritual nature and what some of the better habitual responses to them might be.[68] These rehearsals are therefore intended to help the individual further reflect on the role and effects of their various schemas as well as to help them to prepare for living more fully out of their spiritual self-schemas.

The third central approach is recording. This simply "involves keeping a record of your reflections, observations, and images, as well as a schedule for, and content of, your behavioral practice."[69] For each one of the Phases, there are worksheets in the appendices that the participant can use to keep track of the results of the reflections and rehearsals as well as the plans and commitments that are an intricate part of this program.[70] Such record keeping is therefore intended to help the individual to track and plan for the transformations that they are intentionally committed to engaging in.

In addition to these, there are six other approaches that these authors briefly address at various points throughout this text. One is the use of guided mediations and visualizations. In addition to the TV show visualizations used for rehearsals, these authors also encourage the use of such practices as breath meditation, insight meditation, other multisensory guided visualizations, and "Metta" (or compassion) meditation.[71] These are intended to help with concentration and reflection, to give distance from one's self, and to nurture compassion in one's life.[72]

65. Ibid., 16, 18, 20, 23–24.
66. Ibid., 28, 34, 36, 38, 49.
67. Ibid., 41–44, 47, 52.
68. Ibid., 57–58.
69. Ibid., 13.
70. Ibid., 17, 19, 20, 21, 23, 24, 29, 33, 35, 36, 38, 53, 58–59, 60.
71. Ibid., 44, 45–46, 57, 63–66, 67–70.
72. Ibid., 15, 16, 27, 40, 41, 46.

Another approach is the "self-schema check-in," which is intended to help "identify the habitual self-schema that was active just before you stopped."[73] Students are encouraged to engage in this practice on stopping and noting what schemas they have been engaging in recently at least three times per day.[74]

A third additional approach that is mentioned is the need for ethics, as was mentioned above. On this, they write, "one needs a code of conduct or foundation in ethics that above all seeks to do no harm to self or others, in speech, action, and livelihood."[75] Self-knowledge is still another important part of the approaches they discuss. "To travel a Spiritual path," they assert, "one needs to acquire the insight into one's true nature that purifies the mind; such insight requires right thought and understanding."[76] Such understanding not only involves knowledge of one's true nature, but also insight into the habitual schemas that one currently has so that they can act out what they envision in this program.[77]

Fifth, these authors assert the necessity of having adequate support systems in place. Such support should at the very least take the form of mentors, sacred texts, and a community.[78] Finally, mindfulness in daily life activities is yet another additional approach that these authors discuss. On this, they write, "The Spiritual path you are constructing, with its moment-by-moment destinations, requires that you are fully aware of each moment"[79] because mindfulness is a way of "regaining control over the Path you take habitually."[80] Such mindfulness should address the inner self-talk of our lives as well as our engagement with actions as simple as peeling and eating an orange.[81]

These six additional approaches are therefore intended to further undergird the three primary approaches discussed above. Taken collectively, these nine personal transformation approaches will, they claim, empower each person to intentionally and systematically proceed along the spiritual path that they are committed to walking. This path, as we can see from

73. Ibid., 22.
74. Ibid., 38, 52, 59.
75. Ibid., 27; see also ibid., 39.
76. Ibid., 27.
77. Ibid., 44, 45, 53.
78. Ibid., 34.
79. Ibid., 40–41.
80. Ibid., 47.
81. Ibid., 48, 49, 50.

these approaches, is one that progresses only to the extent that we intentionally and mindfully engage our life with them.

Discernment

Ideally, it seems, discernment for this sacred system is intended to happen in every moment of one's life. One of the ultimate goals is for the participant to ever be aware of what is arising within them, in relation to their surroundings, and to then freely and deliberately choose what schemas to use based upon the spiritual nature they are pursuing. From this perspective, then, every moment is a discerning one. The process is quite simple and systematic. One compares the schemas that have emerged, or are emerging, against those that they have identified to be congruent with their own spiritual path. If there is a match, then they allow the schema to be enacted. If not, then they choose a different schema. This seems to be the primary discernment process that is articulated in this text and the approaches that are discussed above seem to have the purpose of empowering and strengthening such moment-by-moment discernment.

Evaluative Techniques

Clearly, with so much reflecting going on, the evaluative techniques are numerous. The primary one is the self-observations that one makes during the course of each Phase of the program. These mainly focus on the cognitive and behavioral dynamics of one's life. There are also the observations that one's mentor and one's community might make of us in relation to how well we are attuning to our spiritual path. Finally, one can evaluate one's self in relation to the ethics that one has as well as in relation to the sacred texts that they turn to for guidance and support. Each one of these is therefore intended to help the individual to better know how well they are expressing and progressing in their spiritual nature.

Summary/Reflections

Overall, this spiritual formation system is one that is most centrally focused around mindfulness practices. By knowing what one's spiritual nature and true self should look like in terms of thought, feeling, and behavioral patterns or schemas, they can use this system to take intentional

PART SIX: Contemporary Movements

and systematic steps to move toward the expression of these. Emerging out of cognitive-behavioral psychotherapy's views of schemas, this program turns primarily to Buddhism for additional insights and practices for how such "practice makes perfect" progress can be made. This system is almost completely intra-personally focused and is more aligned with a secular humanistic, or other related, non-theistic theological frameworks.

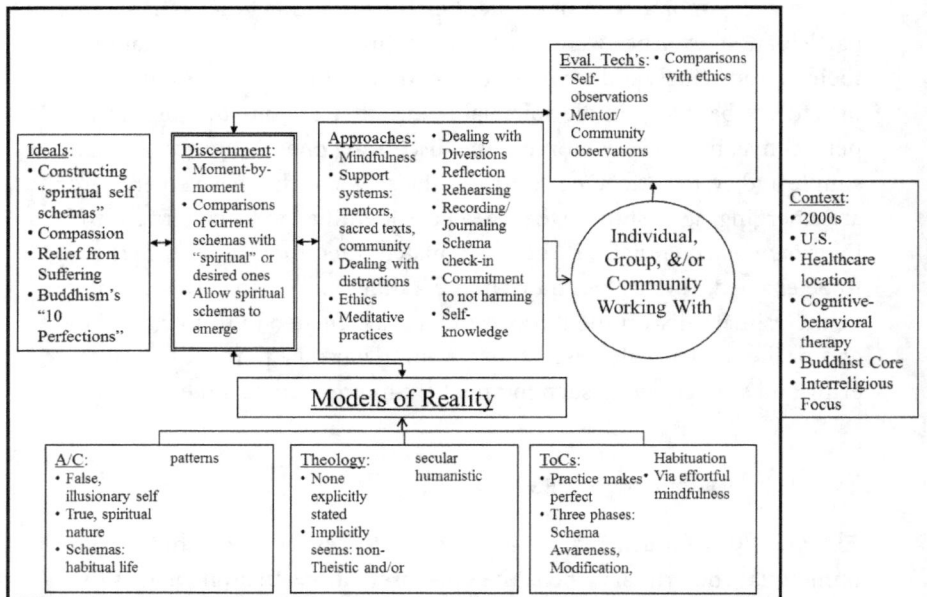

As the West is becoming increasingly diversified religiously, it behooves us to better understand how personal transformation is being conceptualized and embodied in light of other religious traditions and our predominantly secular, science-oriented society. This system is an example of one that seeks to blend another religious tradition, Buddhism with modern science. Coming from a similar psychology location as May, this system presents a different view of and approach to personal transformation. It is therefore imperative that we continue to study these increasingly diverse personal transformation systems.

We can also note that this sacred system sounds very much akin to what we saw in both the *Conferences* as well as in the *Philokalia*. All of three of these systems emphasized the need to mindfully track and work with one's ever emerging inner movements on a moment-by-moment basis. As mentioned above, I believe that this program could very easily be applied to specific religious traditions, though some modifications to the approaches would need to be made, and it would be very exciting to see what a distinctively Christian version of this sacred system might look like. We might also note that their "practice makes perfect" theory of change is also very reminiscent of the *Didache's* view of personal transformation, with its heavy emphasis on working with its constituents to live the "Way." With these observations, as we move into the final part of this book, we will next be stepping back to look more closely at some of the similarities and differences that there are between these various sacred systems. In the end, our hopes are to better understand the personal transformation systems that we and our communities use in more systematic ways.

PART SEVEN

Synthesizing & Summarizing

WITH THIS, OUR JOURNEY through these ages ends but a contemporary one now begins. For unlike most historical explorations, the goal here is not just knowledge and exposure but transformation for the sacred systems of our own lives and communities. It is here that we hope ministers such as Alfred will find some level of guidance and insights for the ministries that they are engaged in with God. We can therefore utilize the information presented herein in at least one of two ways.

First, as stated, we can view this text as a referential work. We can learn more about each of the various eras throughout Western Christian history and a couple of the different views of and approaches to personal transformation found in each. We can look to these specific sacred systems to learn more of the cultural and contextual views they held as well as some of the various practices they admonished. We can see some of the great diversity that this great religious tradition has birthed and nurtured on our planet. In short, we can view this book from a historical perspective that merely informs and educates.

For ministers working actively in congregations and non-profits, however, this is not enough. Like Alfred, there is a need for insights into the nature and dynamics of human transformation. We can all use more help and guidance in learning best practices and more effective ways of formatively engaging with the individuals and communities to which God calls us. For us, knowing the range of formation approaches that have been used, gaining a deeper understanding of the nature of change, learning about spiritual discernment and assessments, and more can be fruitful. The second way to use this text is to therefore look back over the entirety of the historical journey and see what we might glean by comparing these various and diverse sacred systems side-by-side.

PART SEVEN: Synthesizing & Summarizing

This is what we shall be doing in this final section. We shall be seeking to learn from these systems so that our own ministries might be strengthened and more empowered in our quest to partner with God in them. In the first chapter, we will be conducting such a comparative synthesis. By looking at these systems through three different lenses, our hopes are to better understand personal spiritual formation as it has been embodied by these many communities. In the second chapter, we will close out our journey together by summarizing some the key insights that have emerged but also by acknowledging some of the inherent limits of this project. From these critiques will emerge a calling for many more research projects to be conducted in this contemporarily emerging academic field of spiritual formation. Overall, then, the goal of this final section is to further encourage the work and growth of this sacred craft that is as old humanity itself.

16

Synthesizing—
The Sacred Systems
through Three Lenses

Introduction

As it relates to one historical journey through Western Christian spiritual formation, we come into the final phase. We will now look back over these fifteen different systems and reflect upon some of the patterns and trends that can be seen to emerge from among them related to the framework that we having been using throughout. To help us to do this, we will be reviewing these various systems through three different lenses: Vertical, Horizontal, and Historical. Diagrammatically, these three lenses may be depicted as follows:

PART SEVEN: Synthesizing & Summarizing

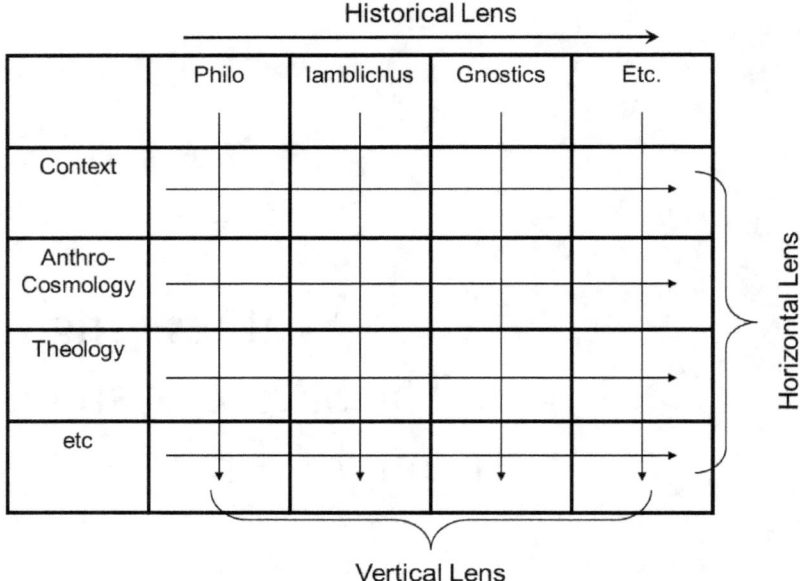

Through the vertical lens we will view each system overall in its own right and seek to ascertain what some of the possible ways are for grouping and categorizing them in hopes that further insights into the nature of personal transformation will be gleaned. In the horizontal lens, we will be considering each part of the framework across these various systems to see what we can learn about these different categories. We will also be considering how these various categories of the framework seem to connect together and influence one another in systematic ways. Finally, through the historical lens, we will be glancing across the history we have just traversed to see if there are any trends that we may highlight. We will finally close with a brief summary/reflection on this phase of the book and reflect on how practitioners might begin to locate their own personal transformation systems in light of this historical journey. The primary purpose of these reflections, then, is to help us in the systematic constructions of our own personal spiritual formation frameworks in light our own unique contexts. By seeing how the sacred systems of others have come together, and what some of the general trends and patterns of these frameworks are, we will be in a better position to work with our own.

Vertical Synthesizing

Through this lens, the primary goal is seek to capture the core backbone of each one of the systems that we have considered. The guiding questions for doing this, therefore, are: What is the core element of each system that it cannot do without? What is its most primary and essential focus? What is the backbone without which it would cease to be the system that it is? By seeking this essential core, I believe that we will be in much better position to categorize them and then reflect on what some of the insights that such categorizations may have for spiritual formators and religious educators as they engage with their own sacred systems in their unique contexts. I also note and assert that such "boiling-down" processes are somewhat reductionistic and are in no way intended to capture the whole of each system's beautiful and complex characteristics; only a life-long experiential engagement with each of these can capture that. Instead, such a reflective and reducing process is intended to help us gain some better insights into what might give rise to various systematic approaches to personal transformation and how we might better engage with our own.

In light of the summaries that have been provided in each of the chapters, whose main points are captured by the summary figures that are located at the end of chapter above, we might summarize the core backbone for each one of the systems as follows:

- Philo of Alexandria: Overall, the system is focused on the neoplatonic view of the soul being enslaved to the passions and senses of the world and the way to freedom is then through the use of knowledge, reason, and asceticism.
- Iamblichus: Focused around our coming to participate in the divine energies and light of the higher gods and natures, which thereby liberates us from our own lower natures. Hence, all of the theurgic practices and rituals have the intended effect of mixing our natures with the natures of the higher gods.
- Gnostics: Focuses primarily on their cosmology of the soul being imprisoned and needing to be liberated by *gnosis* or knowledge that is sent from God via the various rituals, ascetical practices, and prayers.
- *Didache*: This system emerges from its Apocalyptic views of the End Times being imminent and a belief in the two ways: of life and of death. Hence, in order to be saved in the last days and counted as among the "Elect," we must follow the rules and ways that lead to life.

PART SEVEN: Synthesizing & Summarizing

- Cassian: Overall, this system shares the anthro-cosmology of other neoplatonic systems. In this case, mindfulness is given the highest priority and focus, with the intellect and one's will as being the gate to salvation that helps to overcome the flesh.
- *Philokalia*: This system emerges from their central focus on stillness of the intellect. All thoughts are seen as being worldly, and the world is seen as being evil, so stillness is a safe sanctuary. Mindfulness is therefore given a high priority so that we can watch that things of demons don't affect us and make us impure. Again, the neoplatonic worldview is central here in this sacred system.
- Bonaventure/Franciscan: At its core, the Franciscan system of spiritual formation more fundamentally emerges out of its theology of immanence and the love and humility that was emphasized in relation to it. Its most central and special emphasis was on imitating Christ's life of poverty and giving help to the poor and marginalized.
- Erasmus: His is very much a "hunker down and endure the battle" kind of a system. It seems that he is primarily interested in making sure that we choose and follow the pathways of life rather than those of the world and the flesh.
- de Sales: This system seems to be very affectively based, though it is also very comprehensive in terms of cognitive and contextual factors. But the system primarily seeks to cultivate a love of God which then leads to changed action.
- Quakers: Overall, the Quaker system of personal transformation articulated in this text is one that seems to center almost completely around their theological anthropology—the presence of God within each and every human being that is found in the silence of one's heart.
- Law: This system seems to be focused on cultivating the intentions with which one engages their life. These intentions, when oriented toward the glory and service of God, are ultimately what makes one "devout."
- Willard: It is one that seeks to intentionally nurture each one of the six anthropological aspects of his model, with a Scriptural model of "Christlikeness" being its basis and focus. It has a special emphasis on the will/spirit/heart of a person.
- CST's: Spiritual formation is a matter of compassionately and non-judgmentally engaging with all that is so that the deeper, truer Life

within all of creation, especially one's self, can be accessed. We can also note the extensive intrapersonal emphasis that this system has, specifically as it relates to the affective life of the individual.

- Gerald May: This system focuses on helping one to work more effectively with the energies within themselves as they arise, and to willingly be united as One with the "Life Force" of all creation.
- Yale's 3-S: Overall, this personal spiritual formation system is one that is most centrally focused around mindfulness practices specifically as it relates to schemas—it is almost all about monitoring and working with the habitual patterns of one's life.

With these very coarse summaries laid out, there are at least three different ways that I can see categorizing them according to. Each one of these different ways offers insights in how our own systematic personal transformation systems might be better constructed. Our hopes are that they will help us to better understand and locate our own systems in relation to them. The first way is according to the following three categories:

- Habit Forming, Embodying a Way, Conforming to Christ's Image
  - Imitation of Christ
    - Bonaventure/Franciscan
    - Willard
  - Pursuing Specific Ways of Life
    - Yale
    - *Didache*
    - Erasmus
- Inner, Affective, God Within
  - CST
  - Quakers
  - May
  - De Sales
  - Law
- Neoplatonic Cosmology, Liberation of the Soul From Lower Realms
  - Through Direct Divine Intervention

PART SEVEN: Synthesizing & Summarizing

- Iamblichus
- Gnostics
- Through the Intellect
  - Cassian
  - *Philokalia*
  - Philo of Alexandria

From these categories, it seems that these systems have at least partially arisen out of three different origins. The first category above is primarily related to the belief that there is a set of ways that have either been passed on to us from others or that we can discover for our own lives. One of the primary goals of these sacred systems, then, is to help their constituencies to come to embody and integrate these ways ever more fully into their own life and ways of being.

The second category is primarily related to the firm assertion of these systems that God may be directly found within one's inner life and experiences. These systems therefore intentionally seek to enable one to connect to and live in harmony with these inner movements. Such inner movements can take the form of the affections and emotions that one has, or the intentions and motivations that one engages their life with. One of the primary goals of these systems, then, is for us to cultivate and work with such inner stirrings and motivations.

The third category above is most centrally focused on the Neo-Platonic cosmology that these early Christian sacred systems embrace. This worldview depicts the soul as an imprisoned entity that is in need of liberation. Such liberation comes, according to these systems, via one of two methods: direct divine intervention or through the use of one's intellect. These systems then seek to help their disciples to pursue one of these two pathways that then lead to the liberation of their imprisoned souls.

These three categories, then, are essentially External, Internal, and Cosmological ones. For someone working with their own systematic framework, in light of these, they could then ask themselves whether their system is more primarily one that looks to outside means, inner movements, or to their worldviews as the more primary basis for construction. In actuality, any such sacred system (be it personal, relational, or otherwise) will include facets of all three, as each of these systems do. Nevertheless, one seems to be more of the center pole and backbone for their sacred systems and perhaps ours too. We can therefore reflect on our systems in light of these three categories.

Synthesizing—The Sacred Systems through Three Lenses

A second possible way to categorize these, which directly emerges out of our reflections on the one above, is according to one's own anthro-cosmology. For example, my own personal transformation system asserts that creation is essentially comprised of three deeply interrelated layers: Intrapersonal, Interpersonal, and Transpersonal. As it relates to humans, the intrapersonal aspects include such dynamics as body, mind, emotions/affections, and transcendent capacities. The interpersonal aspects are related to the direct interactions that we have on one another and includes such dynamics as political, social, economic, cultural, et cetera influences. Finally, the transpersonal aspects includes such all-pervading and other-worldly influences as energy, parapsychological dynamics, and interactions with other realms of existence and celestial beings (such as angels, demons, etc.). The primary assertion here is that who we are, what makes us, are complex and layered interactions between each one of these aspects in my own theological anthropology.

As I look at each one of these sacred systems, it seems that they can also be categorized according to this theoretical anthropological framework. Based on this, I would categorize these systems as follows:

- Intrapersonal
    - Affective/Intentions
        - CST
        - Quaker
        - De Sales
        - Law
    - Cognitive/Mindful/Intellect
        - Cassian
        - *Philokalia*
        - Philo of Alexandria
        - Yale
- Interpersonal
    - Political/Rules/Ways
        - *Didache*
        - Erasmus
    - Social/Imitation/Modeling

PART SEVEN: Synthesizing & Summarizing

- Bonaventure/Franciscan
- Willard
- Transpersonal
  - Other Realms
    - Iamblichus
    - Gnostics
  - Energy
    - May

For me, these categories not only capture what the backbone and core is for each of the systems, but they also offer a profound insight into the nature of personal transformation. What this suggests to me is that the core of each of these sacred systems is primarily centered on where they find the Presence of God to most directly be encountered for a person. For some, God is found most fully in their inner affective and intuitional stirrings. For others, God is embodied in the rules and ways that have been passed on via their tradition. While still for others God is most directly engaged in the heavenly realms that seem to peak through the transpersonal veils of our otherwise earthly existence. What these categories seem to suggest, then, is that our personal spiritual formation systems may primarily arise out of the mediums through which we most directly experience the Divine in our lives. Having found this medium, these sacred systems then seem to cultivate entire ways of life that nurture not only this most primary core. Hence, another possible way that practitioners might think about their own sacred systems is via the theological anthropologies that they assert and reflect on which part of this anthropology their system most centrally focuses.

Finally, a third possible way that these systems might be categorized is according to one's own theology. Again using my own theology as an example of how such categorization might happen, I assert three different ways that I find God to be manifest in creation, which closely parallel Bonaventure's own theology: Transcendently, Incarnationally, and as a Deity. The Transcendent aspect of God is the God that is "beyond God," or at least all of our expectations, images, experiences, et cetera of God. It is the God who is groundless, no-"thing," and has no-Being, who is completely incorporeal and beyond all of creation. Some might refer to this aspect of the Sacred as "potentiality" or the as yet to be actualized aspect of God.

Synthesizing—The Sacred Systems through Three Lenses

For me, it is quite simply the God of Christian apophatic mysticism as is found in such thinkers as Bonaventure, Pseudo-Dionysius, Eckhart, and many others.

The Incarnational aspect of God, in my theological formulations, is the panentheistic God is who really, truly, and substantially present within and through every part of creation. It is the God who moves through our emotions, works in our institutions, and is energetically alive in every subatomic particle in the material universe. This is the God of "infinite names" of Psuedo-Dionysius for this aspect of God is to be found and therefore imaged everywhere. This is the aspect of God that was found be so central to Francis of Assisi and his spirituality.

Finally, the Deity aspect of God is the ontological God, the God who is experienced as having personhood that is distinct from creation. Many of our Christian concepts of Jesus and the Holy Spirit reflect these Deity views of God, as these two Deities are called upon via prayer to come and bless and heal just as a person would. This aspect of God has will, memory, intention, et cetera as we would expect a Deity to have.

These are the three aspects of God that I currently assert theologically for my own personal transformation system. Based on these, the sacred systems we have explored in this book might be categorized accordingly:

- Transcendent
  - *Philokalia*
  - Cassian
  - Philo of Alexandria
- Incarnational
  - Quaker
  - CST
  - May
  - De Sales
  - Law
  - Bonaventure/Franciscan
  - Yale (a non-theistic system)
- Deity
  - Willard

PART SEVEN: Synthesizing & Summarizing

- Iamblichus
- Gnostics
- Erasmus
- *Didache*

Using these categories is quite a bit more challenging than the other two because for some of these systems it is not clear as to where they might be placed. For instance, Cassian's system has a very strong theological view of God's everywhere Presence, and might therefore be categorized as Incarnational. But in its approaches, with its abundant emphasis of being every mindful of the God who is distinct from us, it might also be categorized under Deity. However, I have categorized it under Transcendent because of its emphasis on God as being incorporeal and the goal of attaining inner purity and stillness. Similarly, for the *Didache*, with its abundant focus on preparing for the Apocalypse, we might categorize it as being under Deity. However, its primary focus is on nurturing people in the "Ways of Life" which might also be construed as being Incarnational based on the assertion that God works in a person's life within and through these Ways. Also, while I have placed the Quakers in the Incarnational category above, it might also be placed under the Transcendent category because of their emphasis on silence. However, their actual conceptions and experiences of God in themselves and in the world seem more Incarnational in nature, which is why I categorized this system there. As we shall see below in the Horizontal Lens, many of these systems have more than one of these theological conceptions as a central part of their systems. Hence, this way of categorizing these various systems is more problematic and less clear than are the other two. Nevertheless, some may find this theology-based way of categorizing these sacred systems, as well as their own, more insightful.

While we will not do so here, a possible fourth way to categorize these sacred systems, and therefore better understand one's own, is the one that we found in the CST system: Contemplative, Creative, or Socially Engaged paradigms. Following this paradigm, each system would then be placed according to whether their core was mostly on the experience of the Sacred as a downward, upward, or outward movement. Again, they basis for categorization seems to be on *how* the Divine is most directly encountered in each system. Hence, in seeking to locate one's own personal transformation system in relation to these other sacred systems, one might choose one of these paradigms or even one of their own construction. The overall point here is that such vertical categorizations will help each of us

Synthesizing—The Sacred Systems through Three Lenses

as we reflect on our own systematic approaches and where they are located in relation to the larger history of Western Christian spiritual formation at the level of the individual.

Horizontal Synthesizing

In this section, we will now turn our attention to each of the various parts of the framework that we have been viewing these various sacred systems through. We will consider each one of these parts in light of what each of the systems offered for them. We will try to balance brevity here with rigor, for our hopes are to glean what insights we can from these various systems so that our own systematic formulations might be better informed. We will therefore not be engaging each of these sections as systematically as we did with each of the chapters above. Rather, we will more simply be seeking a few key insights and general themes/trends that might help us in the construction of our own personal transformation systems and their various parts.

We will be reflecting on each of the parts of the framework in the order that we have been up until now, with the exception that we will not be considering the Context part of the framework. Instead, we will revisit the contextual considerations in the next section of this chapter when we briefly reflect on these systems through a historical lens.

Anthro-Cosmologies

The anthro-cosmologies are as diverse as the systems are in and of themselves. Rather than try to categorize or discuss the details and nuances of these many and various perspectives, I believe that it would instead be more helpful to simply note the primary topics and core questions that most of these systems address and wrestle with. By doing so, we can better know what subjects our own sacred systems should be addressing. The following are the primary topics that I find most of these systems to address, as well as a few brief observations:

- Regarding the World
    - Nature of it
        - Is it primarily seen as negative or positive? (almost every single one of these systems holds a negative view of the world in one way or another)

PART SEVEN: Synthesizing & Summarizing

- What our stance toward it should therefore be?
- God's and the Angel's relation to it
  - How are they present to it? How do they express themselves within it? How are we to know whether they are truly present and active in the world?
- Evil in the world
  - What are the sources and origins of evil and sin in the world?
    - Two primary categories seem to emerge here are:
      - Evil as a substantive reality that must be rejected and avoided altogether (For instance, see: neoplatonic systems, Law, Erasmus, etc.)
      - Evil is the result of poor choices or distortions (see: Willard, May, CST, and Yale)
  - How can we respond to it and deal with it?
- Regarding Humans
  - What is the Nature of Humans?
    - Is it primarily negative or positive? (seems to be, historically speaking, mostly negative up through Erasmus and then turns more positive after that)
    - What are the various parts that make up a person? How do these interact with one another? With the world? With God?
    - What are some of the purposes of humans? Why are we here? What is our life for?
  - God's and the Angel's relation to humans
    - How are they present to us? How do they express themselves to and/or within us? How are we to know whether they are truly present and active within and around us?
  - Evil in Humans
    - What are the sources and origins of evil and sin in us?
    - How can we respond to it and deal with it?
  - Salvation and Liberation
    - What are they? What do they mean and look like in a person's life?

- What are some of the means, processes, mediums (inner and/or outer) through which they can be attained?
- Interrelationship Between These Two
  - How does the world affect humans and vice versa?
  - What should the proper relationship between them be?

As we can see, the anthro-cosmological considerations are fairly extensive. More fundamentally, they seem to focus on unpacking four basic questions: What is our starting point (i.e., What is the nature of things)? Where are we headed (i.e., salvation/liberation)? What are some of the means by which we can go there (internally and externally)? And what are some of the obstacles in our way and how can we deal with them (i.e., evil/sin)? Answering these questions, then, is laying a theoretical foundation upon which we can then more robustly construct our personal spiritual formation systems.

As far as the details of these goes, I would recommend that if a spiritual formation practitioner finds one of the models of these systems to be appealing, that they pursue it more fully. I would encourage each formator to find not only historical models that resonate with their own, but also similarly-minded contemporary ones as well to help them to more fully develop their own version that works for them in their current contexts. Nevertheless, the questions and categories posed above are the primary ones that emerge from across the sacred systems we have considered in this book. In constructing one's own systematic anthro-cosmology, these areas can be taken as a starting framework for what to address.

Theologies

Unlike the anthro-cosmologies, these views are not quite as diverse and varied. Overall, there are at least five different topics that seem to come up repeatedly for this part of the formative framework. The first three are related to the aspects of God that I discussed earlier: God's Immanence, Transcendence, and Ontological Being (or Deity). Incarnationally or Immanently, God is asserted by many of these sacred systems to be present within all things, especially within the thoughts, feelings, and imaginations of people. God's immanent Presence is asserted to be the Ground of all existence and connects all that is.

God is likewise found in some of these systems, particularly in some of the neoplatonic ones, to be utterly transcendent and totally beyond both world and human capacities to know God. Finally, God is also posited as having ontology, particularly in Bonaventure's where God is partially conceived of as having "memory, intelligence, and will," as we might expect a Deity to have. It is one or more of these three aspects of God that many of these systems seek to interact with via their systematic approaches to personal transformation.

The nature of God is also discussed at length by a majority of these systems. God's nature is abundantly described with such concepts as: goodness, charity, love, compassion, new life, vitality, creativity, wisdom, as well as God being contemplative and having a centering effect on humans. God is also viewed repeatedly as being active, helping, and guiding, even one who dances and sings with creation as CST's systems holds, throughout all of creation. Some of these systems also assert that all things, positive or negative, good or evil, either come from God or are at least allowed by God. God is also viewed by many of these systems as one who chastises and reproves, who rewards only those who strive for God.

Finally, many of these systems, being Christian, discuss Jesus. He is repeatedly viewed as being a messenger and/or model of God, one who is the "light of the world." Jesus is the power and wisdom of God who "shatters earthly folly" and liberates and redeems humanity and the world. Overall, the image of Jesus that emerges, then, is one who restores life, and leads creation to God.

As it relates to one's own systematic personal spiritual formation constructions, then, these theological themes can challenge us to reflect on each of these. How do we find God present in creation immanently, transcendentally, and as Deity? What do we assert is the nature and essence of God? As Christians, what is Jesus' place and role in our sacred system? The goal here is not so much for us to become systematic theologians (though such reflections can be helpful), but rather to lay enough of a theological foundation that we are intentional about who we think God/Christ is and how we are to both relate to and grow in our lives with God/Christ via our personal transformation frameworks.

Theories of Change

As we can note from each of the systems that we have considered, the understandings of how transformation comes about in one's life are quite extensive. While some of these discussions are particular to specific systems, many of them do uphold a fairly common view relating to change; namely, that it happens gradually over the course of many years of habitual forming, repatterning, and conditioning. Overall, we can summarize and categorize these discussions via the following questions. The responses are many of the ones found in the sacred systems:

- What is needed for change to happen? What are its foundational elements? (some overlap with Approaches)
    - Internally
        - The use of reason
        - Harnessing the will and mind, steadfastness, a strong intellect, watchfulness, intention, self-determination, mindfulness, commitment, vigilance, attentiveness
        - Humility, willingness, desire, love
    - Externally
        - Education, knowledge of the ways of life, visions of where one is going
        - Apprenticing, mentoring, means to make the journey
        - Practicing righteousness, embodying the virtues, asceticism, hating the world (when it is viewed as "sinful" by an author), purification, uprooting sin
    - Theologically
        - Interactions with the gods/God
        - Receiving the light, *gnosis,* and help that God sends
        - Christ's blood for our sins, Him as the purchase price for us
        - The grace of God
        - Ultimately, it is God who makes transformation happen
        - The help of angels
- What are the processes and phases by which long-term change comes?
    - How does change come about?
        - By a long-hardening and testing process
        - It is like "growing a crop"

PART SEVEN: Synthesizing & Summarizing

- Basic dynamic of transformation = the more something (positive or negative, good or bad) is nurtured, the more that it grows in one's life
  ◊ Habit formation is therefore essential (see: Philo of Alexandria, *Philokalia*, Erasmus, Law, Quakers, Willard, Yale, and CST for this specific assertion)
- What is happening in this change process?
  - There are at least two categories of response:
    1. It is an awakening and ascending process, like the rise of the dawn (see: Iamblichus, Gnostics, de Sales, and Yale)
    2. Or it is viewed as a process of overcoming the weaknesses of the flesh, where we are purged and purified by destroying the passions and desires of the flesh (see: Cassian's *Conferences*, *Philokalia*, and Bonaventure)
  - Note: a difference between these two views seems to partly be a difference in whether we cosmologically believe that
    a. We have been born into a sinful/distorted/false realm and must rise up out of it, or
    b. We have fallen into this realm and must therefore be purged of it
    ◊ Which one we adhere to seems to affect some of the means by which we approach personal transformation
- What are some of the stages/phases by which this change happens?
  - In Bonaventure's scheme, the three primary stages were:
    ◊ 1) Finding God via sensible things,
    ◊ 2) Finding God via the use of reason and intellect, and
    ◊ 3) Finding God who is beyond all concepts
  - For one of the Quakers, the three stages discussed were:
    ◊ 1) Purifying one's self,
    ◊ 2) Habitually orienting one's self toward God, and
    ◊ 3) Coming a state where it becomes God who prays through us

Synthesizing—The Sacred Systems through Three Lenses

- How does short-term change happen?
    - Stages of personal spiritual formation for short-term change:
        - In the *Didache* communities, short-term change was nurtured through the following stages: Calling => Apprenticeship => Transformation => Acceptance into the community
        - In Yale's system, the three phases for beginning to re-orient one's life were:
            - ◊ 1) Becoming aware of one's current schemas,
            - ◊ 2) Constructing/modifying new spiritual schemas, and
            - ◊ 3) Making these new schemas to become more dominant in one's life
    - How does evil arise in one's self and how does one deal with it?
        - Evil thoughts, feelings, etc. are proposed to enter one's self, then we consider it, next we accept it, and finally we act on it (see: *Philokalia* and de Sales). A similar view of how energies unfold within us is provided by May.
        - In order to deal with such tendencies, and therefore better transform one's life, we can:
            - ◊ Cultivate the reverse disposition (de Sales)
            - ◊ Seek to forsake and ignore it (*Philokalia*)
            - ◊ Or we can contemplatively sit with it (CST)

We can see, again, that the discussions on how change happens were quite extensive and complex. This is no surprise as the whole of one's personal transformation system seems, based upon the above, to hinge on what one believes about the nature of change is as well as on what some of the foundational elements that we believe are needed in order better facilitate such change. While the specifics of how such change happens varies, it was noted that more than half of these sacred systems explicitly asserted that habit-forming is a necessary and integral part of one's growing personal spiritual life.

We can also note that some of the foundational elements listed above seem to be dependent on what the goals of one's system are. For instance, in the *Philokalia* system, one of the primary goals is stillness of mind and tranquility of heart because it is only in such silence that one, this system asserts, can most assuredly and un-distortedly encounter God. As a result,

PART SEVEN: Synthesizing & Summarizing

a great emphasis was given in their system to cultivating a "strong intellect" through the many mindfulness practices that this system proposed. Hence, such mindful vigilance is a central and foundational element for their theory of change.

Overall, as we think about and work to construct/modify our own sacred systems of personal transformation, we can look to these change theories for additional insights and guidance. The categories of questions outlined above can serve as guidelines for some of the necessary areas that our own theory of change needs to address in Christian formation. In pursuit of our own answers to them, these sacred systems not only help us to see some of the core elements of how personal transformation that endures across them, but we can also see some of the diversity that is present as well. Finally, we can note how our own views of nature of human nature and the cosmos, as well as the Ideals that we are striving toward, can influence the Theory of Change that we assert. Indeed, we are beginning to see more clearly how thinking about personal spiritual formation systematically can help us to design sacred systems that are more internally consistent and logically unified.

Ideals & Goals

These systems also offer an array of diverse ideals and goals that their constituents are intended to pursue. Dividing these up into categories, we can find the following sets of ideals to be articulated by one or more of these systems. Again, readers are referred to the figures at the end of each chapter where each of these system's summaries are provided, focusing on the boxes that list the Ideals for each sacred system.

- Internally-Focused Ideals
  - Those related to parts of ourselves
    - Gaining knowledge, coming to know ourselves, attaining wisdom
    - Making an effort in one's personal spiritual life, intending toward the divine with all of one's life
    - Honesty, righteousness, humility, willingness, passion, flourishing, being nonjudgmental
  - Those related to whole of ourselves
    - Begin free from enslavements, being pure

- Love, peaceful, goodness, compassion, relief from suffering
- Attaining a tranquility of heart and mind, achieving a state of stillness
- Wholeness, balance, harmony in one's life, loss of self-definition, willingness
- Externally-Focused Ideals
  - Those related to what we can receive from the world
    - Living the "Way," imitating Christ and the Saints/Models
  - Those related to what we should give to the world
    - Living skillfully, working for peace, giving to others, charity, service
    - Being inclusive, seeking reconciliation
- Theological/Religious Ideals
  - Union with God
    - Seeking union with gods/God, Finding God
  - Pursuing God
    - Being led by God/Christ, doing God's will, obeying God, preparing for the coming of God's kin-dom

These goals might also be divided up according to various other categories as we explored with the vertical lens. For instance, in my own system, I might instead seek to divide these up according to the intra-, inter-, and trans-personal aspects of my anthro-cosmology and then seek to expand on what these systems upheld. The main point here is that our personal spiritual formation systems need not have to have a narrow, or even singular, focus. Instead, they can use a broad brush stroke of many of the Ideals listed above in order to better paint the picture of where our particular sacred system is seeking to take its disciples. The overall picture that these systems collectively depict, I assert, is one that is quite magnanimous and holistic.

Spiritual Formation Approaches

These systems, as the figures at the end of each chapter clearly show, offer a very diverse set of spiritual formation approaches that they admonish their followers to engage in. Indeed, the history of Western Christian personal

PART SEVEN: Synthesizing & Summarizing

transformation has and continues to generate a wide range of spiritual practices that we can draw from and engage in. Being aware of this rich history can therefore help us to better discern which sets of interventions we might engage our own communities with.

Again turning to my anthro-cosmology discussed above, I categorize these many different approaches as shown below. Again, it must be noted that this paradigm works well for shaping how I have engaged with these many sacred systems and it may therefore not be best suited for others who find a different paradigm to be more meaningful when engaging with them. For instance, adherents of the CST paradigm might look at this same list of practices and divide them up quite differently (i.e., according to their Contemplative, Creative, and Socially Engaged Movements). In light of this, an important set of questions to reflect on, for those seeking to further construct their own sacred system, is: What is the guiding/dominant paradigm that you seem to work out of as you read and engage with this material? How, then, would you categorize these approaches, and even the rest of the material contained in this chapter? For our purposes here, however, I turn to my own paradigm as an example of how such categorizations might transpire:

- Internal/Intrapersonal
  - Use of reason and reflection
    - Examination of Conscience
    - Honest self-expression
    - Shadow, Parts prayers
    - Mediations, Guided imagination prayers
  - Using one's body
    - Walking meditation, Labyrinths
    - Body, Focusing prayers
  - Vigilance in one's practices
    - Mindfulness
    - Watchfulness
    - Desiring perfection, having a sincere longing and intention in one's practices
    - Choosing the ways of life over the ways of death
    - Praying regularly throughout one's day

- Intending to stay active throughout one's life
  - Guarding self
- Education
  - Morality, ethics, the commandments
  - Scriptures
  - Lectio Divina
  - Having a continuous life of study and devotion
  - Acquiring knowledge in the "ways of life"
  - Learning the wisdom of the "ancients"
  - Self-knowledge and understanding
- Pursuing the virtues
  - Enduring persecutions, forbearance
  - Detachment
  - Humility
  - Courage
  - Gentleness
  - Compassion
  - Hating the vices
  - Cheerfulness, joy
  - Purity
  - Honesty
  - Forgiving
  - Peace, tranquility
- Asceticism
  - Fasting
  - Body deprivations
  - Self-mortifications
  - Solitude
  - Chastity and abstinence from that which tempts
  - Penance

PART SEVEN: Synthesizing & Summarizing

- "Death to Self"
- Releasing one's body to God
- External/Interpersonal
  - Community
    - Accountability, watching over one another
    - Offering guidance to one another
    - Supporting each other, caring and nurturing one another
    - Reconciliation
    - Growth/small groups
    - "Beholding" one another with love
    - Praying for enemies
  - Having a Spiritual Guide, Mentors
    - Looking to the "elders" of one's community
    - Being mentored in the "Ways of Life"
    - Being an example to one another
    - Imitation of Christ, the Saints, and other holy persons
    - Seeing one's self as an apprentice of Jesus
  - Following a "Way"
    - Moral codes
    - Being non-violent in every part of one's life
    - Accepting a life of poverty
    - Being cautious of the ways one chooses
    - Crafting a Rule for one's life
    - Service, giving to those in need, sharing one's gifts
    - Preaching in word and deed
    - Pursuing one's vocation, using one's time and talents appropriately
    - Recording, tracking one's own spiritual growth
- Transpersonal
  - Prayer Practices

Synthesizing—The Sacred Systems through Three Lenses

- Home shrines
- Awareness Examen
- Supplication
- Intercession
- Turning to God in all things, seeking God's guidance
- Lord's Prayer
- Thanksgiving
- Divine Office
- Private and Public prayers
- Rituals
  - Theurgy rituals
  - Baptism
  - Exorcism practices
  - Eucharist
  - Confession
  - Vigils
  - Silent prayers and meetings

We can see that these approaches really encompass most of one's life. Taken collectively, then, it seems that we can look at every single part of our life as a spirituality; with where the Spirit is active and thereby seek to partner with God. Some of the differences in the specific practices that a particular sacred system chooses appear to be dependent on what their unique anthro-cosmology and main foci are. For instance, Iamblichus' system draws more heavily on transpersonal theurgy practices because of their views of creation as essentially being a prison that one needs divine intervention and energies in order to escape. Similarly, the *Philokalia* system focuses more heavily on mindfulness and ascetical practices because of its beliefs that liberation of the soul most fully comes with the silencing of one's soul via the intellect. As one further example, the CST system seems to favor practices that focus more heavily on inner affective movements because of its views that there is a deep Source within one's soul that must be followed. Each system therefore appears to choose and cultivate practices that conform more fully to their own Models of Reality and their deepest and most direct experiences of the Divine. Here, again,

PART SEVEN: Synthesizing & Summarizing

can we see how these various elements of our framework influence one another. This is yet another example of how such systematic reflections can be helpful for both clarifying and strengthening the sacred systems of our community.

Such insights are therefore important for us to remember as we strive to construct our own systematic approaches to spiritual formation at the level of the individual because there are so many diverse and varied practices to choose from, especially in the West's increasingly pluralistic context. Rather than randomly picking and choosing from among the list above, or from the immediate contexts/traditions to which we are exposed, we must be intentional about what approaches we choose and why we are choosing those specific practices. In pursuit of this, we can ask such questions as: What does the specific practice do? How is it transforming the person? Does it seem to support and move them toward the Ideals of our system? Does it seem to be consistent with our Models of Reality? How can it be modified to better fit with our system as a whole? Reflecting on such questions in relation to our approaches can help us to strengthen their impact on our constituents.

Given this, the main categories listed above (such as Reason, Education, Community, Asceticism, Rituals, etc and/or others that we consider essential) should be a part of our system, for they have shown themselves in this historical exploration to be common across these many and diverse sacred systems. This is one of the main benefits of engaging such a research project as this, and many more such projects are needed as we will discuss in the final chapter. By exploring spiritual formation in many different communities, we are better able to look for dominant and recurring patterns and themes that can then help us with our own systematic efforts, making sure that we are not overlooking important aspects of a growing spiritual life at any of the levels (i.e., personal, relational, communal, organizational, etc.).

Discernment

As we look back over and compare the various approaches to discernment, which are summarized in the figures at the end of each chapter, there seems to be a fairly consistent model that emerges. This model appears to have, or can be categorized according to, four stages and roughly follows the "praxis" approach to discernment that was discussed for the CST system. While the details of each of these stages vary from one sacred

Synthesizing—The Sacred Systems through Three Lenses

system to the next, the overall stages themselves seem to be fairly consistent across many of these them.

In the first stage of spiritual discernment, most of these systems emphasize the necessity and centrality of knowledge for one's growing spiritual life. Such knowledge may include being educated in sacred laws, commandments, rituals, codes, etc. It might also include knowing what the ways of both life and death are, which can come from one's community, its elders/saints, and from the sacred texts of one's tradition. Such knowledge, it was noted again and again, should also include knowing one's self. Overall, the purpose of such knowledge is to help each individual to have a clearer image and understanding of the Divine, so that they can follow after God's movements in their lives.

In other words, in order for one to follow God, one must first know who God is, how God manifests within and/or to creation, etc. If this is true, it yields more insights into the Lord's Prayer where we pray, "Hallowed be Thy Name," for one can only rise to the level of the conceptions of what they worship and actively pursue in their growing personal spiritual lives. Hence, education and learning comprise a first stage of most of these approaches to discernment and such knowledge becomes the basis for comparison and reflection in the second stage.

In the second stage of discernment, the primary task is one of comparing the actions and movements that one is considering against the knowledge base of stage one in light of one's context. This stage therefore has at least three aspects to it. First, one can use their cognitive-reasoning faculties to compare what they are considering and how things are going against the knowledge of the ways of life and the images of God that they have. One can think about whether their progress and their actions are "good" or "evil" according to what they have learned. It was also asserted, by Erasmus, that Christ is the most logical way. Hence, use of one's reason is seen by many of these sacred systems as a necessary facet of spiritual discernment.

A second aspect of this stage is related to the affective movements and underlying intentions that one has in relation to what they are discerning. Some of the systems that asserted the presence of God in the inner affections of one's life (such as CST, the Quakers, Law, and de Sales) claimed that one additionally needs to reflect on these inner movements. If an action is truly in accord with God's will and ways, it was claimed, then one's affections and motivations should be consoling, resonant, and oriented toward the glory of God. However, we should also note that some of these systems, particularly the *Philokalia* system, rejected this assertion because of its views that all such passions are potential temptations of demons. As a result, the discernment model being presented here will not automatically apply to every spiritual formation system; though the overall stages seem to. Nevertheless, being aware of one's inner affects and intentions during discernment is seen by many of these systems as being integral to the process of discerning the presence and movements of God in one's life.

A third aspect of this second stage is related to contextual considerations. Some of these authors, such as the *Philokalia*, Cassian's *Conferences*, and de Sales, noted that the knowledge that one has must be modified in order to fit with the local conditions of one's current context. In other words, we cannot just mindlessly take what we have learned and apply to our current lives regardless of what is happening. Instead, we must be ever mindful and reflective of the nuances that each moment brings and the adaptations that it requires. This second stage, then, is a stage of making a decision based upon the foundation of knowledge that we acquired in the first stage, but filtered through our cognitive, affective, and contextual reflections.

Once a decision is made, the next stage is one of action where we embody and live out what we believe is right. Such action is to be embodied mindfully (as we particularly saw in the *Conferences*, *Philokalia*, and Yale systems). This means that each thought, feeling, schema, et cetera that arises is to be continually subjected to the rigorous comparisons and reflections found in stage two. This stage is therefore a stage of discerning while acting.

Finally, in stage four, one is to then look back and reflect on how the actions went. As we saw above, the examination of conscience was a central practice for many of these systems, and this practice is particularly helpful here. The primary purpose here is for one to now reflect on what specifically unfolded, what choices were made, what actions were taken, and how it went. There is to be a specific focus on whether these unfoldings embodied the ways of life or death, and whether they were reflective of the images of the Divine from the first stage or not. As May asserted, the growing spiritual life is one of trial and error, and this stage is intended to help us to look back and learn from what has happened, to what leads us toward greater life, and what leads us toward greater sin and disorder. Feedback from one's mentors and community is therefore an essential part of this stage as well. Not only can they provide us with additional support and guidance, but they can also help to hold us accountable to our spiritual path.

As noted above, these four stages are very reflective of the praxis approach to discernment discussed with the CST system. Again, while the four stages themselves seem to be fairly common to many of the various systems that we have considered to one degree or another, the specifics of each stage might change depending on one's particular Models of Reality. Graphically, we can depict these stages, and some of their various attributes, as follows:

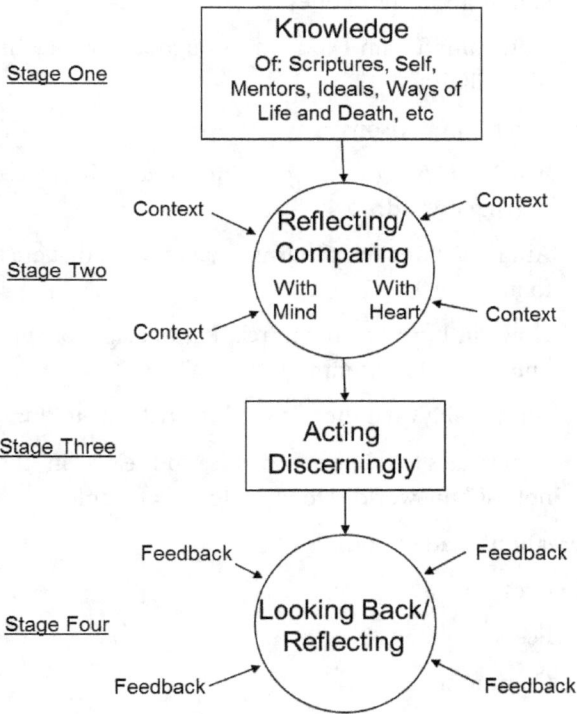

Evaluative Techniques

Finally, looking at the evaluative techniques, there are a number of different ways to categorize these as well just as for some of the other areas above. Again, I could use my own anthro-cosmology because we can look to each one of these aspects as a basis for evaluating the current status and overall directions of our personal spiritual lives just as Willard did in his system. However, I will present them less systematically according to the way that they seemed to be expressed in many of these systems:

PART SEVEN: Synthesizing & Summarizing

- Observations made by one's self
  - Internal observations
    - Reflections on our own life and how we think that it is going
    - Outcomes of such practices as: Examination of Conscience, Awareness Examen, Compassion Practice, etc.
    - Reflecting on the inner dynamics and underlying intentions and motivations of one's life
    - How mindful am I of God throughout my day in every part of my life?
  - External Comparisons
    - Am I achieving or progressing toward the ideals that I am striving toward?
    - Am I matching the patterns, images, ways that are being given to me?
    - How am I progressing in relation to stages of spiritual development that my community uses?
    - Am I doing what the ways of life invite me to do?
    - As it relates to the wider world: Am I really "in" the world and not "of" the world? Do my values really differ from theirs?
- Observations made by others
  - Sources
    - Peers
    - Community
    - Mentors
    - Society-at-large
  - Questions to consider
    - How am I viewed through their eyes?
    - What advice and direction are they giving to me?
    - What impact is my life having on them and they on me?

We can see that evaluation, which is closely tied to discernment, is largely a matter of observations and feedback made by one's self as well as by others. The heart of these techniques seems to be centered on one being

Synthesizing—The Sacred Systems through Three Lenses

able to accurately assess how one's progress in the spiritual life is going, how closely one is pursuing God in their life, and what one should do as they continue on their journeys.

My own personal experiences as a pastor have shown me that we don't always seek to intentionally track and monitor the success or impact of our church activities and programs. Most of these sacred systems make it very clear that such evaluative and monitoring techniques are essential for any person's or community's growing spiritual life. For me, they therefore stand as a both a challenge and a testimony to what is needed for effective and continually progressive personal transformation to transpire. As we heard in a few of these systems, just because one has been journeying in the spiritual life for an extended period of time, does not mean that they can strive any less diligently than they did in the beginning, for back-sliding is ever a possibility. It would seem, then, that these evaluative techniques are therefore necessary throughout one's entire journey for it never ends, at least in this lifetime.

HISTORICAL REFLECTIONS

This last set of lenses are intended to now help us step back and reflect on any overall trends that might emerge across the historical timeline that we have been journeying on during the course of this book. To help with these reflections, I have reserved my reflections on the Context part of the framework for this section. Reading across these various systems, the main observation that can be made is related to the Models of Reality that these sacred systems used. As was noted above, these models varied widely and looking at the contextual aspects, they seemed to be very much related to the dominant worldviews of their time periods.

With the exception of the *Didache*, which was predominantly a Jewish-Christian movement, all of the systems up until the fifth century were heavily influenced by Platonism and Neo-Platonism (Philo, Iamblichus, gnostics, Cassian's *Conferences,* and the *Philokalia*). The Bonaventure/Franciscan movement, with its central emphasis on the imitation of Christ, was heavily influenced by the mendicant movement of that era which emphasized a return to a life of poverty and simplicity. With Erasmus and de Sales, we find the newly emerging humanistic influences to weigh heavily in their systems. Next, we find Law and the Quakers to be fully expressive of the Protestant Reformation movements of their times and locations. Finally, with the exception of Willard who embodies a contemporary evangelical spirituality, each of the other contemporary systems (May, Yale, and CST) are all deeply steeped in modern science insights as well as having an openness to the increasingly interreligious views that are becoming common today in the West.

Each of these different worldviews then seemed to give rise to the specific approaches, discernment processes, et cetera that they utilized. Hence, the primary historical observation that can be made is that each of the worldviews of these systems is deeply connected to and emergent from the contexts in which they are located. From a theological perspective, one might assert that the Spirit has been and continues to be fully conversant with local trends and movements of each generation, seeking to foster its Life amongst the dominant worldviews of the day.

One of the lessons that we can take from this, in pursuit of our own systematic constructions, is for us to be reflective of our own unique contexts and how they might give rise to and be shaped by our spiritual formation systems, particularly in terms of our Models of Reality. One of the purposes of these models is to help provide people with a framework of understanding through which they can vitally grow in their spiritual lives. As we saw above, these models can vary widely while the impact of the spiritual formation system remains deeply transformative for the people and communities that they are utilized with. Again, it can be theologically asserted that God nurtures each part of creation in accordance with its near infinite diversities.

Some questions that we might then ask of our own sacred systems in relation to this are: What Models of Reality will best help the people that I am currently working with to grow more effectively? Through which models does the Spirit seem to be most operative within and through in our local community? Such reflections should consider the unique personalities, stages of development, autobiographical histories, cultural and theological locations, et cetera of our communities. I am not suggesting that any anthro-cosmology will work; this is not a "relativism" of sorts. Rather, I am suggesting that some models may work more profoundly than others in each local and unique context; it is therefore more of a "relative absolutism" if you will (i.e., that there are some models, and maybe even only one model, that works in one specific context that does not work as well, or even at all, in others). If this is the case, then why would we not embrace these models, models through which the Sacred can and does work? Spiritual discernment is therefore an essential aspect to the construction of our sacred systems. This observation of the historical location of these systems can therefore help us to contextually locate our own.

Synthesizing—The Sacred Systems through Three Lenses

Summary/Reflections

Reflecting on each one of these lenses for each of the fifteen sacred systems that we have considered in this project has yielded some very useful insights into the nature and purpose these sacred systems. The Vertical lens has helped us to better understand how we might locate our own systematic constructions in relation to each of these. By choosing a paradigm to categorize the core foci for each system, we are in a position to better understand where the central thrust of our own system might lie.

For the Horizontal Lens, numerous additional insights have also emerged. The anthro-cosmologies and theologies, for instance, were found to map out for us what some of the key issues to address in our own systems, such as: What the nature of the world is? What evil is and how we can respond to it? Who is God transcendentally, incarnationally, and as Deity? What is God's nature? Et cetera. Highlighting each of these, it was noted, can help us to better define and unpack the Models of Reality that inform our own sacred systems. For the ideals and goals, we found a similar mapping, but we also found listings for what many of our own ideals might include. Having such a list can be helpful for us when thinking about the directions that we feel the Divine might be wanting to take people in via our own framework.

Next, for theories of change, spiritual formation approaches, discernment processes, and evaluative techniques, we discovered some fairly common and consistent models that we can draw from for use in our sacred systems. While not all of these historical systems, it was noted, would support these common models in their entirety, the basic framework of them does seem to hold across many of these systems. The challenge for our own system is therefore to reflect on these models, return to the specific sacred systems that appealed to us, and adapt them to our own framework in light of the unique contextual considerations, as the final Historical Lens revealed, that we find ourselves within. These adaptations, it was asserted, should be always be made intentionally and in spiritually discerning ways.

17

Final Insights, Critiques, and Callings

Key Insights & Summaries

As we round out our journey, there are three keys insights that have emerged from this historical exploration of personal transformation in the West. The first, which comes from our vertical reflections, is the insight that personal spiritual formation systems seem to emerge and be systematized primarily around the central means by which they meet God through. In other words, such systems seem to be more focused on and designed around the means than they are the ends. This insight is important for practitioners because it suggests that, in constructing our own sacred systems, we must understand what the core means by which we ourselves, as well as the people/communities we are working with, encounter and engage with the Divine through. Knowing this explicitly will help us to further define and focus our system hopefully making it all the more effective.

The second key insight, which comes from our horizontal reflections, is that the more concept-based and theoretical aspects of the framework (particularly the anthro-cosmologies, theologies, and ideals) vary much more than do the more practically-focused aspects (i.e., theories of change, approaches, discernment, and evaluative techniques). The concept-based aspects provided us with mappings of areas to address as well as some possible content for these parts. For instance, the anthro-cosmologies yielded a series of questions and areas (such as the nature of the world, humans,

Final Insights, Critiques, and Callings

evil, etc.) that our own systems should address, while the ideals gave lists of possibilities that we might set as goals for our constituents. The practical parts of the formative framework, on the other hand, offered us some basic models that we can work with for our own systematic constructions. For instance, spiritual discernment was presented a series of four stages. Such models should help to ensure that our own systems are not missing any major aspects that these fifteen systems seemed to either partially or collectively address. In the end, then, the reflections we made for each of the various parts should help us with the construction of our own sacred systems of personal transformation.

A third and final key insight comes from our historical reflections and it asserts that context is key. Every one of these systems, it is claimed, was deeply rooted in and emergent from the contexts in which they found themselves. As each one of these systems is assumed to have had a major and transformative impact on people's lives, this insight is quite a challenging one for the West. In the West, where the secular/humanistic and scientific paradigms currently dominate, there have been and continue to be many efforts to uncover "universals" and "absolutes" in various fields of study. In spirituality and spiritual formation, I believe, these efforts are being hotly pursued by such persons as Ken Wilber,[1] Wayne Teasdale,[2] and Dorothy Soelle,[3] all of whom assert that there is a universal spirituality and synthesis that we can all share in.

The historical reflections above, however, seem to suggest something somewhat alternative, or even contrary, to these views. Namely, perhaps transformative spiritual formation lies in its ability to become fully embodied in the contexts in which it finds itself. As I asserted previously, this is not necessarily a form of relativism. As noted, there do seem to be models and patterns that repeat themselves across these sacred systems (e.g., the practically-based parts of the framework as discussed above). However, how these models/patterns are specifically expressed seems to deeply depend upon the unique contexts of which they are a part.

So, perhaps, rather than there being universals that are unchangeably applicable across contexts, maybe it is that each local context has its own set and version of absolutes and forms that are needed in order for people to thrive within each unique context. Instead of our seeking after absolutism or relativism in their extremes, perhaps we should instead be

1. Wilber, *Integral Spirituality*.
2. Teasdale, *Mystic Heart*.
3. Soelle, *Silent Cry*.

PART SEVEN: Synthesizing & Summarizing

looking for "relative absolutes"; i.e., those absolutes that each relative context needs to embody in contextually adapted ways in order for spirituality to thrive knowing that these absolutes will look quite different when they are actually embodied from one context to the next. Again, the theological assertion behind such a claim is that the Spirit ever adapts Itself to meet the current developmental and contextual realities. At any rate, and wherever we personally lie in this debate, the role of context is a crucial consideration for one's systematic constructions and much more research is needed in order to better understand this relationship between context and the various parts of the framework as we shall now see.

Closing Critiques & Callings

In addition to these more practically oriented reflections, there are a few theoretical critiques that need to be addressed as well. These are primarily intended to identify some of the inherent limitations of this work so that we better understand how to apply its insights to our own ministries. They are also intended to help further support the more contemporarily emerging academic field of spiritual formation. It is appropriate to end this book on these final notes, for in each ending we can usually find new beginnings.

First, we have spent a great deal of time exploring spiritual formation at the level of the Individual. In the opening chapter, it was noted that this level is a common way that some contemporary thinkers view this field: as only occurring for an individual person. However, when our theology asserts that the Spirit is present and transformatively active within every part and level of creation, and our understanding of spiritual formation is being "formed in the Spirit," then spiritual formation can be engaged for every part of our life and our world. Noting this, we can therefore realize just how limited these explorations are.

Essentially what needs to happen now is for similar historical explorations to be conducted at many of the other levels and arenas of our life, all of which the Spirit is seeking to manifest Its Life to and through. In other words, we need researchers to conduct similar projects that study the spiritual formation of relationships, community building, organizational development, governments, etc. These projects would then provide practitioners with a much fuller and robust understanding of how the Spirit has and continues to transformatively work in each of these different parts of our world.

Final Insights, Critiques, and Callings

For some, however, a second fundamental critique might be raised in relation to these more systematically oriented and intellectually-based endeavors. There are those who would assert that the Spirit's work in our world to be "very complicated, seemingly ineffable, ephemeral, inscrutable, invisible, diffusely interwoven into all human beings and their behavior, and so transcendent that we cannot observe it directly with the human senses."[4] We have already seen Willard's definition of "spiritual" to simply be that which is non-physical. Others, particularly our Neoplatonists, understand God to be completely beyond any of the happenings of this world.

The critique that can therefore emerge from these kinds of views is the question of how can we use many of the parts of the formative framework? If God is utterly transcendent and unknowable, how can we possibly know what Ideals God wants us to strive toward? How can we possibly observe or assess spiritual progress, these dualistic positions wonder, if the realm of the Spirit lies completely beyond the material realm? In short, these questions would seem to ask, how can we possibly formulate and track spiritual formation in more systematic and intentional ways if the Spirit is so ineffable?

To respond to critiques such as this, we look back to our syntheses of the theologies that we encountered across this historical trek. As we saw, there are three ways that God was primarily conceived of as: Transcendent, Immanent, and as Deity. In being conceptualized as transcendent or as Deity, the above views might hold depending on how God's interactions with creation are asserted to be. This doesn't necessarily hold for these, however, and certainly not for God as being immanent, if the Spirit's life is claimed to truly be a part and parcel of every movement and manifestation of creation. Quite often God's work in the world is thought of as happening primarily via miraculous and extraordinary interventions. However, if God truly is immanent as the Creator and Sustainer of every part of creation, then it logically follows that God is also present within and has an influence on the more mundane and routine parts of our lives as well.

Herein lies the response to the critique raised above and is the theological basis for the academic, systematic, and even scientific study of spiritual formation. It now all hinges upon whether or not there are enduring patterns that can be observed in this work. Our historical journey and subsequent synthesis seems to suggest that there is. Similarly, the fact that there are religious traditions that have been passed on from one

---

4. Moberg, "Aging and Spirituality," 213.

PART SEVEN: Synthesizing & Summarizing

generation to the next for thousands upon thousands of years further supports this claim. In other words, all of this would seem to assert that the Spirit, while ineffable, transcendent, spontaneous, and even miraculously moving at times, also works in patterned, repeatable, and observable ways that can be formatively passed on via our religious education and spiritual formation programs.

While it is true, I assert in line with our traditions, that God can never be fully known, it also seems to be the case that God also works in ways that can be discerned, understood to a limited extent, and overtly pursued in cooperation with God—otherwise there is no basis for spiritual discernment, the very center and core of all that we do as theists. Such is therefore one of the primary goals of this text and the academic field of spiritual formation: to identify and more systematically understand the enduring patterns of human transformation that God has and continues to use so that we might more closely partner with our all-wise and ever-loving Parent.

A third central critique relates to the grouping of texts that were chosen and explored and is one that subsequently leads to further callings for more research. As we look over these authors and communities, it can be noted that all of the single authored texts are male and predominantly Western ones, which is why this is a project that is primarily focused on Western Christianity. Even those texts which are collections of writings or thoughts of a larger community, were male-dominated. The feminist perspective is therefore not captured in these writings, nor are the perspectives and approaches of other ethnicities, such as African-American, Asian, South American, African, etc., all of which are a growing part of the Christian global community as we heard in the opening statements to Part VI.

We must know that these other-gendered and ethnic perspectives are quite different from the ones captured by the authors we have explored herein. These alternative views of and approaches to spiritual formation are important because the West has been multiethnic and interreligious throughout its history and is increasingly so today. Texts such as *A Many Colored Kingdom: Multicultural Dynamics for Spiritual Formation*, edited by Elizabeth Conde-Frazier, S. Steve Kang, and Gary A. Parrett,[5] can therefore help us to better understand some of the diversities that lie along these gendered and multiethnic lines.

---

5. Conde-Frazier et al., *Many Colored Kingdom*.

A fourth critique would be that all of these writings are more of a systematic, rationally reflective, prescriptive, and manual type of writing style. For the purposes of this book, which sought a more systematic approach to personal transformation, this may be fine but we must also acknowledge that we could have taken very different routes as well. For instance, we could have focused on how the spiritual journey has been described through poetry, as found in the works of saints such as John of the Cross or Francis of Assisi. Or, we could have focused on narratives/images that have been used to describe the spiritual journey, as in the book *The Way of the Pilgrim* (which uses the climbing of a mountain as a metaphor for spiritual development) or even Bonaventure's *Journey of the Soul/Mind to God* (which, as well saw, uses a six winged seraph for its metaphor). Or, we could have even focused on autobiographies, such as Thomas Merton's or Teresa of Avila's.[6] Views of spiritual formation are embodied in so many different perspectives, and these more systematic/rational-like texts only focus on one way of exploring and expressing the nature and means of personal transformation.

In addition, a fifth critique is that each of these writings was written by and is primarily intended for certain functionally abled adults. There were no discussions of how personal transformation might differ for other developmental differences such as age. Are they appropriate for children? Would they be really helpful for persons in their elder years? I believe that, while somewhat insightful, something more and/or different is needed to help ministers working with these populations.

In might also be argued that these texts may not be appropriate for persons with "disabilities" who are developmentally different cognitively, emotionally, socially, etc. Furthermore, this text has not acknowledged, as many others have, the place and role of personality type differences, charisms, and other similar theories. These models have observed that different groupings of people and communities seem to have fundamentally different foci of interests and ways of processing the world, which then influence the kinds of spirituality that they have. This is why contemporary texts such as Robert Clark's article, "Spiritual Formation in Children,"[7] Lewis Richmond's *Aging as a Spiritual Practice*,[8] books on Myers-Brigg and

---

6. Merton, *Seven Storey Mountain*; Teresa of Avila, "Book of Her Life."
7. Clark, "Spiritual Formation in Children."
8. Richmond, *Aging as a Spiritual Practice*.

PART SEVEN: Synthesizing & Summarizing

the Enneagram,[9] Richard Foster's *Streams of Living Water*,[10] and Stephanie Hubach's *Same Lake, Different Boat*[11] are so important. They can help us to better understand how personal transformation differs in relation to such developmental and type differences.

Furthermore, as Yale's system helps us to see, there is also a need to explore how human transformation is being embodied by other faith positions, which is a sixth area of opportunity for further research and development. Obviously, this includes other religious traditions where similar systematic spiritual formation approaches have been developed and embodied for thousands of years. We have much that we can learn from one another in terms of spiritual formation partly because our formative palette is the same: humanity. However, as we saw increasingly with most of our contemporary authors, there is also still much to learn from and offer to the many disciplines of modern science that study human dynamics in part or in whole.

Collectively, these essentially represent a fuller range of how we might view and approach human transformation. The underlying assumption here is, of course, the claim that the more we can systematically learn about the individuals and communities we are called to work with, the better will we be in partnering with the Spirit's formative work in our midst. Hence, turning to the work and findings of these other faith traditions and comparing and contrasting one another's formation work can give us even further insights into this vocation.

Moreover, another possible set of future research projects could be related to the formative framework that we have used throughout this text. Each one of its elements (Models of Reality, Discernment, Ideals, etc.) needs to be taken up as a set of specific research projects. We can and should be exploring each one across various systems and contexts as we have done to a very limited extent in this book. To further complicate matters, such research therefore needs to be done across each of the diverse communities and populations that have been named in this closing section. Doing so should give practitioners greater insights into the nature and dynamics of each part of the formative framework and ideally help them to improve their vocational craft in light of this framework.

---

9. Examples include: Richardson, *Four Spiritualities*; Riso and Hudson, *Wisdom of the Enneagram*.
10. Foster, *Streams of Living Water*.
11. Hubach, *Same Lake, Different Boat*.

Final Insights, Critiques, and Callings

Finally, as was noted in the CST chapter, this exploration was mostly a literature-based one. The use of other and more ethnographic-based research methodologies are needed for there may be significant differences between what a single author reflects on and what internal and external observers note for a specific community. For instance, as a youth pastor, I may have my own ideas of how the spiritual development of my youth is unfolding, but observations made by outside researchers coupled with the personal reflections of my youth will likely yield significant additional or even alternative insights. Gathering this type of data can therefore help us to better know how spiritual formation is conceived of and embodied in many diverse contexts.

Given all of these limitations, perhaps this book really should have been more appropriately subtitled: *A Brief Literature-Based History of Systematic/Rational Views of Christian Personal Spiritual Formation According to Western Males*—but perhaps this is too long. Because of these limits, again the call for further and continuing research in this field is heard: Research at the other levels of spiritual formation; Research to better understand the differences between personal transformation for women and men in different cultures; Research to better understand how Christian spiritual formation varies from one ethnic group to another in different geographical contexts; Research to explore whether and how spiritual formation is viewed and embodied in diverse forms of expression such as poetry, autobiographies, narratives, et cetera; Research for different developmental stages, types, and abilities; Research that learns from and contributes to human transformation as it is being embodied in various other faith traditions; Research into the different elements of the formative framework; and Research using non-literature based approaches such as ethnography, case study, and other modern research methodologies. To summarize, we can categorize this need for research along at least the following lines:

- Cultural Location—age, gender, ethnicity, geographic region, functional ability, religious tradition, personality type, functional/developmental ability, etc.
- Framework Elements—ideals, models of reality, approaches, etc.
- Level/Formative Foci—individual, relational, communal, ecosystem, government, etc.
- Research Methods—ethnography, literature based, case study, etc.

PART SEVEN: Synthesizing & Summarizing

These can essentially represent different dimensions along which research can be conducted, making the future of research in this field quite extensive and complicated. For instance, we might pursue a research project to study how communal spiritual discernment is carried out by a Samoan congregation in the South Pacific using ethnographic methods. This project would be quite different from doing a literature-based approach or from studying a Samoan-American community residing in Los Angeles. In other words, each of the above can represent different combinations of possibilities along which our research endeavors might unfold.

Indeed, the field of spiritual formation as a formal and contemporary academic and research-oriented discipline is still in its infancy even though human transformation, in all of its diverse manifestations, is as old as humanity. As we come to the close of this limited historical exploration, then, let us hope that such research endeavors will continue thereby expanding and improving upon the knowledge base that better enables us to work ever more systematically and effectively with our communities in partnership with the Spirit who is the ultimate beginning and end of all truly spiritually formative ways.

Bibliography

Abe, Masao, and William R. LaFleur. *Zen and Western Thought*. Honolulu: University of Hawaii Press, 1985.
Allan, J. David. "Population Growth over Human History." January 4, 2006. Online: http://www.globalchange.umich.edu/globalchange2/current/lectures/human_pop/human_pop.html.
Anderson, Rosemarie. "Intuitive Inquiry: A Transpersonal Approach." In *Transpersonal Research Methods for the Social Sciences: Honoring Human Experience*, edited by William Braud and Rosemarie Anderson, 69–94. Thousand Oaks, CA: Sage, 1998.
Avants, S. Kelley, and Arthur Margolin. *The Spiritual Self Schema (3-S) Development Program*. New Haven: Yale University School of Medicine, 2003.
Bilgrave, Dyer P., and Robert H. Deluty. "Stanislavski's Acting Method and Control Theory: Commonalities across Time, Place, and Field." *Social Behavior and Personality* 32/4 (2004) 329–40.
Bonaventure. *The Journey of the Mind to God*. Translated by Philotheus Boehner. Indianapolis: Hackett, 1993.
———. "Major Life." In *St. Francis of Assisi: Writings and Early Biographies*, 627–788. Chicago: Franciscan Herald, 1991.
Booty, John. "Preface." In *A Serious Call to a Devout and Holy Life; the Spirit of Love*, edited by Paul G. Stanwood, 1–5. Mahwah, NJ: Paulist, 1978.
Burridge, Richard. "Jesus and the Origins of Christianity." In *The Story of Christian Spirituality: Two Thousand Years, from East to West*, edited by Gordon Mursell, 11–30. Minneapolis: Fortress, 2001.
Butler, Judith. *Gender Trouble: Feminism and the Subversion of Identity*. Thinking Gender. New York: Routledge, 1990.
Carmichael, Liz. "Catholic Saints and Reformers." In *The Story of Christian Spirituality: Two Thousand Years, from East to West*, edited by Gordon Mursell, 201–44. Minneapolis: Fortress, 2001.
Carver, Charles S., and Michael Scheier. *On the Self-Regulation of Behavior*. Cambridge: Cambridge University Press, 1998.
Cassian, John. *John Cassian: The Conferences*. Translated by Boniface Ramsey. Ancient Christian Writers. Mahwah, NJ: Paulist, 1997.
Chidester, David. *Christianity: A Global History*. 1st American ed. San Francisco: HarperSanFrancisco, 2000.
The Claremont School of Theology. "About CST—21st Century Theological Studies." http://www.cst.edu/about.
Clark, Robert. "Spiritual Formation in Children." In *The Christian Educator's Handbook on Spiritual Formation*, edited by Kenneth O. Gangel and Jim Wilhoit, 234–46. Grand Rapids: Baker, 1994.

Bibliography

Conde-Frazier, Elizabeth, S. Steve Kang, and Gary A: Parrett, editors. *A Many Colored Kingdom: Multicultural Dynamics for Spiritual Formation.* Grand Rapids: Baker Academic, 2004.

Dales, Douglas. "Celtic and Anglo-Saxon Spirituality." In *The Story of Christian Spirituality: Two Thousand Years, from East to West*, edited by Gordon Mursell, 73–88. Minneapolis: Fortress, 2001.

"The Didache." In Aaron Milavec, *The Didache: Faith, Hope, & Life of the Earliest Christian Communities, 50–70 C.E*, 12–48. New York: Newman, 2003.

Dispenza, Joe. *Evolve Your Brain: The Science of Changing Your Mind.* Dearfield, FL: Health Communications, 2007.

Downs, Perry G. *Teaching for Spiritual Growth.* Grand Rapids: Zondervan, 1994.

Dreitcer, Andrew. "IS 201—Spiritual Growth Group." Class lectures, Claremont School of Theology, Claremont, CA, Fall 2008.

Dreitcer, Andrew, and Frank Rogers Jr. "RE 451—Spiritual Formation for Personal and Relational Vitality." Class lectures, Claremont School of Theology, Claremont, CA, Fall 2008.

———. "RE 453—Spiritual Formation for Compassionate Social Engagement." Class lectures, Claremont School of Theology, Claremont, CA, Spring 2009.

Dupré, Louis K., Don E. Saliers, and John Meyendorff. *Christian Spirituality: Post-Reformation and Modern.* World Spirituality 18. New York: Crossroad, 1989.

Erasmus, Desiderius. "The Handbook of the Militant Christian." In *The Essential Erasmus*, 28–93. New York: New American Library, 1964.

Farmer, David. "Saints and Mystics of the Medieval West." In *The Story of Christian Spirituality: Two Thousand Years, from East to West*, edited by Gordon Mursell, 89–124. Minneapolis: Fortress, 2001.

Fitzgerald, John T. *Passions and Moral Progress in Greco-Roman Thought.* Routledge Monographs in Classical Studies. London ; New York: Routledge, 2008.

Foster, Richard J. *Streams of Living Water: Celebrating the Great Traditions of Christian Faith.* San Francisco: HarperSanFrancisco, 1998.

Francis de Sales. *Introduction to the Devout Life.* 1st ed. Vintage Spiritual Classics. New York: Vintage, 2002.

Franklin, Gene F., J. David Powell, and Abbas Emami-Naeini. *Feedback Control of Dynamic Systems.* 3rd ed. Addison-Wesley Series in Electrical and Computer Engineering Control Engineering. Reading, MA: Addison-Wesley, 1994.

Graham, Stephen R. "The Protestant Tradition in America." In *The Story of Christian Spirituality: Two Thousand Years, from East to West*, edited by Gordon Mursell, 274–304. Minneapolis: Fortress, 2001.

Grisbrooke, W. Jardine. "The Nonjurors and William Law." In *The Study of Spirituality*, edited by Cheslyn Jones, Geoffrey Wainwright, and Edward Yarnold, 452–54. New York: Oxford University Press, 1986.

Hart, Tobin. "Opening the Contemplative Mind in the Classroom." *Journal of Transformative Education* 1 (2003) 1–19.

Hellmann, J. A. Wayne. "The Spirituality of the Franciscans." In *Christian Spirituality: High Middle Ages and Reformation*, edited by Jill Raitt, Bernard McGinn, and John Meyendorff, 31–49. New York: Crossroad, 1987.

Hill, Clifford, Akbar Ali Herndon, and Zuki Karpinska. "Contemplative Practices: Educating for Peace and Tolerance." *Teachers College Record* 108/9 (2006) 1915–35.

Bibliography

Holmes, Thomas R. *Parts Work: An Illustrated Guide to Your Inner Life.* Kalamazoo, MI: Winged Heart, 2007.

Holt, Bradley P. "Spiritualities of the Twenieth Century." In *The Story of Christian Spirituality: Two Thousand Years, from East to West,* edited by Gordon Mursell, 305–65. Minneapolis: Fortress, 2001.

Hubach, Stephanie O. *Same Lake, Different Boat: Coming Alongside People Touched by Disability.* Phillipsburg, NJ: P. & R., 2006.

Iamblichus. *The Mysteries of the Egyptians, Chaldeans, and Assyrians.* Translated by Thomas Taylor. 3rd ed. San Diego: Wizards Bookshelf, 1984.

Jonas, Hans. *The Gnostic Religion: The Message of the Alien God and the Beginnings of Christianity.* 2nd ed. Beacon Paperback. Boston: Beacon, 1963.

Jones, Cheslyn, Geoffrey Wainwright, and Edward Yarnold. *The Study of Spirituality.* New York: Oxford University Press, 1986.

Kegan, Robert. *The Evolving Self: Problem and Process in Human Development.* Cambridge, MA: Harvard University Press, 1982.

Law, William. "A Serious Call to a Devout and Holy Life." In *A Serious Call to a Devout and Holy Life; the Spirit of Love,* edited by Paul G. Stanwood, 41–352. Mahwah, NJ: Paulist, 1978.

Linn, Dennis, Sheila Fabricant Linn, and Matthew Linn. *Don't Forgive Too Soon: Extending the Two Hands That Heal.* New York: Paulist, 1997.

Logan, Alastair H. B. *The Gnostics: Identifying an Early Christian Cult.* London: T. & T. Clark, 2006.

Louth, Andrew. *The Origins of the Christian Mystical Tradition: From Plato to Denys.* 2nd ed. Oxford: Oxford University Press, 2007.

Malherbe, Abraham J. *Moral Exhortation: A Greco-Roman Sourcebook.* Library of Early Christianity. Philadelphia: Westminster, 1986.

May, Gerald G. *The Dark Night of the Soul: A Psychiatrist Explores the Connection between Darkness and Spiritual Growth.* 1st ed. San Francisco: HarperSanFrancisco, 2004.

———. *Will & Spirit: A Contemplative Psychology.* San Francisco: Harper & Row, 1982.

McGinn, Bernard, John Meyendorff, editors. *Christian Spirituality: Origins to the Twelfth Century.* World Spirituality 16. New York: Crossroad, 1985.

McGuckin, John A. "The Early Church Fathers (1st to 6th Centuries)." In *The Story of Christian Spirituality: Two Thousand Years, from East to West,* edited by Gordon Mursell, 31–72. Minneapolis: Fortress, 2001.

———. "The Eastern Christian Tradition." In *The Story of Christian Spirituality: Two Thousand Years, from East to West,* edited by Gordon Mursell, 125–50. Minneapolis: Fortress, 2001.

Merton, Thomas. *The Seven Storey Mountain: An Autobiography of Faith.* Orlando: Harcourt Brace, 1948.

Milavec, Aaron. *The Didache: Faith, Hope, & Life of the Earliest Christian Communities, 50–70 C.E.* New York: Newman, 2003.

Moberg, David O. "Guidelines for Research and Evaluation." In *Aging and Spirituality: Spiritual Dimensions of Aging Theory, Research, Practice, and Policy,* edited by David O. Moberg, 211–24. New York: Haworth Pastoral, 2001.

Modras, Ronald E. *Ignatian Humanism: A Dynamic Spirituality for the 21st Century.* Chicago: Loyola, 2004.

———. "The Spiritual Humanism of the Jesuits." In *An Ignatian Spirituality Reader,* edited by George W. Traub, 4–15. Chicago: Loyola Press, 2008.

Bibliography

Moorman, John R. H. "The Franciscans." In *The Study of Spirituality*, edited by Cheslyn Jones, Geoffrey Wainwright, and Edward Yarnold, 301–8. New York: Oxford University Press, 1986.

O'Connor, Michael. "Spiritual Dark Night and Psychological Depression: Some Comparisons and Considerations." *Counseling and Values* 46/2 (2002) 137–49.

O'Reilley, Mary Rose. *Radical Presence: Teaching as Contemplative Practice*. Portsmouth, NH: Boynton, 1998.

Paul, St. "Letter to the Romans." In *The Study of Human Nature: A Reader*, edited by Leslie Forster Stevenson, 56–68. New York: Oxford University Press, 2000.

Philo of Alexandria. "Every Good Man Is Free." In *The Works of Philo: Complete and Unabridged*, translated by C. D. Jonge, 682–97. Peabody, MA: Hendrickson, 1993.

———. "On the Contemplative Life or Supplicants." In *The Works of Philo: Complete and Unabridged*, translated by C. D. Jonge, 698–707. Peabody, MA: Hendrickson, 1993.

The Philokalia: The Complete Text. Vol. 1. Translated by G. E. H. Palmer, Philip Sherrard, and Kallistos Ware. London: Faber & Faber, 1983.

Raitt, Jill, Bernard McGinn, and John Meyendorff, editors. *Christian Spirituality: High Middle Ages and Reformation*. World Spirituality 17. New York: Crossroad, 1987.

Rausch, Thomas P. *Radical Christian Communities*. Collegeville, MN: Liturgical, 1990.

Richardson, Cyril Charles. *Early Christian Fathers*. New York: Touchstone, 1996.

Richardson, Peter Tufts. *Four Spiritualities: Expressions of Self, Expressions of Spirit: A Psychology of Contemporary Spiritual Choice*. Mountain View, CA: Davies-Black, 1996.

Richmond, Lewis. *Aging as a Spiritual Practice: A Contemplative Guide to Growing Older and Wiser*. New York: Gotham, 2012.

Riso, Don Richard, and Russ Hudson. *The Wisdom of the Enneagram: The Complete Guide to Psychological and Spiritual Growth for the Nine Personality Types*. New York: Bantam, 1999.

Rogers, Frank, Jr. "RE 437—Advanced Seminar in Spiritual Formation." Class lectures, Claremont School of Theology, Claremont, CA, Spring 2008.

Sarath, Ed. "Meditation in Higher Education: The Next Wave?" *Innovative Higher Education* 27/4 (2003) 215–33.

Sartre, Jean-Paul. *Nausea*. Penguin Modern Classics. New York: Penguin, 1996.

Schwartz, Richard C. *Internal Family Systems Therapy*. Edited by Michael P. Nichols. Guilford Family Therapy. New York: Guilford, 1995.

Selderhuis, Herman J. "The Prostestant Tradition in Europe." In *The Story of Christian Spirituality: Two Thousand Years, from East to West*, edited by Gordon Mursell, 165–200. Minneapolis: Fortress, 2001.

Seymour, Jack L. "Approaches to Christian Education." In *Mapping Christian Education: Approaches to Congregational Learning*, 9–22. Nashville: Abingdon, 1997.

Sheldrake, Philip. *A Brief History of Spirituality*. Blackwell Brief Histories of Religion. Malden, MA: Blackwell, 2007.

Soelle, Dorothee. *The Silent Cry: Mysticism and Resistance*. Translated by Barbara and Martin Rumscheidt. Minneapolis: Fortress, 2001.

Stanwood, Paul G. "Foreword." In *A Serious Call to a Devout and Holy Life; the Spirit of Love*, edited by Paul G. Stanwood, 7–8. Mahwah, NJ: Paulist, 1978.

Stanwood, Paul G., editor. *A Serious Call to a Devout and Holy Life; the Spirit of Love*. Mahwah, NJ: Paulist, 1978.

Steere, Douglas V., editor. *Quaker Spirituality: Selected Writings*. New York: Paulist, 1984.

Stopp, Elisabeth. "Francois De Sales." In *The Study of Spirituality*, edited by Cheslyn Jones, Geoffrey Wainwright, and Edward Yarnold, 379–85. New York: Oxford University Press, 1986.

Teasdale, Wayne. *The Mystic Heart: Discovering a Universal Spirituality in the World's Religions*. Novata, CA: New World Library, 1999.

Teresa of Avila. "Book of Her Life." In *Saint Teresa of Avila: The Collected Works of St. Teresa of Avila*, 1:53–368. Washington DC: ICS, 1976.

United States Census Bureau. "U.S. & World Population Clocks." http://www.census.gov/main/www/popclock.html.

Wakefield, Gordon S. "The Quakers." In *The Study of Spirituality*, edited by Cheslyn Jones, Geoffrey Wainwright, and Edward Yarnold, 445–48. New York: Oxford University Press, 1986.

Warren, Austin. "William Law: Ascetic and Mystic." In *A Serious Call to a Devout and Holy Life; the Spirit of Love*, edited by Paul G. Stanwood, 11–37. Mahwah, NJ: Paulist, 1978.

Wilber, Ken. *Integral Spirituality: A Startling New Role for Religion in the Modern and Postmodern World*. Boston: Integral, 2006.

Willard, Dallas. *Renovation of the Heart: Putting on the Character of Christ*. Colorado Springs: NavPress, 2002.

Woods, Richard. *Christian Spirituality: God's Presence through the Ages*. Rev. ed. Maryknoll, NY: Orbis, 2006.

Index

à Kempis, Thomas. *See* THOMAS à Kempis
Absolute, 103, 157, 214, 259
Affective, 144, 276, 278
Affliction, 100
Angels, 10, 31, 33, 41, 53, 77, 90, 99, 111, 157, 171, 180–81, 193, 278, 286
Anglican, 15, 145, 179, 180, 197
Anthropological, 9–10, 20, 32, 48, 58, 75, 89, 111, 128, 147, 163, 180, 203, 222, 244, 255
Apophatic, 104, 108, 116, 235, 247, 250, 280
Appetites, 20, 49, 112, 117, 120, 133, 155
Aquinas, Thomas, *see* Thomas Aquinas
Asceticism, 27, 28, 53, 191, 274, 286
Augustine of Hippo, 74, 238
Awakening, 49, 52, 259, 287

Baptism, 54, 61, 66, 131
Beliefs, 2, 17, 32, 55, 67, 203, 210, 212, 294
Benedict of Nursia, 74, 238
Bernard of Clairvaux, 149
Bible, 1, 143, 144, 169, 202, 218
Biola University, 202
Black Death, 107, 310
Boehme, Jacob, 179
Bonaventure, 107, 109–26, 275, 276, 279, 280, 285, 287, 301, 307

Brethren of the Common Life, 127
Buddhism, 201, 253, 254, 260, 262, 267
Byzantine Empire, 72

Calvin, John, 127
Carver, Charles, 6, 307
Cassian, John, 7, 73–89, 92, 104, 181, 227, 275, 277, 278, 280, 281, 287, 297, 301, 307
Catholic, 9, 14, 15, 109, 127, 143–46, 180, 197, 222, 307
Celestial Beings, 33, 111, 278
Centering Prayer, 235
Ceremonies, 36, 39, 54
Charism, 119, 123
Chastity, 79, 82, 154
Christ, 1, 11, 51, 54, 59, 77, 79, 95, 98–101, 114, 118–22, 125, 126, 129, 132–39, 144, 150, 153, 156, 162, 164–73, 182, 183, 188, 190–92, 200, 206–19, 223, 275, 276, 285, 286, 290, 293, 296, 301, 311
Christlikeness, 202, 207–11, 275
Chrysostom, John, 74
Claremont School of Theology, 220, 307, 308, 310
Clark, Robert, 307, 309
Clement of Alexandria, 18
Close Relationships, 3–5
Cognitive, 7, 87, 159, 160, 201, 253–57, 260–63, 266, 267, 275, 296, 297

313

Index

Commandments, 94–96, 101, 292, 296
Communion, 37, 38, 41, 51, 54, 56, 99, 235
Compassion, 5, 100, 110, 118, 121, 172, 225, 226, 229, 231–37, 257, 262, 264, 285, 290
Conde-Frazier, Elizabeth, 308
Confession, 63, 94, 123, 155
Consciousness, 12, 160, 223, 244, 254
Constantine, 71
Contemplation, 23, 28–31, 81, 94, 110–13, 117, 120, 151, 158
Contemplative, 7, 18–29, 233, 235, 241, 242, 250, 254, 281, 291, 308–10
Corporeal, 31, 33, 40, 41, 111, 115, 128
Corruptible, 36, 111
Creator, 9, 22, 29
Critical Thinking, 213, 217
Crusaders, 107

Dark Ages, 73, 107
Dark Night of the Soul, 12, 309
de Caussade, Jean-Pierre, 146
de Sales, Francis, 7, 145–61, 179, 217, 275, 287, 288, 297, 308
Deity, 49
Democracy, 145
Demonic, 42, 48, 54, 102, 103, 225
Devil, 76, 79, 84, 138, 163, 165, 180
Devotio Moderna, 14
Devotion, 28, 83, 147, 150–53, 157–60, 167, 179, 182, 184–93, 292
Devout, 19, 25, 114, 116, 146–53, 179, 182–87, 192–95, 196, 275
Didache, 7, 2, 46, 54, 57–69, 73, 133, 140, 268, 274, 276, 278, 281, 288, 300, 308, 309

Discernment, 7, 11–13, 29, 41, 42, 67, 84–86, 102, 103, 124, 138, 139, 158–60, 168, 175, 194, 195, 217, 240, 248, 266, 270, 296–302, 305
Disciples, 17, 45, 55, 58, 97, 133, 211, 277, 290
Discipleship, 3
Discretion, 64, 82, 85, 102, 121, 124
Distortions, 33, 84, 181, 182, 186, 217, 223, 224, 283
Divination, 31, 38, 41
Doctrine, 46, 169
Dogma, 168
Dominicans, 109
Double-Mindedness, 59
Dreams, 38, 41, 102
Dreitcer, Andrew, 220, 222, 308
Dualistic, 11, 20, 35, 47, 48, 52, 227, 244, 248

Early Christian, 7, 14, 45, 46, 48, 50, 52, 54–68, 309, 310
Eckhart, Meister, 226, 280
Ecumenical, 15
Education, 3, 174, 254, 286, 292, 308, 310
Ejaculatory Prayer, 157
Elders, 26, 27, 85, 102, 157, 293, 296
Elect, 58, 59, 62, 67, 68
Emotion, 247
Energy, 35–38, 92, 96, 206, 229, 244, 245, 278
Engineering, 6
Enneagram, 310
Erasmus of Rotterdam, 2, 127
Eternal, 39, 81, 84, 115, 129, 131, 134–37, 169, 170, 192, 213
Ethics, 84, 253, 260, 265, 266, 292
Eucharist, 43, 54, 58, 63, 66, 294
Evangelical, 15, 200, 220, 222

Index

Evil, 21, 29, 33, 34, 42, 76, 90–103, 121, 122, 129, 133–37, 142, 149, 150, 154, 157, 165, 173, 180–83, 203–13, 228, 237, 244, 247, 248, 275, 283–85, 288, 296, 302, 305
Examination of Conscience, 291, 299

Faith, 1, 57, 60, 78, 92–95, 102, 116, 146, 160, 168, 172, 214, 239, 258
Fasting, 28, 39, 64, 82, 85, 94, 99, 155, 158, 214, 216
Feedback Theory, 9, 6
Flesh, 49, 75–84, 89, 112, 129, 133–37, 150, 181, 214, 221, 223, 275, 287
Forbearance, 100, 154, 292
Foreknowledge, 38
Forgiveness, 100, 158, 166, 227, 232
Formative Framework, 8
Formless, 37
Foster, Richard, 202, 218, 308
Fox, George, 145, 162–74
Francis of Assisi, 280
Franciscans, 110, 119–25, 308, 310
Free Will, 24, 76, 90
Freedom, 19–30, 86, 93, 97, 99, 212, 274
Friendship, 40, 157, 159, 172

Galileo, 145
Gentiles, 17
Gentleness, 99, 119, 134, 153, 154, 206
German Pietism, 144
Globalization, 199
Gnosticism, 14, 46–48, 51, 52, 55
Gospel, 5, 85, 114, 118, 122, 123, 128, 144, 188
Grace, 76–78, 91, 92, 95, 96, 116, 117, 133, 148, 149, 175, 189, 190, 207–10, 223, 226–29, 286
Greco-Roman, 14, 17–19, 23, 30–32, 43, 46, 75, 308, 309
Gregorian Reforms, 14
Gregory the Great, 74

Happiness, 25, 38, 117, 118, 134, 135, 139, 180
Harmony, 5, 9, 12, 34, 51, 116, 118, 204, 211, 224, 226, 229, 233, 277, 290
Heaven, 29, 38, 59, 74, 80, 95, 116, 117, 129, 131, 135, 149, 153, 156, 206
Hellenistic, 19, 27, 47, 48, 53, 63
Hermetic, 46, 72
Hesychast, 15
Higher Nature, 21, 23
Higher Power, 257
Holiness, 26, 62, 67, 79, 81, 146, 155, 186–88, 223, 230
Holmes, Tom, 221–25, 309
Holy Poverty, 120
Hubach, Stephanie, 309
Human Nature, 1, 34, 111, 176, 222
Humanism, 9, 14, 147, 309
Humility, 85, 94, 100, 116–25, 138, 150, 154, 173, 188, 190, 191, 212, 215, 275, 290

Iamblichus, 7, 18, 31–43, 48, 49, 55, 274, 277, 279, 281, 287, 294, 300, 309
Idolatry, 59
Ignatian, 9, 145, 147, 155, 159, 160, 177, 235, 309
Ignatius of Loyola, 9
Illumination, 41, 50, 52, 88, 111, 115–17
Imagination, 112, 119, 144, 145, 189, 229, 236, 291
Imitation, 63, 118, 193, 301

Index

Immanence, 52, 113, 122, 125, 140, 142, 160, 233, 275
Immaterial, 32, 35, 40, 97
Immortal, 24, 29
Imperishable, 29
Incarnational, 219, 241
Incorporeal, 31, 39, 77, 280, 281
Industrial Revolution, 145
Inspiration, 22, 38, 39, 42, 124, 151
Insular Traditions, 14
Intellect, 21, 34, 37, 41, 89, 90, 93–102, 112, 118, 275, 286, 287, 295
Intercession, 82
Interfaith, 15
Internal Family Systems, 221, 310
Interreligious, 200, 220, 221, 253, 301

Jacob's ladder, 151
James, William, 248
Jesuits, 9, 144, 146, 147, 309
Jesus, 5, 9, 14, 17, 19, 45, 54, 60, 62–66, 83, 92, 95, 98, 99, 114, 117, 118, 131, 132, 144, 149, 157, 173, 191, 202, 206–15, 231, 280, 285, 293, 307
Jewish, 2, 14, 17, 18, 30, 32, 45–48, 57–59, 63, 64, 66, 253, 258
Johnson, Samuel, 180
Jonas, Hans, 46–55, 309
Jones, Rufus, 18, 145, 163, 173, 308–11
Jungian, 221–25, 236
Justice, 5, 26, 27, 64, 101, 117, 190, 198, 227, 237

Kang, S. Steve, 308
Kegan, Robert, 221, 309
Kelly, Thomas, 162
Kingdom Of God, 58, 202, 208, 212

Labyrinth, 236

Lady Poverty, 120
Last Days, 59, 62, 67, 274
Law, William, 7, 145, 179, 180–97, 201, 207, 212, 275–78, 280, 283, 287, 297, 301, 308–11
Laypersons, 2, 107, 108, 197
Lectio Divina, 236, 292
Liberation, 15, 276, 284
Little Brothers of Jesus, 144
Logan, Alastair, 52–55, 309
Love, 22, 25–28, 38, 41, 61, 64, 80–83, 88, 94–97, 100, 116–18, 123, 125, 136–39, 146, 150–54, 157, 158, 160, 166, 171–73, 180, 183, 184, 188, 190–95, 206, 214–16, 226–28, 231–37, 244–48, 275, 285, 286, 293
Luther, Martin, 127, 128, 143

Madame Guyon, 179
Magic, 31, 63, 248
Marcion, 51
Markarios of Corinth, 88
Martyrdom, 14, 144
May, Gerald, 8, 12, 200, 219, 221, 242–52, 267, 276, 279, 280, 283, 288, 298, 301, 309
Meditation, 28, 135, 138, 153, 156, 248, 250, 253, 254, 263, 264, 291
Memory, 9, 79, 112, 113, 118, 123, 124, 256, 280, 285
Mendicants, 14
Mentoring, 5, 65, 68, 83, 101, 103, 123, 157, 174, 286
Merton, Thomas, 223, 309
Methodism, 144
Milavec, Aaron, 46, 57–67, 308, 309
Mind, 21, 28, 29, 50, 62, 74–85, 94–98, 112–17, 131–39, 148, 156, 159, 163, 167, 170, 185, 190, 195, 204, 244, 250, 259,

Index

Mind (*cont.*)
    261, 264, 265, 278, 286, 289, 290
Mindfulness, 79–82, 87, 97, 100, 261, 262, 265, 267, 275, 276, 286, 289, 294
Miracles, 110, 114, 122
Missionaries, 72
Modern Science, 145, 200, 201, 251, 267, 301
Modernity, 15
Monasticism, 14
Monks, 19, 22, 23, 26–28, 73, 74, 78–88, 92, 96, 101–04, 125, 135
More, Thomas, 127
Mother Mary, 114
Mysticism, 14, 310

Nayler, James, 165
Neo-Platonism, 111, 300
Neuroscience, 6
New Age, 15
Newman, John Henry, 180, 308, 309
Newton, Issac, 145,
Newton, John, 179
Nikodimos of the Holy Mountain, 88
Non-Dualistic, 11
Nonjudgmental, 234, 290
Nonjuror, 179
Non-Theistic, 10, 254, 258, 267, 280

Obedience, 95, 154, 168, 175, 193
Omnipotence, 182, 183
Omnipresence, 160, 165, 183, 206
Ontological Being, 284
Oracles, 38
Origen of Alexandria, 17, 18
Orthodoxy, 71

Parapsychological, 278

Parrett, Gary A., 308
Parts Work, 221, 236, 309
Pascal, Blaise, 145
Passions, 9, 20, 21, 27–29, 33, 37, 38, 49, 50, 54, 55, 75, 76, 84, 89–96, 101–04, 133, 136, 139, 225, 236, 274, 287, 297
Paul of Tarsus, 9, 213
Peace, 5, 27, 81–84, 96, 116, 118, 128, 131–35, 149, 171, 173, 214, 216, 227, 233, 237, 257, 290
Penn, William, 162, 164
Pennington, Isaac, 145, 171
Perfection, 25, 28, 33, 36, 38, 41, 50, 61–67, 81–85, 88, 89, 114–19, 133, 135, 150–54, 158, 184, 189, 292
Petrarca, Francesco, 127
Philo of Alexandria, 7, 17–29, 274, 277–80, 310
Philokalia, 7, 73, 88–105, 109, 124, 163, 177, 181, 227, 268, 275–80, 287–89, 294, 297, 301, 310
Philothea, 146
Piety, 26, 64, 137, 138, 157, 183–88, 193
Pilgrim's Progress, 180
Pilgrimages, 108
Plato, 19, 309
Platonism, 17, 19, 111, 300
Pleromas, 35
Plotinus, 31
Porphyry, 31, 32, 38
Post-Modern, 15
Post-Structuralist, 9
Poverty, 99, 118, 120–25, 154, 191, 275, 293, 301
Prayer, 28, 39, 41, 42, 64–66, 78–85, 92–103, 108, 111, 117–25, 134, 135, 156, 157, 169, 171, 185, 188–90, 195, 197, 248, 280

Index

Prodigal Son, 225
Prophetess, 39
Prophetic, 39
Protestant Reformation, 7, 9, 126, 143, 162, 197, 301
Psychology, 6, 201, 219–22, 228, 242–47, 250, 252, 267
Purification, 32, 37, 40, 54, 83, 88, 94, 95, 115–17, 151, 286
Puritans, 162
Purity Of Heart, 74, 81

Quaker, 7, 145, 162–77, 226, 242, 275, 278, 280, 311
Queries, 173, 176

Rationality, 107, 144
Reason, 20, 22, 23, 29, 32, 47, 112, 134, 139, 150, 181–84, 193–96, 274, 286, 287, 291, 296
Reconciliation, 66, 224, 290
Relational Vitality, 11, 230, 236
Religion, 30, 45, 51, 52, 71, 145, 147, 157, 160, 167–72, 183, 188, 190, 191, 194, 199, 221, 232, 243, 248
Religious Education, 2, 3, 174
Renaissance, 7, 2, 14, 107, 109
Revelation, 22, 50, 88, 128, 164, 165, 213
Rhineland, 108
Richmond, Lewis, 310
Righteousness, 61, 63, 67, 68, 81, 84, 133, 167, 172, 173, 202, 210, 211, 214, 286, 290
Rituals, 31, 39–43, 52, 54, 65–68, 274, 294, 296
Rogers, Frank, Jr., 9, 220, 222, 308, 310
Roman Catholic, 9, 14, 15, 109, 127, 143, 144, 180, 197
Roman Empire, 17, 46, 72

Sacred Heart, 144
Sacrifices, 37, 39, 40, 41, 42
Saints, 66, 108, 136, 139, 149, 157, 160, 192, 193, 207, 215, 219, 296
Salvation, 43, 47, 49, 50, 52, 77, 81, 84, 85, 93, 131, 135, 138, 184, 208, 209, 275, 284
Satan, 59, 205
Scheier, Michael, 6, 307
Schemas, 253–67, 276, 288
Scholasticism, 14, 107, 144
Schwartz, Richard, 221–25, 310
Scupoli, Lorenzo, 144
Secular, 47, 153, 158, 163, 199, 243, 245, 254, 255, 258, 267, 305
Self-Examination, 192
Self-Reflection, 176, 261, 263
Sensible, 33, 34, 115, 133, 134, 287
Shadow side, 225, 227
Sin, 34, 59, 89–94, 112, 136, 148, 151, 155, 156, 164, 173, 175, 180, 181, 184, 189, 203, 205, 214, 217, 227, 228, 233, 244, 283–86, 298
Slavery, 20, 29, 60, 133, 162, 172
Socrates, 139
Soelle, Dorothy, 305, 310
Solitude, 82, 120, 214
Sophistry, 21
Soul, 2, 12, 19–24, 32–42, 49–54, 61, 75, 76, 79–82, 89–96, 100, 112, 117–24, 129–38, 142, 146–57, 166–73, 182, 185–90, 194, 195, 204, 205, 208–16, 234, 236, 240, 242, 274, 277, 294, 295
Spirit, 1, 3–9, 13, 54, 58, 75, 90–96, 113, 148, 155, 156, 164–70, 175, 191, 200, 207, 221–26, 229–51, 280, 294, 301, 306–11
Spiritual Discernment, 12, 175, 302, 305

Index

Spiritual Exercises, 9, 146
Spiritual Formation, 1–14, 18, 20, 30, 38, 41, 42, 52, 55, 58–61, 65–68, 73, 74, 77, 82, 83, 86, 91, 97, 103, 108–13, 119, 123, 136, 140, 141, 149, 153, 156–59, 163, 168, 170, 173, 174, 185, 186, 191–94, 199, 200, 202, 207, 210–17, 220–22, 231, 238–42, 246, 247, 250, 251, 267, 271–73, 282, 285, 288–91, 295, 297, 301, 304–06
Spirituality, 4, 13, 17, 18, 45, 46, 71–73, 107–10, 143–45, 163, 164, 177, 198–200, 222, 233, 236, 261, 305–11
Steere, Douglas, 162–69, 174, 311
Stigmata, 120
Stillness, 82, 83, 88, 93–97, 102–4, 171, 247, 250, 275, 281, 289, 290
Stoics, 74
Suffering, 21, 64, 100, 121, 138, 180, 189, 231, 256, 262, 290
Supreme Being, 257

Tauler, John, 179
Taylor, Jeremy, 146, 309
Teasdale, Wayne, 305, 311
Temperance, 27, 28, 121, 153
Temptations, 24, 77, 119, 121, 132–34, 148–55, 165, 173, 223, 297
Teresa of Avila, 311
Theistic, 12
Theodosius, 71
Theurgy, 31, 36, 294
Thirty Years War, 143
Thomas à Kempis, 179
Thomas Aquinas, 74, 107
Transcendence, 52, 113, 226
Transpersonal, 11, 254, 278, 294
Tribulations, 45

Trinitarian, 66, 212
Tyndale, William, 143
United States, 143, 311
Unitive, 246–50
Unity Movements, 15
University of Paris, 127

van Ruysbroek, Jan, 179
Vices, 26, 79, 80, 133, 136, 137, 142, 150, 151, 154, 155, 185, 192, 195, 292
Vigils, 82, 94
Vincentians, 144
Virtue, 20–30, 53, 79, 80, 83, 91, 100, 102, 121, 132–34, 138, 139, 150–54, 159, 188, 190
Virtuous, 21, 25–29, 172–76
Visions, 114, 120, 210, 286

Watchfulness, 82, 94–99, 102, 104, 137, 213, 286
Way, The, 57, 61–68, 237, 268, 276, 290, 293
Welcoming Prayer, 236
Wesley, John, 144, 180, 308
Wholeness, 41, 238, 246
Wickedness, 20, 25, 149
Wilber, Ken, 305, 311
Willard, Dallas, 2, 3, 200–22, 251, 275, 276, 279, 281, 283, 287, 299–311
Wisdom, 21, 23, 26–28, 84, 86, 101, 116, 117, 129, 133, 135, 173, 183, 194, 206, 229, 253, 255, 260, 285, 289, 292
Woolman, John, 145, 162, 163, 171, 172
Works Righteousness, 61, 67, 133
Worship, 12, 39, 64, 167–70, 183, 214, 216, 296

Yale University, 201, 307

Zen, 11, 307

www.ingramcontent.com/pod-product-compliance
Lightning Source LLC
Chambersburg PA
CBHW050618300426
44112CB00012B/1562